Approaching Language Transfer through Text Classification

SECOND LANGUAGE ACQUISITION
Series Editor: Professor David Singleton, *Trinity College, Dublin, Ireland*

This series brings together titles dealing with a variety of aspects of language acquisition and processing in situations where a language or languages other than the native language is involved. Second language is thus interpreted in its broadest possible sense. The volumes included in the series all offer in their different ways, on the one hand, exposition and discussion of empirical findings and, on the other, some degree of theoretical reflection. In this latter connection, no particular theoretical stance is privileged in the series; nor is any relevant perspective – sociolinguistic, psycholinguistic, neurolinguistic, etc. – deemed out of place. The intended readership of the series includes final-year undergraduates working on second language acquisition projects, postgraduate students involved in second language acquisition research and researchers and teachers in general whose interests include a second language acquisition component.

Full details of all the books in this series and of all our other publications can be found on http://www.multilingual-matters.com, or by writing to Multilingual Matters, St Nicholas House, 31–34 High Street, Bristol BS1 2AW, UK.

SECOND LANGUAGE ACQUISITION
Series Editor: David Singleton, *Trinity College, Dublin, Ireland*

Approaching Language Transfer through Text Classification

Explorations in the Detection-Based Approach

Edited by
Scott Jarvis and Scott A. Crossley

MULTILINGUAL MATTERS
Bristol • Buffalo • Toronto

Library of Congress Cataloging in Publication Data
A catalog record for this book is available from the Library of Congress.
Approaching Language Transfer through Text Classification: Explorations in the Detection-Based Approach/ Edited by Scott Jarvis and Scott A. Crossley.
Second Language Acquisition: 64
Includes bibliographical references.
1. Language transfer (Language learning) 2. English language—Rhetoric—Study and teaching. I. Jarvis, Scott, 1966- II. Crossley, Scott A.
P130.5.A66 2012
401'.93–dc23 2011048973

British Library Cataloguing in Publication Data
A catalogue entry for this book is available from the British Library.

ISBN-13: 978-1-84769-698-4 (hbk)
ISBN-13: 978-1-84769-697-7 (pbk)

Multilingual Matters
UK: St Nicholas House, 31–34 High Street, Bristol BS1 2AW, UK.
USA: UTP, 2250 Military Road, Tonawanda, NY 14150, USA.
Canada: UTP, 5201 Dufferin Street, North York, Ontario M3H 5T8, Canada.

Copyright © 2012 Scott Jarvis, Scott A. Crossley and the authors of individual chapters.

All rights reserved. No part of this work may be reproduced in any form or by any means without permission in writing from the publisher.

Typeset by Techset Composition Ltd., Salisbury, UK.
Printed and bound in Great Britain by the MPG Books Group.

Contents

	Contributors	vii
1	The Detection-Based Approach: An Overview Scott Jarvis	1
2	Detecting L2 Writers' L1s on the Basis of Their Lexical Styles Scott Jarvis, Gabriela Castañeda-Jiménez and Rasmus Nielsen	34
3	Exploring the Role of *n*-Grams in L1 Identification Scott Jarvis and Magali Paquot	71
4	Detecting the First Language of Second Language Writers Using Automated Indices of Cohesion, Lexical Sophistication, Syntactic Complexity and Conceptual Knowledge Scott A. Crossley and Danielle S. McNamara	106
5	Error Patterns and Automatic L1 Identification Yves Bestgen, Sylviane Granger and Jennifer Thewissen	127
6	The Comparative and Combined Contributions of *n*-Grams, Coh-Metrix Indices and Error Types in the L1 Classification of Learner Texts Scott Jarvis, Yves Bestgen, Scott A. Crossley, Sylviane Granger, Magali Paquot, Jennifer Thewissen and Danielle McNamara	154
7	Detection-Based Approaches: Methods, Theories and Applications Scott A. Crossley	178

Contributors

Yves Bestgen is a Research Associate of the Belgian National Fund for Scientific Research (F.R.S.-FNRS) and part-time Professor at the University of Louvain (Belgium) where he teaches courses in Psycholinguistics and Statistics. He is a member of the Centre for English Corpus Linguistics. His main research interests focus on text production and comprehension by native and L2 learners and on the development of techniques for automatic text analysis.

Gabriela Castañeda-Jiménez is a Lecturer in the Department of Linguistics at Ohio University. She holds two Master's degrees from this institution, in Linguistics and Spanish Literature. Her interests include vocabulary acquisition, language transfer and teaching development.

Scott A. Crossley is an Assistant Professor at Georgia State University where he teaches linguistics courses in the Applied Linguistics/ESL Department. His work involves the application of natural language processing theories and approaches for investigating second language acquisition, text readability and writing proficiency. His current research interests include lexical proficiency, writing quality and text coherence and processing.

Sylviane Granger is a Professor of English Language and Linguistics at the University of Louvain (Belgium). She is the Director of the Centre for English Corpus Linguistics where research activity is focused on the compilation and exploitation of learner corpora and multilingual corpora. In 1990, she launched the *International Corpus of Learner English* project, which has grown to contain learner writing by learners of English from 16 different mother tongue backgrounds. Her current research interests focus on the integration of learner corpus data into a range of pedagogical tools (electronic dictionaries, writing aids, spell checkers and essay scoring tools).

Scott Jarvis is an Associate Professor in the Department of Linguistics at Ohio University. He completed his PhD in Second Language Acquisition in 1997 in the Department of Linguistics at Indiana University. Since then, his work has focused particularly on crosslinguistic influence and lexical diversity, with a special emphasis on methodological problems and solutions. Among his better-known works is the book *Crosslinguistic Influence in Language and Cognition*, coauthored with Aneta Pavlenko and published by Routledge.

Danielle McNamara is a Professor at Arizona State University and Senior Research Scientist at the Learning Sciences Institute. Her work involves the theoretical study of cognitive processes as well as the application of cognitive principles to educational practice. Her current research ranges a variety of topics including text comprehension, writing strategies, building tutoring technologies and developing natural language algorithms.

Rasmus Nielsen is an Assistant Professor at the Institute of Language and Communication, University of Southern Denmark. He holds an MA in Applied Linguistics from Ohio University and a PhD in Sociolinguistics from Georgetown University. His work involves crosslinguistic influence, focusing on lexical styles produced by Danish learners of English. His current research is primarily in the area of language and ethnicity with a specific focus on African American English prosody.

Magali Paquot is a Postdoctoral Researcher at the Centre for English Corpus Linguistics, University of Louvain (Belgium). Her research interests include academic vocabulary, phraseology and corpus-based analyses of L1 transfer in second language acquisition. In 2010, she published a book titled *Academic Vocabulary in Learner Writing: From Extraction to Analysis* published by Continuum.

Jennifer Thewissen is a Researcher at the Centre for English Corpus Linguistics at the University of Louvain (Belgium). Her present work involves computer-aided error analysis, that is, error analysis carried out on the basis of error-tagged learner corpora. Her main analyses have involved the study of error developmental profiles across a proficiency continuum, ranging from the lower intermediate to the very advanced levels of English competence. She also explores the benefits of using error-tagged learner corpus data for language teaching, as well as language testing research.

1 The Detection-Based Approach: An Overview

Scott Jarvis

Introduction

The overarching goal of this book is to contribute to the field of transfer research. The authors of the various chapters of the book use the term *transfer* interchangeably with the terms *crosslinguistic influence* and *crosslinguistic effects* to refer to the consequences – both direct and indirect – that being a speaker of a particular native language (L1) has on the person's use of a later-learned language. In the present book, we investigate these consequences in essays written in English by foreign-language learners of English from many different countries and L1 backgrounds. Our analyses focus on the word forms, word meanings and word sequences they use in their essays, as well as on the various types of deviant grammatical constructions they produce. Although some of our analyses take into consideration the types of errors learners produce, for the most part our analyses are indifferent to whether learners' language use is grammatical or ungrammatical. What we focus on instead is the detection of language-use patterns that are characteristic and distinctive of learners from specific L1 backgrounds, regardless of whether those patterns involve errors or not. We acknowledge, however, that what makes these patterns distinctive in many cases is, if not errors, at least underuses and overuses of various forms, structures and meanings.

The novel contribution of this book is seen in its focused pursuit of the following general research question, which has only rarely received attention in past empirical work: is it possible to identify the L1 background of a language learner on the basis of his or her use of certain specific features of the target language? The potential for an affirmative answer to this question offers a great deal of promise to present and future ventures in transfer research, as I explain in the following sections. At a broad level, this area of research encompasses both the psycholinguistic ability of human judges to detect source-language influences in a person's use of a target language, and the machine-learning capabilities of computer classifiers to do the same. In the present volume, we give only brief attention to the former phenomenon because the main focus of the book is the latter. Also, although we are interested in multiple directions of transfer, such as from a second language (L2) to a third language (L3) or vice versa, as well as from a nonnative language to the L1, for practical reasons we have decided to focus almost exclusively on L1 influence in this book, which should be seen as an early attempt to adopt, adapt and further develop new tools and procedures that we hope can later be applied to the investigation of other directions of crosslinguistic influence.

The Aims of This Book in Relation to the Scope of Transfer Research

In a book-length synthesis of the existing literature on crosslinguistic influence, Aneta Pavlenko and I have stated that 'the ultimate goal of transfer research [is] the explanation of how the languages a person knows interact in the mind' (Jarvis & Pavlenko, 2008: 111). Most transfer research to date has not focused directly on this goal, but has nevertheless contributed indirectly to it through work on what can be described as enabling goals, or areas of research that lead to the ultimate goal. Figure 1.1 depicts the four primary enabling goals of transfer research as I see them. The first is the pursuit of empirical discoveries that expand our pool of knowledge and understanding of crosslinguistic influence. The second involves theoretical advances that explain existing empirical discoveries and additionally offer

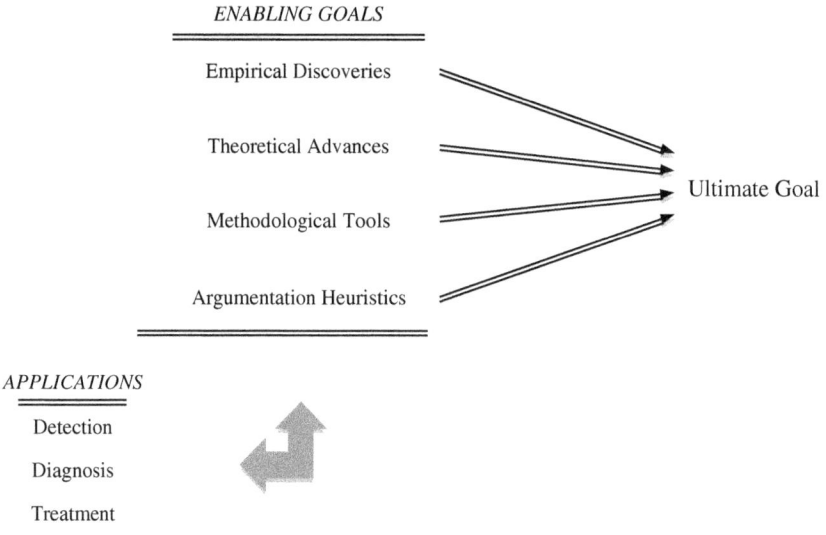

Figure 1.1 The scope of transfer research

empirically testable hypotheses about what transfer is, what its sources and constraints are, what mechanisms it operates through and what its specific effects are. The third enabling goal relates to the development of methodological tools, techniques, procedures and conventions for testing those hypotheses and especially for disambiguating cases where crosslinguistic effects are hidden, obscured by other factors or otherwise uncertain. Finally, the fourth enabling goal involves the development of an argumentation framework that sets standards for (a) the types of evidence that are needed to build a case for or against the presence of transfer; (b) how those types of evidence can and should be combined with one another in order to form strong, coherent arguments; and (c) the conditions under which argumentative rigor can be said to have been achieved. These four enabling goals overlap to a certain degree and also feed into one another in such a way that advances in one area often drive advances in another.

Figure 1.1 shows that the scope of transfer research also includes applications, which are defined as areas of research and other forms of scholarly activity that are not necessarily intended to lead toward the ultimate goal, but instead tend to be directed toward the development of practical applications of what is known about crosslinguistic influence and its effects. Broadly speaking, the applications of transfer research include the detection of instances of crosslinguistic effects (e.g. for forensic purposes), the diagnosis or assessment of transfer-related effects (e.g. for pedagogical or curricular purposes), and the development and implementation of treatments or interventions intended to minimize negative and/or maximize positive crosslinguistic effects (e.g. in order to help individuals or even whole communities achieve their language-related objectives). Progress in the pursuit of these applications often relies on discoveries and developments in research directed toward the enabling goals, but sometimes the inherited benefits are in the opposite direction. Scholarly work on transfer can sometimes also result in simultaneous advances in both areas – enabling goals and applications.

We believe that this is true of the present book, which is dedicated to the advancement of transfer research in relation to three of the enabling goals (empirical discoveries, methodological tools and argumentation heuristics) and one of the applications (detection). The first two of these goals constitute the main focus of this book, whose chapters are dedicated to the *empirical discovery* of new facts about transfer through the adoption and refinement of *methodological tools* that are new to transfer research. The remaining enabling goal also receives a fair amount of attention in this book given that the detection-based approach is strongly motivated by recent work on transfer *argumentation heuristics* (Jarvis, 2010). Although it is not the main focus of this book, argumentation heuristics are discussed at length in the next section of this chapter, and are also given attention by the authors of the empirical chapters of this book, who interpret their results in relation to the extent to which successful L1 detection owes to L1 influence versus other factors that may also coincide with learners' L1 backgrounds. In connection with these interpretations, the authors also consider additional types of evidence necessary to establish the nature and extent of L1 influence in the data. Finally, regarding applications, even though this book is primarily research-oriented, we do give some attention to the practical applications of this type of research. We do this partially as an acknowledgement that the available tools and methods for this type of research – and also many of the relevant previous studies – have arisen largely out of practical pursuits. I describe these in more detail in the section 'Detection Methodology'. Additional practical considerations are brought up in relevant places throughout the book, with a detailed discussion on practical applications given in the epilog.

Argumentation Heuristics

The first point in relation to argumentation heuristics is that any argument for or against the presence of transfer requires evidence, and in most cases, it requires multiple types of evidence. Often, complementary types of evidence combine with one another into premises that serve as the basis for a coherent argument either for or against the presence of transfer. Those arguments can then be used in combination with one another in order to present a case for transfer, where *case* refers to a comprehensive set of arguments resting on all available types of evidence (see Figure 1.2). In Jarvis (2000), I proposed an argumentation framework for transfer that relies on three types of evidence, which I referred to as intragroup homogeneity, intergroup heterogeneity and cross-language congruity. *Intragroup homogeneity* refers to the degree of similarity that can be found in the target-language (TL) use of speakers of the same source language (such as the L1), *intergroup heterogeneity* refers to TL performance differences between speakers of different source languages and *cross-language congruity* refers to similarities between a person's use of the source language and TL. Recently, I have recognized the importance of a fourth type of evidence for transfer, which I refer to as *intralingual contrasts*. This involves

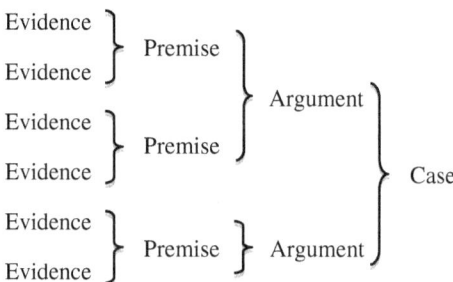

Figure 1.2 Argumentation hierarchy

differences in a person's use of features of the TL that differ with respect to how congruent they are with features of the source language (see Jarvis, 2010).

Figure 1.3 shows how these four types of evidence work together in pairs to form premises, which in turn contribute in complementary ways to the same overall argument. That is, intragroup homogeneity and intergroup heterogeneity combine with each other to demonstrate whether (or the degree to which) learners' behavior in a TL is group based – that is, where a particular pattern of behavior is fully representative of one group (i.e. group representative) and not of others (i.e. group specific). Similarly, cross-language congruity and intralingual contrasts combine with each other to demonstrate whether (or the degree to which) their behavior is also source-language based – that is, reflecting characteristics of the source language (i.e. source like) and/or showing varying patterns of behavior at precisely those points where the relationship between the source and target languages varies (i.e. source stratified). These two premises and the four types of evidence they rest on are derived through a series of comparisons, and they work together to form what I refer to as the comparison-based argument for transfer. Transfer research that collects and presents evidence in this manner follows what I correspondingly refer to as the comparison-based approach.

It is interesting that the same combinations of evidence can sometimes be used to form different premises that serve as the basis for differing (but complementary) arguments for transfer. For example, the pairing of intragroup homogeneity and intergroup heterogeneity can be used not just for comparison purposes, but also for identification and detection purposes. In the comparison-based approach, these types of evidence are used essentially to confirm whether patterns of TL use found in the data are reliably group specific. However, a complementary argument for transfer can be made from exactly the opposite perspective, using exploratory rather than confirmatory procedures. That is, rather than measuring intragroup homogeneity and intergroup heterogeneity with respect to preselected language forms, functions and structures, we can cast our net more broadly over the data and allow patterns of intragroup homogeneity and intergroup heterogeneity to emerge on their own.[1] Any such patterns, if reliable, would be indicative of group-specific behaviors, and the patterns themselves could be treated as artifacts of group membership. Such a technique could potentially be

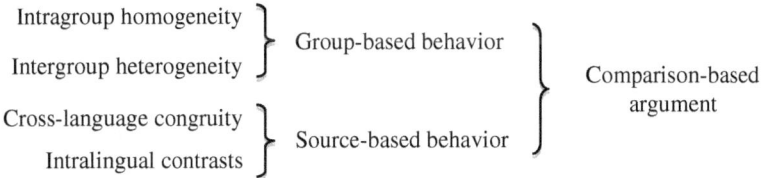

Figure 1.3 The comparison-based argument for transfer

sensitive to (and likewise confounded by) multiple interweaving systems of group memberships (e.g. genders, proficiency levels, L1 backgrounds), but if the technique is tuned to focus narrowly on the artifacts of L1-group membership, and if potentially confounding variables have been controlled, then the accuracy with which learners' L1s can be detected on the basis of those artifacts serves as a valuable indicator of the presence of crosslinguistic effects. Stated in somewhat different terms, it serves as the fundamental premise for what I refer to as the detection-based argument (see Figure 1.4); the methods, techniques, and tools associated with it correspondingly constitute what I call the detection-based approach (see Jarvis, 2010).

Whether the detection-based argument is as strong as the comparison-based argument depends on the nature of one's data and on how well potentially intervening variables have been balanced or controlled. In previous work (Jarvis, 2000; Jarvis & Pavlenko, 2008), I have emphasized that methodological rigor requires the researcher to consider multiple types of evidence and to avoid making claims either for or against the presence of transfer on the basis of a single type of evidence. Further reflection has nevertheless led me to recognize that there are two ways of achieving what I will henceforth refer to as *argumentative rigor*. The most straightforward way of achieving argumentative rigor actually rests on only a single type of evidence, but it also requires showing exhaustively that the presence of that evidence is uniquely due to transfer, and cannot possibly be explained as the result of any other factor. This would constitute a rigorous argument for transfer. However, given the complex ways in which language interacts with other factors, it is rare to find patterns of language use that have only a single explanation. For this reason, I continue to emphasize the value of the previously mentioned route to argumentative rigor, which requires multiple types of evidence, any of which by itself may not be uniquely attributable to transfer, but the collection of which may indeed be difficult to account for as the result of any other factor. Crucially, the rigor of an argument is not determined by the number of types of evidence found, but rather by the researcher's ability to rule out alternative explanations for those pieces of evidence. This means that the strength of a detection-based argument in relation to a comparison-based argument is likely to vary depending on the nature of the data and the degree to which the effects of other, potentially confounding factors have been controlled or otherwise accounted for.

On another level, it is also important to recognize that the comparison- and detection-based approaches have complementary strengths and weaknesses

Figure 1.4 The detection-based argument for transfer

in relation to the types of errors they help us avoid. Statisticians refer to Type I and Type II errors, which can be described as false positives and false negatives, respectively. In the context of the present discussion, a Type I error would be one where the researcher concludes that L1 effects are present when in fact they are not (i.e. a false positive). A Type II error would correspondingly involve the interpretation that L1 effects are not present when in fact they are (i.e. a false negative). In my previous work on argumentative rigor (Jarvis, 2000, 2010; Jarvis & Pavlenko, 2008), I have been concerned mainly (though implicitly) with the avoidance of Type I errors, which the comparison-based approach appears to be especially well suited to prevent due to its reliance on so many types of evidence related to both group-specificity and source-language-specificity. Recently, however, I have become increasingly concerned about Type II errors and the possible real L1 effects that researchers may continually overlook – like fish in a pond that are never seen or caught until the right tools and techniques are used. For reasons that will become clear in the next section of this chapter, the exploratory techniques associated with the detection-based approach are well suited to detecting subtle, complex, and unpredicted instances of L1 influence that can easily be overlooked – and may not even be anticipated – in the comparison-based approach, and these techniques give the detection-based approach certain advantages over the comparison-based approach in relation to the prevention of Type II errors.

The detection-based approach may be particularly useful for investigating indirect L1 effects where source-language-specificity is elusive – that is where learners' TL behavior does not reflect their L1 behavior, but where learners' perceptions and assumptions about the relationships between the L1 and TL do nevertheless affect how they navigate their way through the learning and use of the TL. Such effects might be found, for example, in learners' patterns of avoidance, where they avoid using features of the TL that are different from the L1 in a way that makes those features seem difficult to use (e.g. Schachter, 1974). Indirect L1 effects might also be found in the ways in which the L1 constrains the range of hypotheses that learners make about how the TL works (cf. Schachter, 1992), such as when Finnish-speaking learners of English use *in* to mean *from* – something that learners from most other L1 backgrounds do not do, and also something that Finnish speakers themselves do not do in their L1, but which is nevertheless motivated by abstract principles of the L1 (Jarvis & Odlin, 2000). Indirect L1 effects in which TL behavior is not congruent with L1 behavior also involve cases where learners' TL behavior is neither L1-like nor target-like, but instead either (a) reflects compromises between both systems (e.g. Graham & Belnap, 1986; Pavlenko & Malt, 2011) or (b) involves the relaxing of TL constraints that are incompatible with L1 constraints (cf. Brown & Gullberg, 2011; Flecken, 2011). Other cases of indirect L1 effects in which evidence of cross-language congruity is difficult to find involve cases where the TL has a feature that does not exist in the L1 (e.g. articles or prepositions), or where corresponding structures of the L1 and TL form a one-to-many relationship (e.g. English *be* versus Spanish *ser* and *estar*). In such cases, learners' use of TL features often goes well beyond any possible L1 model, but nevertheless exhibits L1-group-specific patterns in a way that suggests that the L1 does indeed have an effect on the acquisitional trajectory of those features (e.g. Jarvis, 2002; Master, 1997; Ringbom, 2007; Tokowicz & MacWhinney, 2005). Other types of L1 effects that do not involve a direct reliance on the L1 include L1-induced overcorrections and similar L1-induced novelty effects, where learners avoid structures that seem too L1-like and are instead drawn to TL structures that they perceive as being sufficiently novel (Sjöholm, 1995). Again, the detection-based approach may be a very useful way of drawing out these types of indirect, subtle, complex and often unanticipated L1 effects, where evidence of cross-language congruity and/or intralingual contrasts may be difficult or even impossible to find.

As it has been described so far, the detection-based approach focuses solely on evidence of group-specificity and does not take into consideration source-language specificity at all. This raises questions about whether the detection-based approach is sufficiently robust in relation to Type I errors, or whether it will be predisposed to over-identifying as L1 influence other possible factors by which learners can be grouped (e.g. gender, proficiency level, age, educational background, characteristics of their language instruction, types and amounts of extra-curricular TL input). The answer to these questions is multifaceted and begins with a note that there is nothing inherent to the detection-based approach per se that prevents it from using all of the same types of evidence as the comparison-based approach. It is true, nevertheless, that the existing detection-based methods – including the ones used in the empirical chapters of this book – rely only on intragroup homogeneity and intergroup heterogeneity (i.e. the identification of group-specific behavior) without consideration of cross-language congruity or intralingual contrasts (although intralingual contrasts are implicitly addressed through the examination of multiple features of the TL that are likely to vary with respect to how congruent they are with L1 features). In principle, this means that the detection-based approach could lead to the identification of TL patterns that are indicative of speakers of particular L1s but turn out not to be related to their L1 knowledge per se, and would therefore not constitute instances of L1 influence. Cases like this might arise, for example, if learners from one L1 background have all learned one particular variety of the TL (e.g. British English), and learners from another L1 background have all learned another variety (e.g. American English). Similar cases might arise if the data collected from learners of different L1 backgrounds involve different tasks or topics that are not equally distributed across L1 groups. Such cases could pose serious problems for the interpretations of any transfer study, but particularly for those that do not take L1 performance into consideration. This is true of both detection-based and comparison-based transfer research. The best solution, of course, involves the use of careful controls over the data to make sure that factors other than source-language background are either held constant or evenly balanced across groups. When this is done, there is no *a priori* reason to assume that Type I errors will be high in either approach. However, when potentially intervening variables cannot be held constant or evenly balanced across groups, argumentative rigor will be difficult to achieve – especially if evidence of source-language specificity is not provided.

Argumentative rigor is of course not the sole objective of transfer research or of any other field of study. If it were, then very few studies would ever be published. The discovery of empirical and theoretical possibilities and the development of new tools and procedures are equally important, and are ultimately what make argumentative rigor possible in the long run for those relatively few studies that are designed specifically to confirm the facts. In the empirical chapters of this book, we strive for argumentative rigor, but our main objectives are discovery, development and exploration – that is, developing techniques for applying detection-based methodology to the investigation of L1 influence, and seeing what types of empirical discoveries emerge from this approach in relation to the areas of TL use where L1 effects are strongest and most reliable across learners from particular L1 backgrounds. One of the main objectives is also to determine how useful the detection-based approach is for building a rigorous argument for L1 influence. Where it falls short, we point this out and, where possible, introduce other types of available evidence for L1 influence. One of the exciting ventures of this book is its broad-based investigation of L1 influence in learner corpora – particularly in the large *International Corpus of Learner English* (ICLE), which consists of thousands of argumentative and literary essays written in English by learners from 16 different L1 backgrounds (Granger et al., 2009). The use of this corpus also poses a particular challenge for argumentative rigor, however, given that the ICLE does not include L1 data and is not fully balanced across L1 groups in relation to learners' proficiency levels, educational backgrounds, or writing tasks or topics (see Chapters 3 and 5 for more discussion about this). Each of the empirical chapters addresses these challenges in slightly different ways and discusses not only the value of the detection-based approach for transfer research in general, but also its specific usefulness for investigating L1 influence in learner corpora.

Ultimately, if the detection-based approach really is more exploratory while the comparison-based approach is more confirmatory, and if the former is better at avoiding Type II errors while the latter is better at avoiding Type I errors, then an optimal investigation of crosslinguistic influence might involve a combination of both, beginning with the detection-based approach to discover which patterns in the data exhibit potential crosslinguistic effects, and following this with the comparison-based approach to weed out possible false positives and to achieve greater precision and clarity regarding the nature of those effects. The patterns of TL use that both

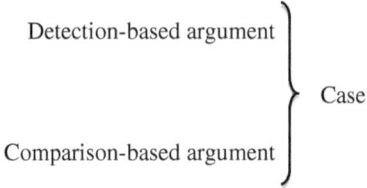

Figure 1.5 A case for transfer based on both detection- and comparison-based arguments

approaches point to as reflecting crosslinguistic influence would thus form the basis of a solid and comprehensive case for transfer (see Figure 1.5).[2] As mentioned earlier, however, either the detection-based or comparison-based argument by itself will achieve argumentative rigor if the potential effects of variables other than crosslinguistic influence have been successfully ruled out.

Detection Methodology

As mentioned in the preceding section, the detection-based approach ultimately extends to methods involving both human judges and computer-based classifiers. In both cases, what we are centrally interested in is whether, when presented with a sample of speech or writing produced by a nonnative speaker of the TL, the human judge or computer classifier is able to predict correctly what the person's L1 is. For purposes of assessing the reliability and generalizability of this predictive power, it is of course necessary to present the human judge or computer classifier with multiple samples of speech or writing produced by nonnative speakers representing a variety of L1 backgrounds. The percentage of samples whose L1 backgrounds are identified correctly can be used as an indicator of one of the following three things, depending on the stage of the analysis and the degree to which the predictive power of the human judge or computer classifier has already been established. First, the overall predictive accuracy can be used as an indicator of the human judge's or computer classifier's ability to learn to recognize patterns of language use that recur across multiple samples produced by speakers of the same L1. Second, the overall accuracy can be used as an indicator of the strength and consistency of the patterns shared within groups of learners having the same L1. Finally, the overall accuracy can be used as an indicator of the number or percentage of samples in the data exhibiting clearly detectable group-specific behavior. In cases where learners' group-specific behavior can be shown unambiguously to be the result of L1 influence, the overall accuracy of the human judge or computer classifier in predicting the L1 affiliation of each sample can serve as a useful indicator of the prevalence of L1 influence in the data.

Concerning the ability of human judges to identify the L1 affiliations of anonymous texts produced by nonnative speakers, I have encountered a number of experienced ESL teachers who have expressed a high level of confidence grounded in a fair amount of anecdotal evidence, that they can take an anonymous text written by any of their students and tell immediately what the student's L1 is. The supporting examples these teachers have given involve a variety of L1s, such as Arabic, Chinese, Japanese, Korean and Spanish, and have also involved a variety of cues, such as specific handwriting styles, spelling errors, grammar errors, word-choice errors, uses of punctuation, overuses and underuses of certain words and constructions and so forth. Although the anecdotal evidence is compelling, we do not know just how strong experienced ESL teachers' ability to predict learners' L1 backgrounds is, and we also do not know whether they consistently rely on the same cues, or even what the most reliable set of cues is and how this might differ depending on the L1. These are important questions for future research, as is the question of whether EFL teachers, who generally teach learners from only a single L1 background, develop an ability to distinguish texts written by learners who are speakers of that particular L1, from learners having different L1s. This latter question is something that I will address in future work with Scott Crossley, Rosa Alonso and other colleagues. In the meantime, as far as I am aware, the only previous studies that have come close to addressing these questions are Ioup (1984) and Odlin (1996). Ioup investigated whether native English speakers could identify the L1 affiliations of texts written in English by speakers of Hebrew and Spanish, and whether they could do the same with taped speech samples produced by speakers of Arabic and Korean. The results show that the English speakers were able to perform L1 detection on the basis of phonological cues but not syntactic cues. However, Odlin (1996) found that L1 detection is possible on the basis of syntactic cues, too. He presented sentences produced by Korean- and Spanish-speaking ESL learners to readers who were bilingual in both English and one of the learners' L1s. The results show that the bilingual judges were successfully able to detect which structural errors were produced by learners whose L1 is one of the languages they know.

The differences in the findings between these two studies highlight the critical need for more research in this area. In the meantime, although it may seem that human judgments have a more natural connection to language use than computers do, and that human judgments should therefore be the starting point for this area of research, it is important to recognize that human judgments are fraught with complexities that limit their reliability and make them difficult to interpret. These complexities include the likelihood that (1) different human judges will show different levels of detection accuracy; (2) no human judge will be perfectly consistent across all judgments; (3) different human judges will rely on different cues; (4) human judges will make judgments based on all cues available to them rather than being able to focus exclusively on certain types of cues while disregarding others; and (5) human judges will not be aware of all of the cues they have relied on or of how they have weighted them in relation to one another. Computer classifiers offer important advantages in relation to these complexities. Above all, the fact that computer classifiers evaluate all texts in the same way, the fact that they rely on the same cues to the same degree across trials, and the fact that the researcher has control over which specific cues they focus on, make computer classifiers very useful for producing precise, reliable and interpretable results concerning which specific combinations of cues – that is, which patterns of language use – in the data are best able to distinguish learners from various L1 backgrounds. Such results highlight the specific cues and combinations of cues where L1 influence is most probable, which can then be confirmed through finer-grained comparison-based analyses of those cues. Results of this type also provide necessary baselines for further L1 detection work, including work involving human judges.

My own interest in computer-based L1 detection began around the year 2002, when I first became aware of the field of authorship attribution and of its statistical techniques for identifying the author of an anonymous text. This field is sometimes referred to as stylometry and is defined by Barr as 'the statistical examination of style through the distribution of language features' (Barr, 2003: 235). In Barr's definition, the term *features* has the same meaning as *cues* in the preceding paragraph: In stylometry, features refer particularly to the use of specific words, word categories (e.g. noun), letters, letter sequences, punctuation, grammatical structures or any indices that might be derived from the language patterns found in a text (e.g. lexical diversity). The term *style* in Barr's definition refers to the specific combination of features that is best representative and distinctive of a particular author. Stylometrists have been successful in showing that authors do indeed tend to have their own unique styles that are relatively consistent across different samples of writing. The uniqueness and consistency of authors' styles has allowed stylometrists to determine with relatively high levels of confidence who the likely author has been in a number of cases of disputed texts, such as in controversial cases involving texts claimed to have been written by William Shakespeare (e.g. Monsarrat, 2002), James Madison (Mosteller & Wallace, 1964), and Civil War General George Pickett (Holmes *et al.*, 2001).

After learning about stylometry and some of its seminal studies, I began to wonder whether the same techniques could be applied to the detection of a person's L1 background rather than his or her specific identity per se. My first attempt to answer this question took the form of a conference paper I presented at the 2004 Second Language Research Forum with Gabriela Castañeda-Jiménez and Rasmus Nielsen (Jarvis *et al.*, 2004). I will say more about this paper shortly, but the main point for now is that, while working on an extended version of that paper, we discovered that stylometry overlaps with another field that had just begun to explore L1 detection through computer classifiers. The field in question is referred to as automated text classification (with any of the following permutations: automated/ automatic document/text categorization/classification), and is part of a larger multidisciplinary endeavor involving artificial intelligence, machine learning, and pattern recognition (see e.g. Alpaydin, 2004; Santini, 2004; Sebastiani, 2002; Stamatatos, 2009; Stamatatos *et al.*, 2000). This larger endeavor is sometimes referred to as machine-learning classification, or simply as classification (e.g. Kotsiantis, 2007), and it cuts across fields as disparate as bioinformatics (e.g. Shen *et al.*, 2007) and geophysical research (e.g. Liu *et al.*, 2003). Common to all areas of classification research is the use of computer programs known as classifiers, which are designed to discover relationships between classes and features that will allow them to predict the class memberships (e.g. L1s) of new cases (e.g. texts) based on the features (e.g. linguistic forms and structures) found therein.

The primary goal of the field of automated text classification is to discover and develop the most effective ways of using machine-learning classifiers to classify texts by either text type or by an attribute of the author (see Figure 1.6). Most of the work in automated text classification so far has focused on classification by text type, including classification by topic or genre, and also the classification of texts according to whether they were originally spoken or written, whether they are fiction or nonfiction, whether they are original or simplified texts and whether they are original texts or translations (see e.g. Baroni & Bernardini, 2006; Crossley & Louwerse, 2007; Crossley *et al.*, 2007). Work on the prediction of whether a text is original or translated has recently been extended to the detection of plagiarism. Unlike traditional approaches to plagiarism detection, which attempt to match strings of words from a suspect text with strings of words in a library (or corpus) of original reference texts, classification researchers approach the problem by examining text-internal features, such as words and vocabulary richness measures, and by analyzing whether the frequencies of these features vary across different parts of the text (Meyer zu Eissen *et al.*, 2007; Stein & Meyer zu Eissen, 2007; Stein *et al.*, 2010). Substantially varying frequencies of multiple features across different parts of the same text are

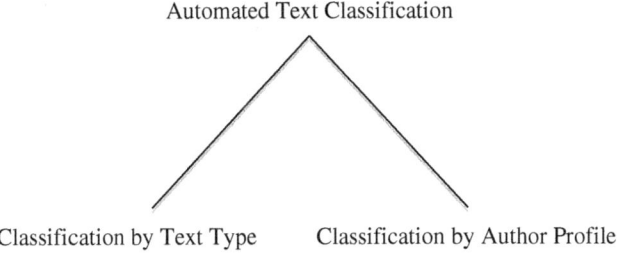

Figure 1.6 Branches of automated text classification

interpreted as reflecting style shifts (or stylistic inconsistencies), which are often indicative of plagiarism.

The other branch of automated text classification involves making predictions about a particular characteristic of the people who produced each text. Studies of this type have attempted to predict the author's sentiment (i.e. whether the author has a positive or negative orientation toward the topic of the text), the author's gender, the author's nationality or dialect (e.g. British versus American), whether the person who produced the text is a native or nonnative speaker of the TL and what the person's L1 background is (see e.g. Baroni & Bernardini, 2006; Crossley & McNamara, 2009; Mayfield Tomokiyo & Jones, 2001). It is of course this last type of automated text classification that is of direct relevance to the present volume, and there have been seven studies I am aware of that have conducted automated text classification by L1 prior to the publication of the present volume. These studies include, in chronological order, Mayfield Tomokiyo and Jones (2001), the 2004 conference paper I mentioned earlier (Jarvis *et al.*, 2004), Koppel *et al.* (2005), Estival *et al.* (2007), Tsur and Rappoport (2007), Wong and Dras (2009) and Jarvis (2011). I will provide a brief summary of the methods and findings of each of these studies in the section 'Previous Studies on L1 Detection', after having first discussed some of the crucial characteristics of classification research.

Classifiers, Features and Cross-Validation

As a general overview, text classification is performed by first splitting a corpus of texts into a training set and a test set. The texts in both sets are reduced to a collection of measurable text-internal features – such as specific words, multiword sequences, word classes, character sequences, punctuation marks, lexical indices or error types. Each text is therefore represented as a feature vector (an ordered set of numbers) where each number in the vector corresponds to a value for one of the included features. Countable features, such as words, word classes and error types, are usually represented as relative frequencies of occurrence (e.g. per 1000 words of text). Once the corpus has been split into training and test sets, and once the texts in both sets have been converted into feature vectors, the feature vector and also the associated class (e.g. L1 background) for each text in the training set are fed into a computer classifier. The classifier then examines relationships among features, and also between features and classes, in order to construct a mathematical model that assigns appropriate weights to each of the features (sometimes even omitting features that do not contribute to the classification model) in a way that maximizes both intragroup homogeneity within and intergroup heterogeneity between the classes of texts. Once the model has been constructed on the basis of the patterns found in the training set, the model is then applied to the test set in order to see how well the model predicts the correct class memberships of each text in the test set on the basis of the features found in those texts, without being given access to the texts' class memberships. The overall percentage of texts in the test set that are classified accurately is taken as a measure of the usefulness of the model and of the prominence and reliability of the group-specific patterns found in the features included in the analysis.

One of the challenges of this type of research is deciding which classifier to use. There are numerous types of classifiers available, each with its own advantages and disadvantages. Some of the most popular types of classifiers include centroid-based classifiers, boundary-based classifiers, Bayesian classifiers and decision trees. Centroid- and boundary-based classifiers are similar in the sense that they represent each feature vector (e.g. each text) as a coordinate in multidimensional space. Where they differ is that centroid-based classifiers calculate a central coordinate – or centroid – for each class (e.g. L1 group) during the training phase, and then classify each text in the testing phase as belonging to the class whose centroid it is closest to. Boundary-based classifiers, by contrast, create new vectors – called support vectors – that represent the boundaries between classes, and then classify each text in the testing phase as belonging to the class whose side of the boundary it is on. One of the most popular centroid-based classifiers is Linear Discriminant Analysis, and one of the most popular boundary-based classifiers is Support Vector Machines.

Bayesian classifiers are among the simplest classifiers. They use a formula to calculate probabilities from feature values. Those probabilities reflect the likelihood that a particular case (e.g. text) might belong to a particular class. During the testing phase, the feature values that were determined to be associated with particular classes during the training phase are applied to the texts in the test set. For each text in the test set, probabilities of belonging to each of the possible classes are calculated for each feature, and then these probabilities are summed together. The text is then classified as belonging to the class for which its probability is highest. The most widely used of the Bayesian classifiers is what is referred to as a Naïve Bayes classifier.

Decision-tree classifiers take a flow-chart approach to classification, creating a series of steps that can be regarded essentially as if–then statements formulated in relation to individual features. For example, the first step in a decision tree might relate to frequencies of occurrence for the feature *definite article*, and the decision at that branch of the decision tree could be formulated as follows: If the value of this feature is less than 95 occurrences per 1000 words, then proceed to branch X; if the value of this feature is between 95 and 110, then proceed to branch Y; if the value of this feature is greater than 110, then proceed to branch Z. The subsequent sets of branches would have similar if–then statements associated with different features, and the very final step (i.e. the leaves of the decision tree) would involve assigning a text to a specific class. A popular decision-tree classifier is the Random Forest classifier, which actually creates a number of alternative decision trees, and makes its final prediction of a text's class membership on the basis of how the text has been classified by a plurality of the trees. More information about these and the broader array of available classifiers can be found in Jarvis (2011), Kotsiantis (2007) and Witten and Frank (2005).

Deciding which classifier to use for a particular classification task is not a straightforward process because there is no one classifier that is superior across all tasks. Support Vector Machines and Random Forest are often touted as exceptionally powerful and accurate classifiers, but they are not always the most accurate. In fact, in a comparison of 20 separate classifiers applied to a single classification task – which happens to be the classification task dealt with in Chapter 3 of this book – Jarvis (2011) found that the most accurate classifier turned out to be Linear Discriminant Analysis (a centroid-based classifier), followed by Sequential Minimal Optimization (a boundary-based classifier based on Support Vector Machines), Naïve Bayes Multinomial (a Bayesian classifier), and Nearest Shrunken Centroids (a centroid-based classifier). Support Vector Machines and Random Forest performed substantially worse than these in terms of the percentage of texts whose L1 backgrounds they predicted accurately.

We have chosen to use Linear Discriminant Analysis (henceforth, DA) in all of the studies in the present volume, not only because of how well it performed in Jarvis' (2011) study – which analyzed the same corpus (i.e. the ICLE) that is the focus of most of the chapters of the present book – but also because DA is widely available in statistical applications such as SAS, SPSS and R, because DA is relatively easy to perform and its results are relatively easy to interpret, and because it has proven to be one of the more robust classifiers available (Hastie *et al.*, 2008: 111). DA does have one very notable drawback, however: unlike Support Vector Machines, Random Forest and many other classifiers, DA is subject to similar statistical assumptions as those that underlie traditional multivariate tests such as factor analysis and multiple linear regression. That is, it requires a robust ratio of cases (e.g. texts) to variables (i.e. features). The convention that we attempt to adhere to throughout this book is to have at least 10 texts for every feature. Some scholars recommend an even higher ratio of cases to features (e.g. Burns & Burns, 2008: 591; Field, 2005), but what really matters are the specific relationships among the features, which will vary from one set of data to the next. In the studies included in the present volume, the rigorous cross-validation (CV) procedures the contributors have implemented give us confidence that our findings are not statistically biased overestimates of the generalizability of our results. I will describe our CV procedures shortly, after saying a few words about the selection of features.

The features employed in the chapters of this book include collections of frequently occurring words, frequently occurring multiword sequences (or lexical *n*-grams), lexical and semantic indices, and error categories. Features that we do not investigate, but which have been included in past studies of

L1 classification, include word classes (or parts-of-speech categories), sequences of word classes and sequences of letters. In an ideal confirmatory study, the collection of features that is used as the basis of one's L1 classification analysis is coherently defined in relation to a theory of language, language use or language competence and is selected in accordance with theoretical principles, assumptions, hypotheses and/or past empirical findings regarding crosslinguistic influence within that particular domain. In truly exploratory studies, on the other hand, although categories of language, language use or language acquisition do still form the basis for defining the domain of features that will be fed into the classifier, additional procedures are used to determine which features should ultimately be included in the model that the classifier constructs of the relationship between features and classes. In exploratory studies that use the DA classifier, it is customary to use the stepwise feature-selection procedure (Burns & Burns, 2008: 604–606). This is what we use in each of the empirical chapters of this book.

The stepwise feature-selection procedure in DA begins by creating a classification model with just one of the many features that have been submitted to the classifier. This feature is generally the one that best separates the classes, or, in other words, is most predictive of class membership. In each subsequent step of the DA, the classifier chooses the feature with the next highest *unique correlation* with class membership until no further feature meets the significance criterion or until the model reaches the maximum number of features set by the researcher (McLachlan, 2004: 412; Burns & Burns, 2008: 604–605). The researcher can adjust the significance criterion and some of the other parameters of the classifier; in an exploratory study, it is usually beneficial to experiment with various different parameter settings in order to determine which provides the optimal results (cf. Estival *et al*, 2007; Witten & Frank, 2005).

I mentioned earlier that one of the drawbacks of DA is that it is subject to restrictions concerning the number of features that can be fed into it. This is not always a disadvantage, however. In fact, the inclusion of too many variables can result in a condition referred to as *overfitting*, which reduces the model's predictive power. Overfitting occurs when the classifier constructs a model that is so tailored to the training data that it does not generalize well to new cases (i.e. the test set). A clothing analogy can perhaps make this clearer: If you buy a shirt off the rack at a department store, it probably will not fit you perfectly, but it probably will fit you relatively well as long as you have chosen the best values for the available parameters, such as collar size, chest size and sleeve length. What is even more important from the perspective of generalizability is that the same shirt will probably fit a very large number of people fairly well. If you have the shirt tailored, however, the more perfectly it is tailored to fit your own specific contours, the less well it will fit most everyone else. This is essentially what happens with statistical overfitting, too, where a classification model is fit too tightly against too many features of the training set; it fits the training set well, but does not generalize optimally to new cases. A classification model will almost unavoidably provide higher classification accuracy for the training set than for the test set, but when the discrepancy between the two is considerable, overfitting will be a problem. This problem is usually dealt with by reducing the dimensionality of (i.e. the number of features in) the model (see e.g. Kotsiantis, 2007). The optimal classification model is one that has the best combination and the right number of predictive features to account for the generalized relationship between features and classes. The CV phase of a classification analysis is critical for arriving at an optimal classification model for a particular classification task.

The main purpose of CV is to determine the generalizability of a classification model – to determine how well it applies to new cases beyond those that were used to create the model. As just mentioned, however, CV is also a valuable way to test for the possible effects of overfitting and to determine the best combination of features for an optimal classification model. CV occurs during the testing phase of the analysis, where the model constructed during the training phase is applied to the test set. When the researcher is performing classification analysis on a truly large corpus, it may be sufficient to use a single training set and a single test set, such as by assigning half the texts to each set, or by assigning two-thirds to the training set and one-third to the test set (Kotsiantis, 2007: 250). If the corpus consists of only a few hundred to a few thousand texts, however, a single split of the data into training and test sets might result in an uneven distribution of features, and this would bias the results either negatively or positively. One way to test for this is to run the training and testing phases once as normal, and then run them again a second time while using the test set as the training set and vice versa. Doing this would constitute a double-fold or twofold CV, and the overall classification accuracy could be reported as the mean accuracy of both folds. It is also possible to run a three-, four- or n-fold CV by splitting the data into three, four or n partitions, and then by running a series of folds where each consists of a training and testing phase. In any particular fold of the CV, all but one of the partitions are combined into the training set for the training phase, and then in the testing phase the remaining partition is used as the test set. Except in cases where a given text has the potential to occur in the test set of multiple folds, such as in the case of multiple-fold CV with random sampling (e.g. Mayfield Tomokiyo & Jones, 2001), each text will occur in exactly one test set during the entire CV. This means that the number of texts used during the testing phases of the CV will be the same as the number of texts in the entire corpus. The overall classification accuracy of the model will thus be the percentage of texts in the entire corpus whose L1s are correctly predicted when those texts occur as part of a test set.

Because, in the case of a limited-size corpus, the specific way in which the data are divided into training and test sets can have important effects on the results, it seems best to divide the data as many ways as possible to counter-balance these effects. The highest number of partitions possible is the number of texts in the corpus, and indeed it is possible to perform a CV whose number of folds equals the number of texts. This is called a leave-one-out CV (LOOCV) because, in each fold, the CV uses all texts but one as the training set, and then uses just the one held-back text as the test set. Across all folds, each text gets its own turn to be left out of the training phase and to be used as the sole text in the testing phase. The overall cross-validated accuracy of the model is, once again, calculated as the percentage of texts whose L1s are predicted accurately when those texts occur in the test set.

Although some researchers have raised concerns about the stability and generalizability of LOOCV (e.g. Gavin & Teytaud, 2002), the empirical comparisons that have been conducted with various types of CV have generally shown that 10-fold CV and LOOCV are both quite stable and unbiased, and are roughly equally superior to other types of CV. Because 10-fold CV is more computationally efficient than LOOCV, the former tends to be preferred over the latter (e.g. Lecocke & Hess, 2006: 315; Molinaro *et al.*, 2005: 3306). The studies reported in Chapters 2 through 4 of this book all use 10-fold CV, whereas the studies presented in Chapters 5 and 6 use LOOCV. The choice between the two was determined mainly by the size of the available corpora. The numbers of texts analyzed in the studies in Chapters 2 through 4 range from 446 to 2033, whereas the number of texts analyzed in Chapters 5 and 6 is only 223 in each study. In a 10-fold CV, the training set in each fold is made up of 90% of the texts in the corpus. For Chapters 2 through 4, this means that each training set consists of over 400 texts, and the authors felt that these training sets were sufficiently large to create useful classification models. For Chapters 5 and 6, however, 90% of the texts would have amounted to only 200 or 201 texts, which the authors felt was somewhat too small to produce an optimal classification model. In order to make use of training sets that were as large as possible (i.e. 222 texts) and thus capture as much of the generalizable information from the data as possible, the authors of Chapters 5 and 6 used LOOCV.

In SPSS, LOOCV is the only CV option available for use with DA. None of the contributors to this book used that option, however. This is because, in exploratory studies such as the ones in the present book, where stepwise feature selection is used in conjunction with DA, the CV process needs to validate not just a classification model, but also the method by which features are selected for inclusion in a model. This is done by embedding the process of feature selection within each fold of the CV. A failure to do this tends to result in classification accuracies that are overly optimistic and not generalizable (e.g. Lecocke & Hess, 2006: 315; Molinaro *et al.*, 2005: 3306). Unfortunately, popular statistical software packages such as SAS and SPSS do not have built-in options for embedding stepwise feature selection within the folds of the LOOCV. Consequently, the researchers contributing to this book created their own programming scripts to help automate this process.[3] One of the outcomes of using multiple-fold CV (either 10-fold CV or LOOCV) with embedded stepwise feature selection is that each fold can potentially construct a different classification model with different sets of features and different numbers of features. Although at first glance this may seem chaotic, on closer inspection it turns out that many of the same features are chosen across most or even all folds of the CV. Multiple-fold CV with embedded stepwise feature selection therefore allows the researcher to assess which features are likely to be the most generalizable predictors of class membership. The features that are selected most frequently across the folds of the CV can, for example, be regarded as the optimal model for the particular classification task at hand (Schulerud & Albregtsen, 2004: 97). The authors of the empirical studies in this book rely on slightly varying instantiations of this principle when arriving at their own optimal L1 classification models.

Previous Studies on L1 Detection

I mentioned earlier that there are seven previous studies on automated L1 classification that I am aware of. In this section I describe each of these studies briefly in chronological order while giving attention to the nature of the texts analyzed, the L1s they represent, the classifiers used, the features fed into the classifiers, the types of CV used, and the overall results as they pertain to automated L1 detection and evidence of crosslinguistic effects.

The first study to perform automated L1 detection appears to have been Mayfield Tomokiyo and Jones (2001). This study was designed primarily to test the ability of a Naïve Bayes classifier to learn to distinguish between transcripts of spontaneous speech produced by native versus nonnative speakers of English. As a secondary focus, it also included an analysis of how well the classifier could learn to distinguish between Chinese- and Japanese-speaking learners of English. However, the groups of nonnative speakers consisted of only six Chinese speakers and 31 Japanese speakers, all of whom appear to have been university students who had received similar types and amounts of English instruction. The study involved several analyses in which differing sets of features were fed into the classifier in order to see which set produced the best results. The features included the relative frequencies of individual words (or lexical unigrams), sequences of two adjacent words (or lexical bigrams), sequences of three adjacent words (or lexical trigrams), the part-of-speech classes of individual words (or POS unigrams), sequences of two adjacent part-of-speech classes (or POS bigrams), and sequences of three adjacent part-of-speech classes (or POS trigrams). The CV was a 20-fold CV, but instead of dividing the data into 20 equal partitions and using each partition once as the test set, the authors ran 20 separate random-sampling trials in which 70% of the texts were randomly assigned to the training set and 30% to the test set. The researchers also tried various types of feature selection, but did not embed the feature-selection procedures into the folds of the CV. The final classification results were averaged over the 20 trials. The highest level of L1 classification accuracy they achieved was 100% accuracy in distinguishing between samples produced by Chinese speakers versus Japanese speakers. It achieved this result with a model constructed from a set of features made up of lexical unigrams and lexical bigrams in which nouns (but no other word class) were converted to their POS identifier.[4] The 100% L1 classification accuracy achieved by this study is quite phenomenal, but the fact that there were only two L1s to distinguish between, and the fact that the two L1 groups were so small and unevenly balanced, casts some doubt on the generalizability of the results. Unlike some of the studies described in the following paragraphs, this study does not provide specific information about the features fed into the classifier nor of which features may have exhibited direct L1 effects.

The second study dealing with automated L1 detection was the conference paper I mentioned earlier, which I presented with Gabriela Castañeda-Jiménez and Rasmus Nielsen at the Second Language Research Forum in 2004 (Jarvis *et al.*, 2004). The purpose of the study was to determine how well a DA classifier could predict the L1 backgrounds of 446 adolescent EFL learners from five different L1 backgrounds: Danish, Finnish, Portuguese, Spanish and Swedish. One of our goals was to make the classification task challenging for the classifier in order to see how sensitive it is to L1-related patterns that differ only subtly between groups and which are also buried in a great deal of variability within each group. To make it challenging, we included pairs of L1s that are closely related to each other (Danish and Swedish, Portuguese and Spanish), and we recruited participants for each L1 group who represented a wide range of English proficiency levels. The texts consisted of written narrative descriptions of a segment of a silent Charlie Chaplin film. Unlike Mayfield Tomokiyo and Jones (2001), whose purpose appears to have been to achieve the highest L1 classification accuracy possible with whatever features were available to them, our purpose was to focus exclusively on lexical transfer, and more specifically on learners' use of highly frequent words. The features we fed into the classifier included the 30 most frequent words used by each group, which gave us an overall pool of 53 words. We ran our DA analysis in SPSS, forcing the classifier to construct a model with all 53 features. Our CV was an 11-fold CV applied to 11 equally sized partitions of the data, where each partition was given its own turn to serve as the test set while all others were used as the training set. Our cross-validated results showed that the L1 classification model correctly predicted the L1 affiliations of 81% of the texts in the test sets of the CV. We found this to be a rather remarkable result given that the classifier had to distinguish among five L1 backgrounds, some of which were so closely related to each other. However, as we have learned more about the field of classification, we have recognized that the CV procedures we used in our 2004 version of the study were overly simplistic and somewhat positively biased. This has prompted us to reanalyze the data using 10-fold CV with embedded feature selection. Our new, expanded analysis appears in Chapter 2 of this book, and it is supplemented with a qualitative discussion on what appear to be direct effects of the learners' L1s on their specific word choices.

The third study on automated L1 detection is Koppel *et al.* (2005), which, similar to Jarvis *et al.* (2004), also focused on a classification task involving five L1 backgrounds. The five L1s in the Koppel *et al.* study were Bulgarian, Czech, French, Russian and Spanish, and the 1290 texts used in the analysis (258 from each L1 group) were essays written on a variety of topics. The essays were extracted from the International Corpus of Learner English (ICLE; Granger *et al.*, 2009). The classifier used was Support Vector Machines (SVM), and the features fed into the classifier included 400 function words, 200 frequent letter sequences (or letter *n*-grams), 185 error types and 250 rare POS bigrams. The researchers used 10-fold CV, but did not use feature selection procedures. The highest level of L1 classification accuracy they achieved was 80%, which they achieved when submitting all 1035 features to the classifier. With the 400 function words alone, they achieved 75% L1 classification accuracy, and with the 200 letter *n*-grams alone, they achieved 71% accuracy. The 80% accuracy they achieved with their combined model is similar to the 81% achieved by Jarvis *et al.* (2004). Both studies included five L1 backgrounds and used similar CV procedures. What is noteworthy, though, is that Jarvis *et al.* achieved this level of classification accuracy with only 53 features, compared with the 1035 features used by Koppel *et al.* It is true, nevertheless, that the film-retell task in the Jarvis *et al.* study was much more controlled than the open-ended essays in the Koppel *et al.* study, which means that the latter study had a good deal more variability to account for. It is also possible that the inclusion of so many features in the study by Koppel *et al.* was a disadvantage; in many cases, better generalizability can be achieved by limiting the number of features in the model, depending of course on which specific features are chosen (see e.g. Mayfield Tomokiyo & Jones, 2001). This is directly related to the problem of overfitting, which I discussed earlier.

The fourth study on automated L1 detection is a study by Estival *et al.* (2007), in which the authors set out to determine which of many classifiers would produce the highest levels of cross-validated classification accuracy on a number of classification tasks, including tasks involving the prediction of the L1s, age ranges, genders, levels of education, countries of origin and so forth, of the 1033 people who produced the 9836 email messages in their database. The emails were all written in English by individuals representing three L1 backgrounds: English, Arabic and Spanish. The classifiers that were compared include eight of the many classifiers available in the Weka toolkit (see Witten & Frank, 2005). The 689 features that were fed into each classifier included punctuation frequencies, word-length indices and relative frequencies of function words, POS categories, paragraph breaks and various HTML tags. Each classifier was run with a 10-fold CV. The researchers also tried out various feature-selection protocols, which were tuned through an extra layer of 10-fold CV. The highest level of classification accuracy in the entire study was 84%, which was achieved by the Random Forest classifier in the classification task involving L1 classification. It achieved this level of classification accuracy when it was given just those features that had passed an information-gain criterion, and after features that were used by speakers of only one L1 background were removed. A cross-validated L1 classification accuracy of 84% is quite impressive, although this is not outside of what one would expect on the basis of Jarvis et al. (2004) and Koppel et al. (2005), whose L1 classification accuracies were nearly this high even though they involved a larger number of L1s.

A study by Tsur and Rappoport (2007) is the fifth study to have conducted an automated L1 classification analysis. This study is in many respects a replication of the Koppel et al. (2005) study in that it also analyzed texts extracted from the ICLE, investigated the same five L1 backgrounds, used the same classifier (i.e. SVM), and used roughly the same features. The main differences between the two studies are that Tsur and Rappoport drew their own random sample of texts from the ICLE – 238 texts per L1 background – which probably overlapped with but was not exactly the same as the sample used by Koppel et al. Tsur and Rappoport used essentially the same categories of features as Koppel et al. did, but delimited them somewhat differently, and also focused primarily on letter bigrams and trigrams. Additionally, unlike Koppel et al., Tsur and Rappoport did not run an overall analysis using all features at the same time. Instead, they ran separate L1 classification analyses involving only 460 function words, only 200 frequent letter bigrams, and only 200 frequent letter trigrams. The researchers attempted certain types of statistically based feature selection, but appear not to have embedded feature selection procedures within their CV. The highest level of L1 classification accuracy they achieved was 67%, which they achieved with a model made up of 460 function words. The model consisting of 200 frequent letter bigrams did only slightly worse, at 66%. Given that this study is essentially a replication study of Koppel et al., it is not clear why the results of Tsur and Rappoport are so much lower than those of Koppel et al. (i.e. 67% versus 75% for function words, and 66% versus 71% for letter n-grams). Possible explanations include the smaller sample in Tsur and Rappoport, differently composed sets of features in the two studies, and the possibility that the two studies used somewhat different classifier settings. From the perspective of the Jarvis et al. (2004) results, it seems that both of these latter studies may have suffered from excessive dimensionality (i.e. too many features).

The sixth study on automated L1 classification is another follow-up study to Koppel et al. (2005). It is a study by Wong and Dras (2009), which, like Koppel *et al.* and Tsur and Rappoport, uses an SVM classifier to analyze texts drawn from the ICLE. The Wong and Dras study includes the same five L1s as the previous two studies, but it also includes texts written by Chinese- and Japanese-speaking learners of English. As of 2009, this study was therefore the most ambitious study of L1 classification in terms of the number of L1s involved. Even though it dealt with more L1s, however, the Wong and Dras study analyzed a smaller sample of texts (95 per L1, 665 total) than either of its two predecessors. Wong and Dras also used a simple-split CV rather than a multiple-fold CV. More specifically, they assigned 70 texts per L1 (490 total) to the training set, and the remaining 25 texts per L1 (175 total) to the test set. They appear not to have used any form of automated feature selection. The features they fed into the classifier were similar to those used by Koppel *et al.* and Tsur and Rappoport, and they included 400 function words, 500 letter n-grams and 650 POS n-grams. They ran separate classification analyses with different combinations of these features. The highest level of L1 classification accuracy they achieved was 74%, which was achieved both through a combination of all three categories of features, and also through a combination of just the function words and POS n-grams. Even though 74% is lower than the 80% achieved by Koppel *et al.*, it nevertheless seems in line with the fact that the analysis of Wong and Dras was more challenging in relation to the number of L1s needing to be distinguished (i.e. seven instead of five). An ability to discriminate among seven L1 backgrounds with a predictive accuracy of 74% is indeed quite remarkable, and is something that would likely be very difficult for a human judge to achieve. There are nevertheless a few problems with the Wong and Dras study that cast some doubt on its generalizability. These problems include the relatively small sample they used and their implementation of a simple-split CV instead of a more robust multiple-fold CV. On the other hand, their 74% L1 classification accuracy might also be an underestimation of the amount of L1 predictive accuracy that is possible, especially if the large number of features they used resulted in overfitting.

The seventh and final study of automated L1 detection that has been presented or published prior to the current volume is Jarvis (2011), which is a companion paper to Chapter 3 of this book. Its point of departure is a recognition that no one classifier is superior across all classification tasks (for a detailed discussion, see Kotsiantis, 2007), and its purpose is to determine which classifier works best for the classification task in Chapter 3 of this book. The classification task in question involves predicting the L1 backgrounds of 2033 argumentative essays written by learners of English from 12 L1 backgrounds. Like the studies by Koppel *et al.* (2005), Tsur and Rappoport (2007) and Wong and Dras (2009), the study in Chapter 3 of this book deals with essays drawn from the ICLE. However, unlike those studies, this study focuses on a single type of feature: lexical n-grams (i.e. single words, two-word sequences, three-word sequences and four-word sequences). The study in Chapter 3 of this book includes several detailed analyses of these different lengths of *n*-grams and different combinations of them, whereas Jarvis (2011) looks only at the overall, combined usefulness of *n*-grams for predicting learners' L1 backgrounds. The study by Jarvis compares 20 classifiers, including DA, SVM, Random Forest and several other popular classifiers. Each classifier was fed a pool of 722 lexical *n*-grams, which included the 200 1-grams, 200 2-grams, 200 3-grams and 122 4-grams that were the most frequent in the data after prompt-specific content words had been omitted. Each classifier was run with 10-fold CV. Most classifiers were run through the Weka toolkit (Witten & Frank, 2005), but DA was run through a combination of SPSS trials (for the training phases of each fold) and self-programmed scripts (for the testing phases of each fold), which allowed me to embed the stepwise feature-selection procedure within each fold of the CV. Various types of feature selection were attempted with the other classifiers, but in most cases, the best results with those classifiers were achieved by including all 722 features in the model. The very highest level of L1 classification accuracy achieved (53.6%), however, was achieved with DA, and it arrived at this outcome with a model constructed from just 200 features, whereas all of the nearest competitors relied on all 722 features. The results of this study therefore validated the decision by Jarvis and Paquot to use DA in the study reported in Chapter 3 of this book, and by extension it motivated the use of DA in all of the empirical studies included in this book. The fact that DA combined with stepwise feature selection produces strong results with a subset of the features fed into it makes it very useful for homing in relatively narrowly on the language-use patterns associated with L1 groups. The L1 classification accuracy of 53.6% achieved by Jarvis (2011) and in Chapter 3 of this book does not seem so striking, but it is considerably above chance (100/12 = 8.3%) and seems to be in line with the results of Koppel *et al.* (2005), Tsur and Rappoport (2007) and Wong and Dras (2009) when one considers the fact that this study involved roughly twice as many L1s as those previous studies did, and also relied on only a single type of feature and a classification model made up of far fewer features than the other studies used.

In this section, I have focused primarily on the methodological dimensions of past studies that have carried out automated L1 classification analyses. I have not given much attention to their interpretations or implications regarding the evidence or implications they have brought to light regarding crosslinguistic effects. Some of these studies (e.g. Jarvis *et al.*, 2004; Koppel *et al.*, 2005) have indeed included qualitative information about the patterns exhibited by each L1 group, but a good deal more of this needs to be done in order to clarify the degree to which L1 classification accuracies actually owe to L1 influence. There is also a need to isolate these influences and define as narrowly as possible the language-use patterns that carry them. Most of the past studies dealing with automated L1 classification seem to have prioritized the maximization of classification accuracy over the identification of narrowly defined L1-related patterns. This is in contrast to the studies included in the present volume. In addition to relying on robust classification methods that overcome some of the methodological shortcomings of previous studies, the studies in the present volume (1) focus on specific areas of language use where L1-related effects are found; (2) present additional qualitative evidence that points unambiguously to some of the direct effects of the learners' L1s; and (3) supplement these results with discussions of the types of influences beyond the L1 that may have contributed to the obtained classification accuracies.

Organization of the Book

It was impossible to organize the chapters of this book in a way that represents a linear progression in all respects, but the way we have ordered them does represent a progression of certain threads. Chapter 2 deals with L1 classification using features that consist of nothing more than single words, or 1-grams (also known as unigrams). Chapter 3 continues with an examination of lexical patterns, but expands the scope of analysis to include not just 1-grams, but also 2-grams, 3-grams and 4-grams. Chapter 4 then takes the examination of lexical influences to a more abstract level, performing classification analysis with features that consist of indices of word concreteness, word imagability, word hypernymy, word meaningfulness, word polysemy, lexical diversity, semantic relatedness and so forth. Another thread that links Chapters 3 and 4 is the fact that they both make use of argumentative essays extracted from the ICLE. This is also true of Chapters 5 and 6. Chapter 5 moves into the domain of errors, performing classification analysis with features consisting of the relative frequencies of various types of errors found in learners' texts. Chapter 6 then brings everything together by performing a series of comparative and combined analyses involving all of the types of features used in Chapters 3 through 5 applied to a single set of texts. The final chapter, Chapter 7, summarizes the main findings of the book regarding both classification and transfer, and points to future directions and applications in both areas. A somewhat expanded description of the contents of each chapter is given in the following paragraphs.

In Chapter 2, Jarvis, Castañeda-Jiménez, and Nielsen reanalyze their 2004 data by using more principled and robust feature-selection and CV procedures than were used in the earlier version of the study. The purpose of the study is to investigate the degree to which learners' word-choice patterns reflect L1-group-specific lexical use tendencies, which may in turn be indicative of L1 influence. The five L1s under investigation include two closely related Germanic languages (Danish and Swedish), two closely related Romance languages (Portuguese and Spanish) as well as Finnish – a non-Indo-European language that is not related to any of the other languages but nevertheless shares geographical proximity with Danish and especially Swedish. The features chosen for analysis include the 30 most frequent words used by each L1 group in their written narrative descriptions of a silent film. Many of these words overlap across groups, so the aggregation of these words renders a pool of 53 words, including both function and content words. These 53 features were submitted to a DA using stepwise feature selection embedded within the folds of a 10-fold CV, and the results of the CV show an L1 classification accuracy of 76.9%, which is somewhat lower than the 2004 result of 81%, but is more generalizable in light of the more rigorous CV that was used. Beyond these results, the authors discuss the specific features that were selected most frequently across the folds of the CV, and show how these features differentiate various L1 groups from one another, and how the learners' use of several of these features in English resembles corresponding characteristics of and patterns in the learners' L1s. The authors also discuss observed effects of L2 proficiency and transfer from a nonnative language.

In Chapter 3, Jarvis and Paquot use as their point of departure some of the questions Chapter 2 raises but does not attempt to answer, such as whether high levels of L1 classification accuracy can also be achieved with less controlled data, with more L1 groups (12 instead of just 5), and with the help of lexical *n*-grams (or multiword sequences). In comparison with Chapter 2, the purpose of the study in Chapter 3 is essentially to make the classification task more difficult while providing the classifier with additional lexical resources in an attempt to make it more powerful. The features used by Jarvis and Paquot include, after topic- and prompt-specific words were omitted, the 200 most frequent 1-grams in the data, the 200 most frequent 2-grams, the 200 most frequent 3-grams and the 122 most frequent 4-grams. The researchers would have used 200 4-grams, too, but there were not enough of these in the data. The researchers performed a series of eight analyses on the data, the first four of which involved submitting the entire set of 1-grams to the classifier, then the entire set of 2-grams, then the entire set of 3-grams and then 4-grams. These first four analyses were carried out using 10-fold CV without any feature selection (i.e. all features submitted to the classifier were used to construct the model). Of these first four analyses, the 1-gram analysis produced the highest level of L1 classification accuracy at 53.0%, and the remaining analyses produced progressively lower accuracies (39.5%, 31.2% and 22.0%, respectively). The remaining four analyses involved progressive combinations of different lengths of *n*-grams, and they were carried out via stepwise feature selection in order to keep the DA classifier from building models with more than 200 features, and in order to discover the most generalizable combinations of L1-predictive features. The first of these analyses included just 1-grams, the second included both 1-and 2-grams, the third included 1-, 2- and 3-grams, and the final analysis included a combination of all four. These final four analyses were conducted using

10-fold CV with embedded stepwise feature selection. The results show that the L1 classification accuracies increase steadily (49.9%, 52.8%, 53.2%, 53.6%) with progressively more diverse combinations of *n*-grams. Some of the most interesting findings of this study relate to the specific *n*-grams selected for the optimal classification model, as well as how the learners' use of several of these *n*-grams can be explained in relation to patterns found in the learners' L1s, and how others might reflect the effects of other factors, such as language instruction.

Chapter 4 digs below the surface of language-use patterns by investigating whether more abstract properties of a text – such as coherence, lexical richness and the types of concepts expressed in a text – are used by learners in such a way that points reliably to their L1 memberships. In this chapter, Crossley and McNamara perform an L1 classification analysis on roughly 900 argumentative essays extracted from the ICLE. The essays were written by learners who were native speakers of the following four L1s: Czech, German, Finnish and Spanish. The researchers fed 19 features into the DA classifier, using 10-fold CV with embedded stepwise feature selection. The features included indices of word concreteness, word familiarity, word hypernymy, word imagability, word meaningfulness, word polysemy, number of motion verbs, number of causal particles/verbs, number of positive temporal connectives, lexical diversity and so forth. These indices were all calculated using the computational tool Coh-Metrix (McNamara & Graesser, in press). The results of the CV are very clear, showing that 14 of the features were selected in all 10 folds of the CV, whereas the remaining five features were selected in only one or two folds, if at all. This leaves little doubt concerning the makeup of the optimal model. The classification results show that the model correctly predicted the L1 affiliations of 66% of the texts. This level of L1 classification accuracy is not as high as has been found in several of the studies mentioned earlier, but it is high nevertheless, and is especially impressive when considering that it was achieved with a model consisting of only 14 features. This study thus highlights the potential value of using these types of abstract lexical and semantic measures in transfer research. In their discussion, the authors describe the profiles of each L1 group in relation to these features, and discuss how strong their evidence is for L1 influence and what additional types of evidence are needed to make the argument stronger.

In Chapter 5, Bestgen, Granger and Thewissen explore the value of error categories for automated L1 identification. Like Chapters 3 and 4, the study in this chapter also analyzes argumentative essays extracted from the ICLE. However, because only a relatively small portion of the essays in the ICLE had been error-tagged, the analysis in this chapter is limited to the 223 essays written by French-, German- and Spanish-speaking learners that had been carefully annotated regarding the types of errors found therein. The features fed into the DA classifier include the relative frequencies of 46 error subcategories representing the following seven broader categories: formal errors, grammatical errors, lexical errors, lexico-grammatical errors, punctuation errors, style errors and errors involving redundant, missing or misordered words. The DA was run using LOOCV (i.e. leave-one-out cross-validation) with stepwise feature selection embedded within each fold of the CV. The results show that only 12 of the 46 features exhibited significant differences across L1 groups and were selected in more than half of the folds of the CV. The results also show that the cross-validated model was able to predict the correct L1 memberships of 65% of the texts, which is noteworthy when considering that the model consisted of only a small set of error categories. After presenting the results, the authors provide fine-grained discussion and analysis concerning the effects of L2 proficiency, developmental factors and crosslinguistic influence on the error patterns in the data that made their L1 classification successful. They also provide helpful advice for follow-up research in this area, and point to important practical applications that it can lead to.

Chapter 6 is a combined analysis that both directly compares all of the types of features used throughout this book against one another, and assesses their ability to work in combination with one another in the detection of L2 writers' L1 backgrounds. In this chapter, Jarvis, Bestgen, Crossley, Granger, Paquot, Thewissen and McNamara use the same 223 texts from the previous chapter in a series of L1 classification analyses involving the 722 *n*-grams from Chapter 3, the 19 Coh-Metrix indices from Chapter 4, and the 46 error categories from Chapter 5. The analyses were run with all of these types of features separately and in combination with one another. In all analyses, features were fed into the DA classifier using LOOCV with embedded feature selection. The analyses performed on separate types of features show that the model built with error categories achieved the highest L1 classification accuracy (65.5%), followed closely by the model constructed from Coh-Metrix indices (64.1%), which in turn was followed closely by the model based on *n*-gram features (63.2%). The combined analysis of all three types of variables resulted in an L1 classification accuracy of 79.4%, demonstrating the combined usefulness of all three feature types. Most remarkable is perhaps the fact that it achieved this result with a model consisting of only 22 features – far fewer than the 1035 features used by Koppel *et al.* (2005). The researchers also conducted one additional analysis to determine whether a comparable level of classification accuracy could be achieved without error categories – a feature whose accurate measurement often requires time-consuming and expensive human intervention. The additional analysis was thus a combined analysis using just *n*-grams and Coh-Metrix indices. This resulted in an L1 classification accuracy of only 67.7%, which is slightly better than the results achieved on the basis of n-grams or Coh-Metrix indices alone, but is significantly and substantially less powerful than a model based on a combination of all three types of features. The authors therefore conclude that this area of research greatly benefits from the inclusion of error categories, and they recommend that more work be done to improve the efficiency with which errors are accurately identified and tagged in learner texts. In their discussion and conclusions, the authors also go into a great deal of depth concerning the nuances and caveats of classification research applied to learner texts, and they provide a realistic and clear appraisal of the contribution that the detection-based approach offers to transfer research both now and in the future.

Finally, in the epilog, Crossley summarizes the main empirical findings of this book and discusses the implications that these findings and the methodology have for future research on crosslinguistic influence and the field of second language acquisition more generally. He also revisits the contribution that the detection-based approach makes to transfer argumentation heuristics, and then focuses on potential future directions in this line of work, including its practical applications in the realms of language pedagogy, language assessment and forensic linguistics. Above all, he demonstrates that this is indeed an exciting and promising area of inquiry that is not just an exercise in computational modeling, but more fundamentally reflects the new discoveries and applications that are achievable when researchers, human raters and teachers competently make use of powerful tools that complement and enhance what they can accomplish through their own expertise.

Notes

(1) Thanks to Yves Bestgen for suggesting the net-casting analogy.
(2) There may also be other types of arguments for transfer that have not yet been considered (see Jarvis, 2010).
(3) The open-source application RapidMiner evidently does have this built-in option, but we have not yet been able to get it to work successfully with multiple linear discriminant analysis.
(4) In other words, the model took into account how many nouns were used by each participant, but did not distinguish individual nouns from one another.

References

Alpaydin, E. (2004) *Introduction to Machine Learning*. Cambridge, MA: MIT Press.
Baroni, M. and Bernardini, S. (2006) A new approach to the study of translationese: Machine-learning the difference between original and translated text. *Literary and Linguistic Computing* 21, 259–274.
Barr, G.K. (2003) Two styles in the New Testament epistles. *Literary and Linguistic Computing* 18, 235–248.
Brown, A. and Gullberg, M. (2011) Bidirectional cross-linguistic influence in event conceptualization? Expressions of path among Japanese learners of English. *Bilingualism: Language and Cognition* 14, 79–94.
Burns, R.B. and Burns, R.A. (2008) *Business Research Methods and Statistics Using SPSS*. London: Sage.
Crossley, S. and Louwerse, M. (2007) Multi-dimensional register classification using bigrams. *International Journal of Corpus Linguistics* 12, 453–478.
Crossley, S.A., McCarthy, P.M. and McNamara, D.S. (2007) Discriminating between second language learning text-types. In D. Wilson and G. Sutcliffe (eds) *Proceedings*

of the 20th International Florida Artificial Intelligence Research Society (pp. 205–210). Menlo Park, CA: AAAI Press.
Crossley, S.A. and McNamara, D.S. (2009) Computational assessment of lexical differences in L1 and L2 writing. *Journal of Second Language Writing* 18, 119–135.
Estival, D., Gaustad, T., Pham, S.B., Radford, W. and Hutchinson, B. (2007) Author profiling for English emails. In *Proceedings of the 10th Conference of the Pacific Association for Computational Linguistics (PACLING 2007)* (pp. 31–39). Melbourne, Australia.
Field, A. (2005) *Discovering Statistics Using SPSS*. London: Sage Publications.
Flecken, M. (2011) Event conceptualization by early Dutch–German bilinguals: Insights from linguistic and eye-tracking data. *Bilingualism: Language and Cognition* 14, 61–78.
Gavin, G. and Teytaud, O. (2002) Lower bounds for training and leave-one-out estimates of the generalization error. In J.R. Dorronsoro (ed.) *ICANN 2002, LNCS* 2415 (pp. 583–588). Berlin: Springer.
Graham, R. and Belnap, K. (1986) The acquisition of lexical boundaries in English by native speakers of Spanish. *International Review of Applied Linguistics in Language Teaching* 24, 275–286.
Granger, S., Dagneaux, E., Meunier, F. and Paquot, M. (2009) *The International Corpus of Learner English. Handbook and CD-ROM*. Version 2. Louvain-la-Neuve: Presses universitaires de Louvain.
Hastie, T., Tibshirani, R. and Friedman J. (2008) *The Elements of Statistical Learning: Data Mining, Inference, and Prediction* (2nd edn). Berlin: Springer.
Holmes, D.I., Gordon, L.J. and Wilson, C. (2001) A widow and her soldier: Stylometry and the American Civil War. *Literary and Linguistic Computing* 16, 403–420.
Ioup, G. (1984) Is there a structural foreign accent? A comparison of syntactic and phonological errors in second language acquisition. *Language Learning* 34, 1–17.
Jarvis, S. (2000) Methodological rigor in the study of transfer: Identifying L1 influence in the interlanguage lexicon. *Language Learning* 50, 245–309.
Jarvis, S. (2002) Topic continuity in L2 English article use. *Studies in Second Language Acquisition* 24, 387–418.
Jarvis, S. and Odlin, T. (2000) Morphological type, spatial reference, and language transfer. *Studies in Second Language Acquisition* 22, 535–556.
Jarvis, S., Castañeda-Jiménez, G. and Nielsen, R. (2004) Investigating L1 lexical transfer through learners' wordprints. Paper presented at the 2004 Second Language Research Forum. State College, Pennsylvania.
Jarvis, S. and Pavlenko, A. (2008) *Crosslinguistic Influence in Language and Cognition*. New York: Routledge.
Jarvis, S. (2010) Comparison-based and detection-based approaches to transfer research. In L. Roberts, M. Howard, M. Ó Laoire and D. Singleton (eds) *EUROSLA Yearbook 10* (pp. 169–192). Amsterdam: John Benjamins.
Jarvis, S. (2011) Data mining with learner corpora: Choosing classifiers for L1 detection. In F. Meunier, S. De Cock, G. Gilquin and M. Paquot (eds) *A Taste for Corpora. In Honour of Sylviane Granger* (pp. 131–158). Amsterdam: John Benjamins.
Koppel, M., Schler, J. and Zigdon, K. (2005) Determining an author's native language by mining a text for errors. In *Proceedings of the Eleventh ACM SIGKDD International Conference on Knowledge Discovery in Data Mining* (pp. 624–628). Chicago: Association for Computing Machinery.
Kotsiantis, S. (2007) Supervised machine learning: A review of classification techniques. *Informatica Journal* 31, 249–268.
Lecocke, M. and Hess, K. (2006) An empirical study of univariate and genetic algorithm-based feature selection in binary classification with microarray data. *Cancer Informatics* 2, 313–327.

Liu, J.Y., Zhuang, D.F., Luo, D. and Xiao, X. (2003) Land-cover classification of China: Integrated analysis of AVHRR imagery and geophysical data. *International Journal of Remote Sensing* 24, 2485–2500.

Master, P. (1997) The English article system: Acquisition, function, and pedagogy. *System* 25, 215–232.

Mayfield Tomokiyo, L. and Jones, R. (2001) You're not from 'round here, are you? Naive Bayes detection of non-native utterance text. In *Proceedings of the Second Meeting of the North American Chapter of the Association for Computational Linguistics (NAACL '01)*, unpaginated electronic document. Cambridge, MA: The Association for Computational Linguistics.

McLachlan, G.J. (2004) *Discriminant Analysis and Statistical Pattern Recognition*. Hoboken, NJ: Wiley.

McNamara, D.S. and Graesser, A.C. (in press) Coh-Metrix: An automated tool for theoretical and applied natural language processing. In P.M. McCarthy and C. Boonthum (eds) *Applied Natural Language Processing and Content Analysis: Identification, Investigation, and Resolution*. Hershey, PA: IGI Global.

Meyer zu Eissen, S., Stein, B. and Kulig, M. (2007) Plagiarism detection without reference collections. In R. Decker and H. J. Lenz (eds) *Advances in Data Analysis* (pp. 359–366). Berlin: Springer.

Molinaro, A.M., Simon, R. and Pfeiffer, R.M. (2005) Prediction error estimation: A comparison of resampling methods. *Bioinformatics* 21, 3301–3307.

Monsarrat, G.D. (2002) A funeral elegy: Ford, W.S., and Shakespeare. *The Review of English Studies, New Series* 53, 186–203.

Mosteller, F. and Wallace, D.L. (1964) *Applied Bayesian and Classical Inference: The Case of the Federalist Papers*. Reading, MA: Addison-Wesley.

Odlin, T. (1996) On the recognition of transfer errors. *Language Awareness* 5, 166–178.

Pavlenko, A. and Malt, B.C. (2011) Kitchen Russian: Cross-linguistic differences and first-language object naming by Russian–English bilinguals. *Bilingualism: Language and Cognition* 14, 19–46.

Ringbom, H. (2007) *Cross-Linguistic Similarity in Foreign Language Learning*. Clevedon: Multilingual Matters.

Santini, M. (2004) State-of-the-art on automatic genre identification [Technical Report ITRI-04-03, 2004]. Information Technology Research Institute, UK: University of Brighton.

Schachter, J. (1974) An error in error analysis. *Language Learning* 24, 205–214.

Schachter, J. (1992) A new account of language transfer. In S. Gass and L. Selinker (eds) *Language Transfer in Language Learning* (pp. 32–46). Amsterdam: John Benjamins.

Schulerud, H. and Albregtsen, F. (2004) Many are called, but few are chosen: Feature selection and error estimation in high dimensional spaces. *Computer Methods and Programs in Biomedicine* 73, 91–99.

Sebastiani, F. (2002) Machine learning in automated text categorization. *ACM Computing Surveys* 34, 1–47.

Shen, C., Breen, T.E., Dobrolecki, L.E., Schmidt, C.M., Sledge, G.W., Miller, K.D. and Hickey, R.J. (2007) Comparison of computational algorithms for the classification of liver cancer using SELDI mass spectrometry: A case study. *Cancer Informatics* 3, 329–339.

Sjöholm, K. (1995) *The Influence of Crosslinguistic, Semantic, and Input Factors on the Acquisition of English Phrasal Verbs: A Comparison between Finnish and Swedish Learners at an Intermediate and Advanced Level*. Åbo, Finland: Åbo Akademi University Press.

Stamatatos, E. (2009) A survey of modern authorship attribution methods. *Journal of the American Society for Information Science and Technology* 60, 538–556.

Stamatatos, E., Fakotakis, N. and Kokkinakis, G. (2000) Automatic text categorization in terms of genre and author. *Computational Linguistics* 26, 461–485.

Stein, B. and Meyer zu Eissen, S. (2007) Intrinsic plagiarism analysis with meta learning. In B. Stein, M. Koppel and E. Stamatatos (eds) *Proceedings of the SIGIR Workshop on Plagiarism Analysis, Authorship Attribution, and Near-Duplicate Detection* (pp. 45–50). Amsterdam: Technical University of Aachen (RWTH).

Stein, B., Lipka, N. and Prettenhofer, P. (2010) Intrinsic plagiarism analysis. *Language Resources and Evaluation* 2010, 1–20.

Tokowicz, N. and MacWhinney, B. (2005) Implicit and explicit measures of sensitivity to violations in second language grammar. *Studies in Second Language Acquisition* 27, 173–204.

Tsur, O. and Rappoport, A. (2007) Using classifier features for studying the effect of native language on the choice of written second language words. In *Proceedings of the Workshop on Cognitive Aspects of Computational Language Acquisition* (pp. 9–16). Cambridge, MA: The Association for Computational Linguistics.

Witten, I.H. and Frank, E. (2005) *Data Mining: Practical Machine Learning Tools and Techniques* (2nd edn). Amsterdam: Elsevier.

Wong, S.-M.J. and Dras, M. (2009) Contrastive analysis and native language identification. In *Proceedings of the Australasian Language Technology Association* (pp. 53–61). Cambridge, MA: The Association for Computational Linguistics.

2 Detecting L2 Writers' L1s on the Basis of Their Lexical Styles

Scott Jarvis, Gabriela Castañeda-Jiménez and Rasmus Nielsen

Introduction

An earlier version of this chapter was presented at the Second Language Research Forum in 2004 (Jarvis *et al.*, 2004) at a time when we, the authors, had recently become aware of the field of stylometry (see e.g. Holmes, 1998) but were not yet aware of the broader field of machine learning and automated classification (see e.g. Alpaydin, 2004). We had learned from stylometry that authors tend to exhibit relatively consistent patterns of word choice – patterns often referred to as *lexical styles* (Youmans, 1990) or informally as *wordprints* (Hoover, 2003). We had also learned from the stylometric literature that, because of the consistency of authors' lexical styles, the authorship of an anonymous text can be determined with relatively high levels of success by comparing the lexical style found therein with the lexical styles of known authors who are thought to be possible authors of the anonymous text (e.g. Holmes *et al.*, 2001). Impressed with these findings, we were eager to determine whether the same approach could be applied to the identification of not just the specific identities of authors but their profiles more generally. The particular element of writers' profiles we were interested in identifying was their native language (L1). Because the successful detection of nonnative writers' L1s on the basis of their lexical styles would be possible only if learners who shared an L1 also shared reliable lexical-style characteristics that were not shared with learners from other L1 backgrounds (cf. Jarvis, 2000), we saw the prospect of being able to identify individual learners' L1s on the basis of their patterns of language use as a fundamental potential source of evidence for L1 transfer that had received very little attention in the past (but see Ioup, 1984; Odlin, 1996).

Previous studies had shown that learners with different L1s do indeed often choose different words in the same contexts (e.g. Ijaz, 1986; Jarvis & Odlin, 2000; Ringbom, 1987), but the prior research tended to analyze L1-related differences in word choice through examinations of only one word at a time (e.g. German-speaking and Urdu-speaking learners' use of the preposition *on*; see e.g. Ijaz, 1986). Although this technique is useful for demonstrating specific L1 effects in learners' use of individual words, it does not take into consideration possible cumulative effects of learners' word choices. For various reasons – including learners' knowledge of collocations and subcategorization constraints, as well as their attempts to strike the right balance between coherence and redundancy (cf. Downing, 1980) – the words learners choose at any given point in a text can have important consequences for the words they choose at subsequent points. Thus, the words a learner deploys in a particular sample of speech or writing should not be thought of as having been selected individually and independently of one another, but should instead be thought of as a constellation of multiple, interdependent lexical choices. This is essentially what the term *lexical style* means in the field of stylometry, where a text is represented as a constellation, or vector, of multiple features (e.g. word frequencies), and where texts are clustered (or classified) according to similarities between vectors rather than in relation to any particular feature within those vectors. Given that we were primarily interested in lexical transfer, and given that the stylometric literature had shown that feature vectors made up of the relative frequencies of the 50–100 most frequent words in a corpus tend to be the most useful indicators of authorship (e.g. Holmes, 1994; Holmes *et al.*, 2001; Stamatatos *et al.*, 2001), we set out to determine whether feature vectors (i.e. lexical styles) made up of roughly 50 of the most frequent words in a learner corpus would similarly serve as successful indicators of learners' L1s.

This is the question we address in the present study, which is a new, more rigorous analysis of the data we originally presented in 2004. We describe the details of the study more fully in the 'Method' section, after discussing more of the literature that informs and motivates the present study. For now, it is relevant to mention that our data are narrative descriptions of a silent film written by foreign-language learners of English in Grades 5 through 11 in Brazil, Denmark, Finland and Mexico. The participants' native languages include Danish, Finnish, Portuguese, Spanish and Swedish. For the purposes of the analysis, each text was converted into a feature vector consisting of the relative frequencies of 53 of the most frequent words in the corpus. These feature vectors were submitted to a linear discriminant analysis, which is one of many methods used in statistics, stylometry and various related fields for purposes of finding linear combinations of features (e.g. word frequencies) that distinguish two or more classes (e.g. L1s) (McLachlan, 2004).

Background

After we presented the results of our initial analysis in 2004, we discovered that there already existed a vibrant field of research dealing with the detection of background characteristics of texts, including the detection of author attributes (e.g. gender, sentiment toward the topic) and the identification of text types (e.g. topic, genre, register). As described in Chapter 1, this field is often referred to as *automated document classification* or *automated text categorization* (Sebastiani, 2002) and is part of a larger multidisciplinary endeavor involving data mining, pattern recognition and machine learning applied to various types of classification problems, including the prediction of disease (Shen *et al.*, 2007) and the charting of geophysical data (Liu *et al.*, 2003). Beginning around the turn of the millennium, the field of stylometry began aligning itself with this larger multidisciplinary endeavor, recognizing that the problems it dealt with involved both identification and classification. The identification of specific authors as well as the classification of texts according to characteristics of the authors and/or the texts are similar problems in the sense that both involve the selection and measurement of certain style markers within a text – such as lexical richness, textual attributes (mean word length), and the relative frequencies of selected words, multiword sequences, and part-of-speech sequences – followed by the use of 'a disambiguation method ... to classify the text in question into a predefined category (i.e. a text genre or an author)' (Stamatatos *et al.*, 2000: 472). In the classification literature, disambiguation methods are often referred to as *classifiers*, and it turns out that the disambiguation method we originally chose for our analysis – that is, linear discriminant analysis – is one of the common, traditional classifiers used in this area of research (e.g. Kotsiantis, 2007).

Because we were unaware of the literature on automated document classification when we presented our initial analysis in 2004, we failed to recognize that there already existed one previously published study whose aims were similar to ours. This was the study by Mayfield Tomokiyo and Jones (2001) mentioned in several chapters of this book. Although the primary purpose of the Mayfield Tomokiyo and Jones' study was to determine how well a computer-based classifier could learn to predict whether a given text was produced by a native or nonnative speaker, a side purpose was to determine how well the classifier could identify the specific L1 of the person who produced the text. It is of course this latter aim that is similar to our own. The data in the Mayfield Tomokiyo and Jones study were collected from 45 participants: eight native English speakers, 31 Japanese-speaking learners of English and six Chinese-speaking learners of English. The nonnative participants had all studied English in their home countries for between six and eight years, had lived in an English immersion environment for between six and 12 months, and had given themselves a self-reported rating of three on a scale of one to five regarding the level of comfort they experience when speaking English. Participants were given two tasks, both in English: a read-speech task and a spontaneous-speech task. Only the latter task was performed by both the Chinese and Japanese speakers, so this is the only task whose data were used for distinguishing learners by L1 background.

The spontaneous-speech data were transcribed and entered into an electronic corpus, where they were submitted to a tagging program that indexed each word according to the part of speech (POS) it represented. The researchers then calculated the relative frequencies of all word unigrams (i.e. individual words), word bigrams (i.e. two-word sequences) and word trigrams (i.e. three-word sequences), as well as all POS unigrams, POS bigrams and POS trigrams for each text. In various different combinations, these values (or features) were fed into an automated classifier in order to determine which type of feature and which combination of features could best differentiate texts produced by Chinese speakers from texts produced by Japanese speakers. Leaving aside a number of important details, the Naïve Bayes classifier they used achieved higher L1 classification accuracy with word unigrams and bigrams (93%) than with POS unigrams and bigrams (86%), but it achieved its highest level of L1 classification accuracy (100%, in fact) when it was fed a combination of unigrams and bigrams where only nouns were replaced with their POS tags. The use of trigrams – whether word trigrams or POS trigrams – together with unigrams and bigrams showed no advantage over the use of unigrams and bigrams alone.

The results of the Mayfield Tomokiyo and Jones study are quite remarkable and seem to suggest, first of all, that perfect L1 detection accuracy is achievable, and second, that near-perfect L1 detection accuracy is achievable on the basis of nothing more than lexical features. There are reasons for caution, however, including the fact that this study attempted a classification analysis of only two L1 groups, one of which was much larger than the other. The Japanese speakers made up 84% of the nonnative participants, which means that the baseline level of accuracy for their study was 84% (i.e. the accuracy that would be attained if the classifier naively categorized all cases as belonging to the largest L1 group). From this perspective, the high levels of classification accuracy achieved in this study are probably not generalizable. Nevertheless, we do take the study's results as support for the possibility that learners' lexical styles carry a good deal of L1 influence, much of which is likely to go unnoticed by human observers due to its subtlety and complexity.

A second reason for caution is that the Mayfield Tomokiyo and Jones study was not designed as a proper investigation of L1 influence. As mentioned, this was not the researchers' main purpose. The researchers were mainly interested in the classifier's ability to distinguish texts written by native versus nonnative speakers, and they approached this problem from the perspective of machine learning rather than from the perspective of second language acquisition. They were essentially probing the power of the Naïve Bayes classifier, and were additionally exploring which sets of features fed into the classifier resulted in the highest levels of classification accuracy. If their study had been designed as a proper investigation of L1 influence, it would have included (1) a more balanced selection of learners from different L1 backgrounds; (2) a consideration of evidence for whether the patterns found in the data can also be found in the learners' L1s; and (3) an attempt to weigh this evidence against other possible differences between the groups – such as their levels of L2 proficiency, educational backgrounds, and types and amounts of exposure to the L2 – that might allow the classifier to discriminate successfully between the L1 groups even in the absence of any direct influence from the L1 itself (cf. Jarvis, 2000, 2010; see also Chapter 1). Given that the study by Mayfield Tomokiyo and Jones was not intended as a study of L1 influence, we do not fault the researchers for neglecting these considerations; we point them out merely as a way of highlighting some of the important differences between our study and theirs.

The present study's focus on lexical transfer points to another important difference between our study and that of Mayfield Tomokiyo and Jones: Their interest in maximizing the power of their classifier led them to feed into the classifier as many available features and as many available types of features as were found to increase classification accuracy. By contrast, our interest in gauging the extent of lexical transfer in our data leads us to restrict our analysis to just words. In the present study, we focus narrowly on lexical styles characterized as constellations of word unigrams. (The usefulness of word unigrams in comparison with bigrams, trigrams and quadrigrams for L1 classification is addressed in Chapter 3.) Because this is an investigation of the potential effects of the L1 on learners' word choices, we turn next to a brief overview of the literature on lexical transfer and, more specifically, word-choice transfer.

Word-Choice Transfer

Over the past several years, lexical transfer has received perhaps more attention than any other type of transfer in the professional literature, and a good deal of the research that has been conducted on lexical transfer has clear implications for word choice. Some of the relevant studies have investigated how the L1 can affect a person's choice of certain categories of words (e.g. phrasal verbs v. one-part verbs), whereas other studies have investigated how the L1 can affect a person's choice of specific words. Investigations of the former include studies on learners' use of relative pronouns, articles, prepositions and various types of verbs (e.g. serial verbs, manner verbs, causatives). The general findings of these studies are (1) that learners often exhibit a measurable tendency to rely on the types of lexical options preferred in their L1s when using the L2 to refer to notions such as motion (e.g. Hohenstein *et al.*, 2006) and causation (e.g. Helms-Park, 2001); and (2) that speakers of L1s that lack certain types of words, such as articles, prepositions, relative pronouns, and serial verbs, tend to omit (or avoid) these types of words when using an L2 (e.g. Dagut & Laufer, 1985; Jarvis, 2002; Jarvis & Odlin, 2000; Laufer & Eliasson, 1993; Master, 1997; Schachter, 1974; Schumann, 1986; Sjöholm, 1995). These studies have left little doubt that the L1 can have a considerable effect on the categories of words that learners are inclined to use or not to use in certain contexts.

The question becomes somewhat more complicated when we talk about the specific words – not just the categories of words – that learners choose in given contexts. This is because the factors that affect the choice of specific words are highly varied and interconnected. To begin with, there are constraints on which words are even available for selection in the learner's lexicon. Foremost among these constraints is vocabulary knowledge, as learners cannot use words that they do not know. Even when they do know the relevant words, however, not all of the words that they know will necessarily be retrievable at all times and in all contexts (e.g. Ringbom, 1987). Thus, retrievability constitutes another important constraint on which words will be available for selection. Problems with retrieval are often intralingual (e.g. Ecke, 2001), but they can also be caused by crosslinguistic processing interference that either blocks the retrieval of a word from the target language (e.g. De Bot, 2004; Green, 1998) or results in the accidental use of a corresponding word from the wrong language, whether the L1 (e.g. Poulisse, 1999) or another L2 (e.g. Ringbom, 2007; Williams & Hammarberg, 1998), or results in the blending and hybridization of L1 word forms with L2 word forms (Dewaele, 1998; Ringbom, 2007).

A third and equally fundamental constraint on word choice is whether a context has been created for certain words even to be relevant. For example, a learner's use or nonuse of the words *walk*, *by*, *the* or *house* is not even worthy of consideration unless the written or spoken text under analysis contains a context where these words might be relevant (at least from the learner's perspective). Context in this case entails not only the semantic elements of the text (i.e. what entities, events, relationships and conditions the text is referring to), but also the situational conditions in which the text was created (including the relationship between interlocutors, and the speaker's/writer's assumptions about what the listener/reader already knows), as well as the linguistic environment in which words are produced, which imposes discursive and grammatical well-formedness constraints on word choice. Crosslinguistic influence can have an important effect on how a learner understands those contextual constraints, but at an even more fundamental level, crosslinguistic influence can affect whether the learner creates the context for certain words to be used in the first place (cf. Hohenstein *et al.*, 2006; Jarvis, 1998, 2002; Pavlenko, 1997; Schachter, 1974; Slobin, 1996; von Stutterheim & Nüse, 2003).

When a person does have the relevant lexical knowledge and ability to access that knowledge, and when a context has been created for certain words to be relevant, it may seem that word choice is very straightforwardly a matter of choosing the one word that best meets the semantic, situational, and linguistic requirements of the context (for a discussion, see e.g. Nilsson, 2006). However, in many cases word choice is not so simple. For instance, languages often provide the speaker with multiple ways of referring to a given notion, not only because of the existence of synonyms and other types of words with overlapping semantic fields, but also because of the options that a language provides its speakers for referring to notions at differing levels of specificity. According to Downing (1980), there is a general tendency for people to refer to objects at an intermediate level of abstractness (e.g. saying *bicycle* instead of *vehicle* or *ten-speed*). She also suggests that what constitutes an intermediate level of abstractness may vary from one language to another (see also Lakoff, 1987), and this clearly has implications for crosslinguistic influence. However, crosslinguistic influence goes far beyond learners' selection of levels of abstractness (cf. Crossley *et al.*, 2009); it also affects the ways learners conceptualize and mentally categorize objects, events and spatial relations (e.g. Graham & Belnap, 1986; Jarvis, 2011a; Jarvis & Odlin, 2000; Pavlenko & Driagina, 2007; Pavlenko & Malt, 2011; von Stutterheim & Nüse, 2003), and additionally affects the ways that learners semantically map words to concepts, which often leads to semantic-extension errors ('He bit himself in the *language*,' Finnish kieli=tongue, language), and calques (*firesticks*, Finnish tulitikut=matches, lit fire sticks) (examples from Ringbom, 2001; see Ijaz, 1986 for related findings).

In addition to semantic and conceptual factors, word choice is also affected by the speaker's attempt to maintain a certain register and level of formality (e.g. Nilsson, 2006), to achieve a satisfactory degree of textual coherence, to develop the plot in a certain way (in narratives), and to avoid unacceptable levels of ambiguity and redundancy (e.g. Downing, 1980). Accomplishing these goals can be especially challenging for language learners because they often have underdeveloped intuitions of the registers, levels of formality and situational appropriateness associated with various words in the target language. Crosslinguistic influence certainly plays a role here (e.g. Strick, 1980), and it probably also has an effect on what learners consider to be acceptable levels of ambiguity and redundancy (e.g. a Czech-speaking learner's decision not to use a definite article with a noun phrase whose definiteness is retrievable from other cues; see Young, 1996), as well as on which words they intuit to sound best in given linguistic and situational contexts (cf. Hiki, 1995).

Finally, the frequency of L2 forms (including words) is sometimes identified as a factor that has potentially powerful effects on whether learners acquire and use these forms. Ellis has pointed out that 'the frequency with which certain items and sequences of items are used profoundly influences the way language is broken up into chunks in memory storage, the way such chunks are related to other stored material, the ease with which they are accessed, and the way linguistic regularities, abstract schematic constructions, default patterns, and central tendencies emerge' (Ellis, 2004: 619). Even though a number of other variables confound the relationship between input frequency and output frequency, as a general rule it seems safe to say that language users, in both their L1s and L2s, adopt patterns of language use they are frequently exposed to, and this relates not only to the forms they produce, but also to the frequencies with which they produce those forms and, concomitantly, to the ways they distribute those forms throughout their language use (cf. Ellis, 2002: 170–171). Even though this line of research deals mainly with intralingual factors (i.e. properties of the target language), cross-linguistic influence nevertheless also plays a role. Frequency (as well as recency and salience) of input affects the strength of the neural pathways associated with forms and structures in the language. The effects of frequency are also cumulative in the sense that the strength of neural pathways acquired through frequent encounters with L1 structures can override or at least moderate the effects of input frequency in the L2 (cf. Ellis, 2002, 2006). Among other things, this means that a learner's word choices in the L2 can reflect L1 lexical preferences (cf. Hasselgren, 1994) – preferences presumably related to the frequency with which L1 lexical patterns have been experienced (cf. Ellis, 2002: 170–171).

As Lado once observed, 'individuals tend to transfer the forms and meanings, and the *distribution* of forms and meanings of their native language and culture to the foreign language and culture' (emphasis ours) (Lado, 1957: 2). When referring to transfer as a distributional phenomenon, Paquot (2007, 2008) uses the term *transfer of frequency*, and describes it as a correlate of the transfer of function and form. Focusing on the use of multiword units in five sub-corpora of the International Corpus of Learner English, Paquot found that learners of English from different language backgrounds differ in relation to how frequently they use multiword sequences such as *to illustrate this, let us take as an example* and *let's consider*. In particular, she found that learners tend to overuse L2 multiword units that have frequently occurring counterparts in their L1s. By taking into consideration the output frequencies for multiword sequences, not only in learners' use of the L2 but also in their L1s, Paquot's study expands on previous work by Ringbom (1998), who analyzed seven sub-corpora of the same learner corpus and found that learners from different L1 backgrounds differ from one another and from native speakers in the frequencies with which they use various individual words (e.g. *do, think, with*) and collocations (involving the verb *get*). Whereas Ringbom showed that learners from different L1 backgrounds display some differences in the use of high-frequency words, Paquot showed that these differences are often statistically significant and that they are also related to the output frequencies of corresponding words and multiword sequences in the learners' L1s.

Despite the fact that crosslinguistic influence has been found to be an important factor in learners' word choice, it is important to point out that none of the studies reviewed here has found transfer to be the sole or necessarily even the most important determinant of learners' word choices. One of the caveats mentioned by Paquot (2007) is that, even when crosslinguistic influence can be shown to affect the frequencies with which learners produce L2 forms, those frequencies can nevertheless differ substantially from the frequencies with which corresponding forms occur in the learners' L1s. Another caveat mentioned by Ringbom (1998) is that there is often quite a bit of variation among learners within the same L1 groups in terms of the frequencies with which they produce individual lexical items. It is in fact precisely this caveat that has led us to adopt a different approach to word choice transfer for the present study. Most of the studies we are aware of that have investigated word choice transfer have analyzed – either directly or indirectly – learners' use of words and multiword sequences one at a time. Although the one-unit-at-a-time approach does reveal group differences in word choice that are often significant, the individual variation that exists within L1 groups renders the predictive power of this type of analysis fairly low. Where L1 transfer exists, we should not only find significant group differences, but ultimately should be able to detect the L1s of individual learners based on their specific patterns of language use. The within-group variation that exists among learners from the same L1 backgrounds renders the detection of individual learners' L1s relatively unsuccessful when learners' language samples are examined in relation to only one lexical unit at a time because it is rare to find cases where most learners from the same L1 background choose the same word in the same context, and where most learners from other L1 backgrounds choose another word in that same context (cf. Jarvis, 2000). We believe that the one-word-at-a-time type of analysis underestimates the effects of crosslinguistic influence on word choice transfer, and we have therefore adopted a classification approach to word choice transfer in order to explore how accurately learners' L1 backgrounds can be identified when their word choices are investigated collectively rather than individually. Our assumption is that even when a learner's use of some words may not be very indicative of his or her L1 background, this may be compensated by his or her use of other words, in a way that may be captured through a classification model of learners' lexical styles.

L1 Classification Studies

Since the publication of the Mayfield Tomokiyo and Jones study in 2001, there have been a handful of additional studies in the field of automated document classification that have explored L1 classification. These studies are discussed in Chapter 1 and also in some of the other chapters of this book, so our discussion of them here will be brief and will focus on their relevance to the purposes of the present study. We will focus particularly on what the prior classification literature shows concerning how well L2 writers' L1 backgrounds can be identified (a) on the basis of feature vectors made up solely of the relative frequencies of highly frequent word unigrams, and (b) in cases involving learners from at least five L1 backgrounds.

Prior to the publication of the present volume, the only other published studies on L1 classification we are aware of, aside from Mayfield Tomokiyo and Jones (2001), are, in chronological order, Koppel et al. (2005), Tsur and Rappoport (2007), Estival et al. (2007) and Wong and Dras (2009). Each of these studies explored the power of various classifiers and sets of features for identifying the L1 backgrounds of texts written in English by speakers of a variety of L1s. Unlike the Mayfield Tomokiyo and Jones study, which included texts produced by only 45 participants, each of these later studies included texts written by several hundred participants. They all explored the efficacy of a variety of textual features for predicting the participants' L1 backgrounds, and one of these types of features in each study included highly frequent word unigrams – more specifically, function words (e.g. articles, conjunctions, prepositions and pronouns). The difficulty of the classification task varied from one study to the next. The study with the lowest number of L1s was the Estival et al. (2007) study, which focused on emails written by speakers of just three L1s – only two of which were the L1s of learners (i.e. Arabic and Spanish). Not surprisingly, this was also the study that produced the highest classification accuracy. Using a Random Forest (a decision-tree) classifier and a mix of various types of features (punctuation frequencies, word length indices, relative frequencies of function words and parts of speech, paragraph breaks, etc.), Estival et al. were able to correctly identify the L1s of 84% of the texts. Unfortunately, they did not report the level of L1 classification accuracy attributable to function words alone.

The studies by Koppel et al. (2005) and Tsur and Rappoport (2007) each attempted L1 classification with over a thousand texts in the International Corpus of Learner English that were written by learners from five L1 backgrounds: Bulgarian, Czech, French, Russian and Spanish. Both studies used a classifier known as Support Vector Machines (or SVM), and both used similar sets of features, including a large set of function words, frequent combinations of letters, error categories and part-of-speech bigrams. Using all features at the same time, Koppel et al. achieved an L1 classification accuracy of 80%. They also found that function words contributed the most: using function words alone, they achieved an L1 classification accuracy of 75%. Due to slight differences in sampling procedures and the selection of features, Tsur and Rappoport, were able to achieve only 67% accuracy using just function words, but they did confirm that function words, as a set, were stronger predictors of L1 background than any other type of feature they examined.

Finally, the study by Wong and Dras (2009) was the most ambitious in the sense that it attempted L1 classification with texts from the International

Corpus of Learner English that were written by learners from *seven* L1 backgrounds. These included the five L1s from the two previous studies, as well as Chinese and Japanese. The number of texts they included for each L1 group was smaller than in the two previous studies (i.e. 70 per group versus 200+ per group) and they also explored a slightly different pool of features, which nevertheless overlapped a great deal with those used in the two previous studies. The features used in the classification analysis by Wong and Dras included 400 function words, 500 combinations of letters and 650 combinations of parts of speech. Like the two previous studies, Wong and Dras also used an SVM classifier, but with a different kernel. The highest level of L1 classification accuracy achieved by Wong and Dras was 74%, which was attained both through the use of all three types of features at the same time, and also through the use of a combination of just the function words and part-of-speech n-grams. They unfortunately did not report the level of L1 classification accuracy achievable on the basis of just function words.

Despite the fact that not all these studies provide levels of L1 classification accuracy achievable on the basis of function words alone, the two that do provide this information (Koppel *et al.*, 2005; Tsur & Rappoport, 2007) show that function words are more predictive of L1 background than is any other type of feature considered. Furthermore, the other two studies (Estival *et al.*, 2007; Wong & Dras, 2009) show that function words are included among the combination of features that produce the highest levels of L1 classification accuracy. Like our study, the studies by Koppel *et al.* and Tsur and Rappoport examined texts written by learners from five different L1 backgrounds. The results of their analyses involving only function words – which make up the bulk of the most frequent words in a language – are informative regarding what we might expect in our own study. If our results are similar to theirs, then the level of L1 classification accuracy we achieve on the basis of highly frequent word unigrams is likely to fall somewhere in the range of 67–75%. However, there are some important differences between our study and theirs that makes this prediction less than straightforward. For one, our analysis will include a variety of highly frequent words made up of not just function words but also content words. Another difference is that their pool of function words included 400–460 words, whereas we are limiting ours to a pool of only roughly 50 (as mentioned earlier). A third difference is that the texts examined by these two previous studies included open-ended essays (primarily argumentative essays) written on a number of topics, whereas our texts are all written descriptions of the same silent film (i.e. a segment from Chaplin's *Modern Times*).

We anticipate that the more controlled task we gave to our participants will reduce some of the noise in the data, thereby enhancing our ability to home in on L1-specific patterns. However, in order to test the sensitivity of the classifier and in order to more fully evaluate the strength of L1 influence on learners' lexical styles, we have added two variables that will make our classification task challenging. First, we have included pairs of L1s that are similar to each other: Danish and Swedish, Portuguese and Spanish. Because of the similarities between these languages – which are to a large degree mutually intelligible – we anticipate that they will produce similar L1 effects that will be difficult to distinguish from one another. If the classifier is nevertheless able to distinguish reliably between the texts written by Danish speakers versus Swedish speakers, and also Portuguese speakers versus Spanish speakers, then this will have important implications for both the sensitivity of the classifier and the uniqueness of L1-related lexical styles. Second, if lexical styles can truly be thought to have an L1-based component, then we should be able to detect certain consistencies in learners' lexical styles that persist across changes in L2 proficiency. In order to determine whether this is true, and as an extra challenge for our classifier, we have recruited learners representing a broad range of proficiency levels in each of our L1 groups. As we will describe more fully in the following section, the proficiency ranges are similar across groups but are quite broad within groups. If, under these conditions, our classifier is able to achieve high levels of L1 classification accuracy based on the learners' word choice patterns, then we can be quite confident that L1-related factors have a powerful influence on learners' lexical styles.

Method

Learner Corpus

The texts used in the present study are written narrative descriptions of the eight-minute 'Alone and Hungry' segment of Chaplin's silent film *Modern Times*. The texts were produced by 446 foreign-language learners of English whose native languages were Danish, Finnish, Portuguese, Spanish and Swedish. The Danish speakers were natives of Denmark, the Finnish speakers of Finland, the Portuguese speakers of Brazil, the Spanish speakers of Mexico and the Swedish speakers of Finland. The Finnish speakers and Swedish speakers were recruited from different areas of Finland. The Finnish speakers all attended Finnish-language schools and lived in municipalities where Finnish is the dominant language. The Swedish speakers all attended Swedish-language schools, and nearly all of them lived in Swedish-dominant municipalities. A questionnaire was used to identify and eliminate bilinguals or learners who were not native speakers of the L1s they were recruited to represent. A breakdown of the participants by L1 background, age, grade level and years of English instruction is given in Table 2.1, and sample texts are shown in the Appendix.

Because of differences in educational policies and opportunities across countries, we were unable to find learners in all of these countries who were

Table 2.1 Breakdown of participants

L1	Age	Grade	Years of English	n
Danish (n = 60)	12–13	6	3	26
	14–15	8	5	34
Finnish (n = 140)	11–12	5	2	35
	13–14	7	4	35
	15–16	9	6	35
	15–16	9	2	35
Portuguese (n = 60)	11	5	2	1
	12–13	6	2–7	4
	13–14	7	2–7	17
	14–15	8	3–7	14
	15–16	9	4–8	8
	16–17	10	2–10	12
	17–18	11	3–6	4
Spanish (n = 116)	11–12	5	5–7	44
	13–14	7	6–10	28
	15–16	9	2–13	44
Swedish (n = 70)	13–14	7	2	35
	15–16	9	4	35

fully comparable in terms of age, grade and years of English instruction. This is not necessarily a disadvantage for the present study, however, because across groups – and particularly between related L1s – we have a similarly broad range of ages, grade levels and years of instruction. More importantly, as far as we have been able to gather through personal experience in the contexts of instruction in question, as well as through discussions with the participants' teachers and through our own examinations of the data, the L2 proficiency levels of the learners in each group were similarly broad, ranging roughly from the level of A2 to C1 on the scale of the *Common European Framework of Reference for Languages* (CEFR), with very few cases that might qualify as A1 or C2. These are our informed impressions, although we acknowledge that only the texts written by Finnish speakers and Swedish speakers were systematically rated for proficiency level. These ratings were performed by two trained raters on a scale of 0–8, with plusses and minuses between levels. The scale was based on the 7-level intensive English program where the raters worked (a large university in the American Midwest). In this program, Level 1 students are not complete beginners, but have (institutional, paper-based) TOEFL scores below 400, whereas, on the opposite extreme, Level 7 students are advanced and have TOEFL scores above 550. Our rating scale was expanded beyond the seven levels to range from 0 for complete beginners to 8 for exceptionally strong writers. The Finnish speakers' and Swedish speakers' ratings ranged from 1– (low beginner, A1 on the CEFR scale) to 8+ (highly advanced, C2 on the CEFR scale), with a mean of 4– (low intermediate, roughly between B1 and B2 on the CEFR scale) and a standard deviation of almost two full levels (or just over one CEFR level). The texts ranged in length from 15 to 608 words, with a mean of 218.00 words, and a standard deviation of 105.68 words.

As mentioned earlier, we deliberately recruited learners representing a wide range of L2 proficiency in order to test the sensitivity of our classifier, and more importantly to test whether clearly measurable L1-related characteristics of learners' lexical styles remain consistent across proficiency levels. Our desire to probe the L1-distinctiveness of learners' lexical styles is also why we intentionally recruited learners whose L1s are similar (i.e. Danish and Swedish, Portuguese and Spanish) and who share a culture and educational system (i.e. the Finnish speakers and Swedish speakers living in Finland). The data were collected in the learners' English classes in their home countries. After giving them a brief introduction to the study, we showed them the eight-minute film segment mentioned earlier, and then asked them to write descriptions of what happened in the film. We later compiled their written narratives into a computer-based corpus, where we determined their frequencies of word use. This is described more fully in the following section.

Classification Analysis

The classifiers used for L1 classification in the studies discussed earlier include Naïve Bayes (NB), Support Vector Machines (SVM) and Random Forest (RF). All of these classifiers appear to be quite useful for L1 classification purposes, but, as described by Jarvis (2011b), they do not work equally well for all classification tasks. In a comparison of the effectiveness of 20 classifiers for identifying the L1 backgrounds of the texts used in Chapter 3 of this book, Jarvis (2011b) found that a classifier known as Linear Discriminant Analysis was far superior to NB, SVM and RF for the given classification task, and that it held at least a slight edge over all other classifiers included in the comparison. Whether this would be true for the classification task we have undertaken in the present study is not certain, but, for comparison purposes, we considered it important to use the same classifier in all the studies contained in the present volume. Thus, we adopted Linear Discriminant Analysis (henceforth, DA) for the present study. DA also has other advantages, including the fact that it is relatively easily accessible (e.g. in statistical software such as SPSS and SAS), relatively easy to learn to perform, and it produces results that are more transparent and interpretable than is the case with many other classifiers, such as SVM (Baayen, 2008: 163).

The inner workings of DA are described at some length in Chapters 1 and 3, and are explained in detail in McLachlan (2004), so we will not attempt to do so here. The essential points for now are that DA creates a statistical model of the relationship between feature vectors and class memberships. Our purpose for using DA was to create a statistical model of the relationship between texts and L1s, so we represented each text as a feature vector, and treated each L1 as a class. The features under investigation in our study were word choices, so we represented each text as a feature vector (or ordered sequence) of the relative frequencies of occurrence for a given set of words. Determining the appropriate number of features (or words) to include in the analysis required several important considerations. In the L1 classification studies we discussed earlier, the researchers included several hundred features in many of their analyses. This seems to have been a successful strategy, but it may have also resulted in an overfitting of the data; that is, the large number of features included in the classification model may have allowed the model to become overly tailored to the data at hand, and thus less generalizable to future cases (e.g. Kotsiantis, 2007). We felt that a better, more theoretically grounded, approach would be to limit our analysis to the 50–100 most frequent words in the corpus, given that the stylometric research had found words in this frequency range to be the most useful indicators of authorship (e.g. Holmes, 1994; Holmes *et al.*, 2001; Stamatatos *et al.*, 2001). This decision was also motivated by statistical constraints. Although the statistical assumptions underlying some classifiers are not violated when the ratio of cases to features is small (see e.g. Kotsiantis, 2007), DA rests on more traditional multivariate statistical assumptions. The conventional rule of thumb in multivariate statistics is that there should be at least 10 cases (e.g. texts) per variable (e.g. word). We adopted this convention for the present study, although we recognize that some statisticians recommend a higher ratio of cases to features for DA (e.g. Burns & Burns, 2008; Field, 2005).

Selecting an appropriate set of features was a multifaceted process. First, in order to maintain a ratio of at least 10 cases per feature, we knew it would be necessary to limit the number of words (i.e. features) in our classification model to no more than 45 words, because our corpus consisted of 446 texts. However, we also recognized the need to cross-validate our results by partitioning our data into training and testing sets. As we will discuss shortly, this meant that our training sets would include only 401 or 402 texts (i.e. 90% of the data), so the number of features included in our classification model would need to be limited to no more than 40. To meet this requirement, we could have simply chosen the 40 most frequent words from our learner corpus. As this might reflect the lexical preferences of some groups more than others, however, we decided to include in our pool of features the most frequent 30 words used by each group. In practice, we found that there was a good deal of overlap in the words used most frequently by each group, so following this selection criterion resulted in a pool of 53 words. These words are listed in Table 2.2 in order of decreasing F values (from a series of one-way ANOVAs using the relative frequencies of each word as the dependent variable and the learners' L1s as the independent variable). As can be seen in the table, only the first 45 of these words differ significantly across groups. It would have been convenient to select from this list the 40 words with the highest F values, but in order to avoid the potential bias this might introduce into our analysis, and allowing for the possibility that a word's F value is not a reliable indicator of whether it will make a significant, unique contribution to the classification model, we decided to use DA's stepwise procedure to select an optimal set of features not to exceed 40 in number.

To perform our classification analysis, we used the Discriminant Analysis feature available in SPSS version 17.0. We selected the participants' L1s as the grouping variable, with all L1s treated as having equal prior probabilities. We submitted all 53 features listed in Table 2.2 into the analysis, using the stepwise feature-selection procedure so that the DA would gradually build its classification model with just those features whose incremental addition to the model contributed significantly to the model's ability to predict the L1s of (the writers of) individual texts. We did this to (1) facilitate our identification of the words with the strongest L1-related effects; (2) further reduce the likelihood of overfitting; and (3) avoid the construction of a classification model consisting of more than 40 features. Our criteria for feature entry and removal during the stepwise procedure were the default values of $p < 0.05$ and $p > 0.10$, respectively. As we will show a little later, this resulted in what appeared to be an optimal number of features.

As described in Chapter 1 and throughout this volume, the predictive power of a classification model can be verified only through the use of a cross-validation (CV) procedure that uses separate sets of data for training and testing. The most common form of CV in the classification literature appears to be 10-fold CV (Lecocke & Hess, 2006: 315), which normally begins with a division of the data into 10 equally sized partitions. In each of 10 successive trials (or folds) of training and testing, nine of the partitions are combined together and used as the training set while one of the partitions is held back as the testing set. During the training phase within each fold, the classifier is given both the features (words) and classes (L1s) associated with each case (text) in the training set, and uses this information to construct a model that best accounts for the relationship between features and classes. During the testing phase within the same fold, the model that was created during the training phase is applied to the testing set in order to determine how well it can predict the classes of these new cases. Because the testing set is not used to construct the model and because the classifier is furthermore blind to the classes associated with each case in the testing set, the accuracy with which the cases in the testing set are correctly classified

Table 2.2 The 53 features selected for inclusion

Feature	F	p
come	40.82	<0.001
bread	36.07	<0.001
the	28.46	<0.001
imagine	22.51	<0.001
Chaplin	21.79	<0.001
into	20.42	<0.001
out	19.96	<0.001
a	19.47	<0.001
away	16.45	<0.001
girl	16.17	<0.001
it	15.34	<0.001
Charlie	15.22	<0.001
do	13.08	<0.001
to	12.91	<0.001
when	12.74	<0.001
bus	11.08	<0.001
take	10.98	<0.001
there	10.86	<0.001
then	10.78	<0.001
man	9.71	<0.001
go	9.28	<0.001
police	9.25	<0.001
say	8.96	<0.001
he	8.62	<0.001
car	8.50	<0.001
that	8.06	<0.001
be	7.92	<0.001
with	7.24	<0.001
one	7.19	<0.001
woman	7.16	<0.001
of	7.01	<0.001
steal	6.30	<0.001
in	5.94	<0.001
tell	5.72	<0.001
policeman	5.63	<0.001
lady	5.54	<0.001

Feature	F	p
she	4.40	0.002
and	4.25	0.002
so	4.09	0.003
sit	3.72	0.005
get	3.18	0.014
down	3.08	0.016
run	2.82	0.025
see	2.75	0.028
have	2.57	0.037
for	2.25	0.063
who	1.97	0.098
but	1.91	0.108
up	1.75	0.138
eat	1.62	0.168
they	1.08	0.368
house	0.83	0.507
live	0.43	0.784

is used as an indicator of the generalizability of the model. Over the course of all 10 folds of a 10-fold CV, each partition serves once as a testing set. The predictive power of the model is calculated as the overall percentage of cases classified correctly across all 10 testing sets. In the present study, this means that the predictive power of the model was calculated as the percentage of correct classification of all 446 texts in our corpus in relation specifically to the folds where each of those texts were part of the testing set.

In order to avoid positive bias (i.e. overly optimistic results) that can arise from the stepwise procedure's ability to take advantage of even incidental statistical relationships in the data, it was necessary to embed the stepwise procedure within each fold of the 10-fold CV (Lecocke & Hess, 2006; Molinaro et al., 2005). Because SPSS does not have built-in automated options for either 10-fold CV or any type of CV that would allow the stepwise procedure to be embedded within the folds of the CV, we created scripts in the Perl programming language to help facilitate our CV. Specifically, we ran the training phase of each fold of the CV using stepwise Discriminant Analysis in SPSS, but then exported the model information (e.g. weights associated with each feature, centroids or idealized vectors associated with each class) from each fold into text files and employed our Perl scripts to access these files and calculate the weighted vectors for each text in the respective testing set and to classify each text as being a member of the L1 class whose centroid it was nearest to (for more information about how DA works, see e.g. McLachlan, 2004). As mentioned earlier, the overall cross-validated classification accuracy was calculated as the percentage of texts – across all 10 testing phases – that were matched with the correct L1.

Results

A summary of the results of the 10-fold CV is shown in Table 2.3. Each row of the table represents a successive fold of the CV. The first row, for example, corresponds to the first fold of the CV, where partitions 2–10 were combined into a training set of 401 texts. For each of these texts, relative frequencies per 1000 words of text were calculated for the 53 features under investigation (see Table 2.2) and were submitted to the stepwise DA procedure described earlier. The third column of Table 2.3 shows that, during this training phase, the stepwise DA constructed its L1 classification model on the basis of just 36 of the 53 features it was fed. The model was then exported and used to calculate weighted vector scores (or discriminant functions) for each of the 45 texts in the test set (i.e. partition 1), and to measure the distance between each text's scores and the group centroid (from the training phase) for each L1 group. As mentioned earlier, each text was classified as representing the L1 whose centroid it was closest to. The final column of Table 2.3 shows that 37 (or 82.2%) of the 45 test-set texts in the first fold of the CV were classified correctly. In the second fold, the training set consisted of the 401 texts from partitions 1 and 3–10, whereas the test set was made up of the texts in partition 2. The number of features selected in the second partition was 40 out of the 53 features fed into the classifier, and the number of texts classified correctly by L1 background was 36 (or 80.0%) of the 45 texts in the test set.

Table 2.3 Summary of the results of each fold of the 10-fold CV

Fold	Texts in training set	Features selected	Texts in test set	Texts correctly classified
1	401	36	45	37 (82.2%)
2	401	40	45	36 (80.0%)
3	401	37	45	34 (75.6%)
4	401	34	45	37 (82.2%)
5	401	37	45	32 (71.1%)
6	401	39	45	32 (71.1%)
7	402	38	44	35 (79.5%)
8	402	36	44	28 (63.6%)
9	402	37	44	36 (81.8%)
10	402	37	44	36 (81.8%)

Table 2.4 L1 classification matrix (raw numbers)

Actual L1	Predicted L1				
	Danish	Finnish	Portuguese	Spanish	Swedish
Danish ($n = 60$)	**38**	7	1	1	13
Finnish ($n = 140$)	8	**93**	1	10	28
Portuguese ($n = 60$)	0	0	**50**	9	1
Spanish ($n = 116$)	1	1	6	**104**	4
Swedish ($n = 70$)	6	3	0	3	**58**

Across all folds, the mean number of features selected ranged from 34 to 40, with a mean of 37.1 and a median and mode of 37. Fortunately, the number of features selected never exceeded 10% of the number of texts in the training set. The percentage of test-set texts classified correctly ranged from 63.6% (fold 8) to 82.2% (fold 1). The total number of texts that were classified correctly across all 10 folds was 343 (out of 446), which represents an overall, cross-validated L1 classification accuracy of 76.9%. This is considerably and significantly higher than the chance level of 20% (df = 16, $n = 446$, $X^2 = 934.82$, $p < 0.001$; *Cohen's Kappa* = 0.705). It is also significantly and substantially higher than the baseline accuracy of 31.4% ($t[445] = 14.18$, $p < 0.001$), which is the accuracy that would be attained if all texts were classified as belonging to the largest L1 group (i.e. Finnish = 140 texts; 140/446 = 31.4%). A breakdown of the overall classification results by L1 background is given in Tables 2.4 and 2.5. Table 2.4 shows the raw numbers of texts from each L1 background that were predicted to have been written by speakers of any of the five L1s. The numbers of texts that were classified correctly for each L1 are highlighted in bold text. Table 2.5 shows the same information in the form of percentages.

The percentages in Table 2.5 show that the L1 classification accuracies for individual L1s ranged from 63.3% to 89.7%. The classification accuracies for texts written by Danish and Finnish speakers were roughly 65%, whereas the classification accuracies for the three remaining groups were well above

Table 2.5 L1 classification matrix (percentages)

Actual L1	Predicted L1				
	Danish	Finnish	Portuguese	Spanish	Swedish
Danish	**63.3**	11.7	1.7	1.7	21.7
Finnish	5.7	**66.4**	0.7	7.1	20.0
Portuguese	–	–	**83.3**	15.0	1.7
Spanish	0.9	0.9	5.2	**89.7**	3.4
Swedish	8.6	4.3	–	4.3	**82.9**

54 Approaching Language Transfer through Text Classification

Table 2.6 Number of folds in which each of the 53 features was selected

Feature	F	p	Folds
come	40.82	<0.001	10
bread	36.07	<0.001	10
the	28.46	<0.001	10
imagine	22.51	<0.001	9
Chaplin	21.79	<0.001	10
into	20.42	<0.001	10
out	19.96	<0.001	10
a	19.47	<0.001	10
away	16.45	<0.001	10
girl	16.17	<0.001	10
it	15.34	<0.001	10
Charlie	15.22	<0.001	10
do	13.08	<0.001	10
to	12.91	<0.001	10
when	12.74	<0.001	10
bus	11.08	<0.001	10
take	10.98	<0.001	9
there	10.86	<0.001	10
then	10.78	<0.001	10
man	9.71	<0.001	–
go	9.28	<0.001	4
police	9.25	<0.001	10
say	8.96	<0.001	–
he	8.62	<0.001	10
car	8.50	<0.001	9
that	8.06	<0.001	2
be	7.92	<0.001	10
with	7.24	<0.001	6
one	7.19	<0.001	6
woman	7.16	<0.001	10
of	7.01	<0.001	–
steal	6.30	<0.001	10
in	5.94	<0.001	9
tell	5.72	<0.001	8
policeman	5.63	<0.001	10
lady	5.54	<0.001	10

Feature	F	p	Folds
she	4.40	0.002	3
and	4.25	0.002	5
so	4.09	0.003	3
sit	3.72	0.005	10
get	3.18	0.014	9
down	3.08	0.016	10
run	2.82	0.025	2
see	2.75	0.028	–
have	2.57	0.037	10
for	2.25	0.063	–
who	1.97	0.098	10
but	1.91	0.108	2
up	1.75	0.138	4
eat	1.62	0.168	–
they	1.08	0.368	–
house	0.83	0.507	–
live	0.43	0.784	1

80%. As expected, misclassification occurred largely between related L1s. Misclassified texts written by Danes were misclassified mainly as having been written by Swedes and vice versa, and misclassified texts written by Portuguese speakers were mainly misclassified as having been written by Spanish speakers and vice versa. What was not expected was the relatively high number of texts written by Danes that were misclassified as having been written by Finns, and the even higher proportion of texts written by Finns that were misclassified as having been written by Swedes. Although Danish and Swedish are closely related to each other, Finnish is not related to either. Finnish is nevertheless linked to Danish and especially Swedish through geographical and cultural proximity, as well as through language contact and language-instruction practices in Finland. We will return to a discussion on the possible effects of these factors in the following section.

In the meantime, we wish to give some additional attention to the features that were included in the L1 classification model in each fold of the CV. As we showed in Table 2.3, the stepwise procedure did not select all 53 features in any fold of the CV, and it selected different numbers of features across folds. One question that immediately arises is how much consistency there was across folds concerning which features were selected. If the consistency was low, then we cannot be confident that we have captured a generalizable relationship between learners' word choices and L1 backgrounds, whereas a high level of consistency would be indicative of a generalizable relationship.

Following conventions similar to those adopted in Chapters 4 through 6 (see also Schulerud & Albregtsen, 2004), we assumed that any features selected in a majority of the folds of a CV are candidates for inclusion in a final solution, or optimal model. Table 2.6 lists the 53 features once again and in the same order they were presented in Table 2.2. The difference between the two tables is that Table 2.6 has an additional column showing the number of folds in which each feature was selected. As can be extrapolated from this table, there were 36 features that were selected in a majority of the folds, 34 of which were selected in at least eight folds, 33 in at least nine folds and 28 in all 10 folds. Depending on the rigidity of one's rationale for determining the final solution, any of these sets of features could be deemed to represent the optimal model for this particular L1 classification problem.

In the section 'Discussion', we will offer our own interpretations regarding the optimal set of features. In the meantime, we wish to draw the reader's attention to two additional patterns in Table 2.6 that are worth noting. The first is that eight of the 53 features were not selected in any of the folds of the CV. These features include the following words, given in the order in which they are listed in Table 2.6: *man, say, of, see, for, eat, they, house*. It is not particularly surprising that the last four of these features were not included in the DA model in any fold of the CV, given that the frequencies of occurrence of these words did not differ significantly across L1 groups. The other four features do differ significantly across groups, however, so their failure to be included in the L1 classification model in even one fold suggests that the distributions (or relative frequencies) of these words is collinear with – or reliably predictable on the basis of – other words already included in the model. Our second observation is similar: It is that a feature's F value is not a particularly strong indicator of its usefulness in a classification model. A Pearson bivariate correlation test shows only a moderate relationship ($r = 0.48$, $N = 53$, $p < 0.001$) between the F values in Table 2.6 and the number of times each feature was selected for inclusion in the L1 classification model across folds of the CV. This is once again presumably an outcome of the types of covariance and collinearity existing in the data, which prevent the stepwise procedure from selecting features that do not make a unique contribution to the model's ability to predict classes. This result is also consistent with the assumption in stylometric and classification research that what is crucial in relation to lexical styles – and patterns of language use more generally – is how features work in combination with one another, rather than how they work individually.

Discussion

The primary research question our study was designed to address was whether the DA classifier we used could create a model of the relationship between learners' lexical styles and their L1 backgrounds with sufficient precision as to predict the L1 backgrounds of new texts with high levels of reliability. In the present study, we operationalized lexical styles as feature vectors made up of 53 highly frequent words from our learner corpus, which included the 30 most frequent words used by each of our five L1 groups. Using 10-fold CV with embedded stepwise feature selection, we found that our classifier was able to create a model that successfully predicted the L1 backgrounds of 76.9% of the test-set texts it encountered. Moreover, it was able to achieve this level of accuracy without using all 53 of the words it was fed; in various folds of the CV, it created its L1 classification model using only 34–40 of these 53 features.

It is useful to compare these results against those of the only two other studies we are aware of that have conducted L1 classification analyses with exactly five L1 groups: Koppel *et al.* (2005) and Tsur and Rappoport (2007). Koppel *et al.* achieved a maximum L1 classification accuracy of 80% when feeding all 1035 features of various kinds (function words, letter combinations, POS combinations, error types) into their SVM classifier, and they achieved an L1 classification accuracy of 75% when feeding just the 400 function words into the classifier. Tsur and Rappoport evidently did not perform a combined analysis, but they reported an L1 classification accuracy of 67% when feeding 460 function words into their SVM classifier. Our L1 classification accuracy of 77% is substantially higher than that of Tsur and Rappoport but is very close to the accuracy rates reported by Koppel *et al.* Our results are nevertheless somewhat more remarkable than those of Koppel *et al.* in the sense that our L1 classification model consisted of far fewer features than theirs (i.e. less than 50 v. 400 or more). Some additional differences between our study and Koppel *et al.* are also worth elaborating on. First, the texts in the Koppel *et al.* study were mainly argumentative texts written in response to a range of prompts, whereas the texts in our study were all narrative descriptions of a single film. The greater range of content in the corpus used by Koppel *et al.* certainly constitutes a better test of the generalizability (across tasks and genres) of the observed L1-related patterns of L2 use. However, their corpus has the disadvantage that certain prompts were written about more by some L1 groups than by others (see Chapter 3), which may have confounded the effects of the L1 itself. Second, even though Koppel *et al.* reported that their texts all represented the same level of English proficiency, more recent evidence shows that this was not the case, and that L2 proficiency was also not evenly distributed across L1 groups (see Chapter 5). This likely facilitated the classifier's ability to predict the L1 backgrounds of L2 texts independently of any direct L1 influence. Finally, another important difference between the two studies is that the only word unigrams they fed into their classifier were function words, whereas we included both function words and content words, which we selected on the basis of frequency rather than on the basis of word class. This was motivated by the findings of authorship attribution research (e.g. Holmes, 1994; Holmes *et al.*, 2001; Stamatatos *et al.*, 2001), and it appears to have been successful.

One of the challenges of using 10-fold CV with embedded stepwise feature selection is that it has given us different sets of features for each fold of the CV. This makes it difficult to say with certainty what the optimal model is for the particular L1 classification task we are dealing with in this study. We mentioned in section 'Results' that the number of features selected in each fold ranged from 34 to 40, with a mean, median, and mode of approximately 37. We also reported that 28 features were selected in all 10 folds, 33 in at least nine folds, 34 in at least eight folds and 36 in at least six folds. Our own interpretation of the optimal model for this particular classification task rests on the assumption that the features included in the model need to work well together and should therefore be selected as a set rather than as separate features whose individual performance indicators look strong. Table 2.2, which was presented earlier, shows that the most successful models in the CV were the ones in fold 1 and fold 4, each of which correctly predicted the L1 backgrounds of 82.2% of the respective test-set texts. The model in fold 1 consisted of 36 features, whereas the model in fold 4 consisted of 34 features. After carefully examining which particular features were included in each of these models, we have chosen the model from fold 1 as the optimal model for the L1 classification task at hand. This model includes all 34 features that occur in at least eight folds of the CV (see Table 2.6), and additionally includes the words *go* and *she*. Although *go* and *she* were selected in only four and three folds, respectively, they were selected in a majority (i.e. three) of the five models whose L1 classification accuracies were higher than 80%. In fact, there were exactly 37 features that were selected in a majority of the most successful models – the 36 already accounted for in our proposed optimal model, as well as the word *with*. For reasons of parsimony, it might be useful to include *with* in the optimal model, but the results of our analysis do not indicate that this feature would make a unique contribution to the model beyond the contributions of the other 36 features. We prefer the model from fold 1 over the model from fold 4 because the former includes all 34 features that were selected in at least eight folds – whereas the latter includes only 31 of these (i.e. all but *take*, *tell* and *get*) – and because the former is closer to the mean number of features selected across all 10 folds.

In order to examine more closely how the 36 features in our optimal model made it possible to identify learners' L1s with such a high level of success, we ran a series of Student–Newman–Keuls (SNK) post-hoc tests. Whereas the ANOVA results we reported in Tables 2.2 and 2.6 indicated that the use of each of these 36 words differed significantly across the means of our five L1 groups, they did not show which specific groups were significantly different from others. This is where the SNK tests were useful, as they produced homogeneity subsets that indicate where significant divisions exist between L1 groups. It is somewhat difficult to interpret the SNK results for 18 of these words due to the fact that the SNK tests placed all L1 groups into a single subset for three words (i.e. *down, sit* and *who*) and created overlapping subsets for 15 other words (i.e. *car, Charlie, get, have, he, in, it, lady, out, she, steal, take, tell, to, when*). However, the SNK results for the remaining 18 words are unambiguous and very telling about how these words contribute to the L1 classification model. A summary of the SNK results for these 18 words is given in Table 2.7. For example, for the word *a*, the table shows that the texts written by Finnish speakers had a significantly lower mean relative frequency for the use of this word than did the texts written by Portuguese speakers. The texts written by Portuguese speakers, in turn, had a significantly lower mean use of *a* than did the texts written by Swedish, Spanish and Danish speakers, but there was no significant difference among these latter three groups. Thus, there are three homogeneity subsets for this word. The first subset includes only the Finnish speakers, the second subset only the Portuguese speakers, and the third subset all the remaining groups.

The results summarized in Table 2.7 show quite clearly how these features work in complementary combination as indicators of specific L1 backgrounds. For example, the Finnish speakers are clearly separated from the

Table 2.7 SNK homogeneity results for 18 words with clear subset divisions

Feature	SNK Homogeneity Subsets
a	Finnish<Portuguese<Swedish, Spanish, Danish
away	Spanish, Portuguese<Danish, Swedish, Finnish
be	Finnish<Spanish, Swedish, Danish, Portuguese
bread	Portuguese<Danish, Swedish<Spanish, Finnish
bus	Danish, Finnish, Swedish<Portuguese, Spanish
Chaplin	Spanish, Danish, Portuguese, Swedish<Finnish
come	Portuguese, Spanish<Finnish, Swedish, Danish
do	Danish, Swedish<Portuguese, Spanish, Finnish
girl	Portuguese<Spanish<Swedish, Danish, Finnish
go	Portuguese, Swedish, Danish, Spanish<Finnish
imagine	Danish, Finnish, Swedish<Portuguese, Spanish
into	Portuguese, Finnish, Spanish<Swedish<Danish
police	Swedish, Danish, Finnish<Portuguese, Spanish
policeman	Spanish<Swedish, Portuguese, Danish, Finnish
the	Finnish<Swedish, Danish<Portuguese, Spanish
then	Portuguese<Danish, Swedish<Spanish, Finnish
there	Portuguese, Spanish<Finnish, Swedish<Danish
woman	Danish, Swedish, Finnish, Spanish<Portuguese

other groups by their use of the words *a, be, Chaplin, go* and *the*. The word *a* also helps separate the Portuguese speakers from the other groups, but the other words that isolate the Portuguese speakers from the other groups are different from the ones that isolate the Finns. They include the words *bread, girl, then* and *woman*. The Spanish speakers, on the other hand, are best distinguished by their use of the words *girl* and *policeman*, whereas the Danes are distinguished by their use of the words *into* and *there*, and the Swedes are isolated simply by their use of the word *into*. Given the relatively high number of clear L1 markers for the Finns and the low number for the Swedes, it may seem surprising that the texts written by Swedish speakers were identified with substantially higher accuracy than the texts written by Finnish speakers (see Table 2.5). However, it is important to recognize that the classifier makes use of all available information when classifying a text, and that all of this information together is fairly reliable in determining not only which class a text probably belongs to but also which classes it probably does not belong to.

The complementary nature of the features included in the classification model can also be seen in another respect: learners' high use of one word often entails a low use of other words. We see in Table 2.7, for example, that the Spanish speakers have the highest use of the word *police* and the lowest use of the word *policeman* – two words that are largely in complementary distribution. Similarly, the Portuguese speakers show the lowest use of *girl* and the highest use of *woman*. Of course, complementarity effects also go beyond the list of words shown in the table. For example, the proper noun *Chaplin*, which is shown in Table 2.7, is to a large degree in complementary distribution with the pronoun *he*, which is not shown in the table; it is interesting to note that the Finnish speakers show the highest use of *Chaplin* and the lowest use of *he*, a point we return to in the following paragraph.

A crucial question is whether these L1-specific word choice patterns are due to direct L1 influence, or whether they might more simply reflect differences in the L1 groups' cultural and educational backgrounds. A fully adequate answer to this question would require us to submit each of the words in our 36-feature model to a series of in-depth, comparison-based analyses of the types described in Chapter 1 (see also Jarvis, 2000, 2010). For reasons of space, we will reserve those analyses for future research, but in the meantime we offer a few observations that suggest that direct L1 effects are indeed quite prevalent in our results. Beginning with the finding that the Finnish speakers show the highest use of *Chaplin* and the lowest use of *he*, it is also true that the Finnish speakers also show the highest use of *girl* and the lowest use of *she*. These patterns quite possibly reflect the fact that Finnish does not have separate pronouns for *he* and *she*, but rather uses a single pronoun (i.e. *hän*) to refer to both. Although this needs to be confirmed empirically, it seems that the ambiguity of this pronoun makes it necessary for Finnish speakers to resort to the use of referential nouns more often in their L1, and this tendency also seems to carry over into their use of an L2. Of the five L1s included in the present study, Finnish is the only one that lacks pronominal gender, and this seems to account quite well for the fact that the Finnish speakers show the lowest use of *he* and *she*.

An even clearer, direct effect of L1 Finnish on the present results is seen in the fact that the Finnish speakers use *a* and *the* significantly less frequently than any of the other groups (see Table 2.7). Finnish lacks articles altogether as a grammatical class, and one of the consequences of this is that they frequently omit articles in the L2 (see e.g. Jarvis, 2002). All four of the other L1s included in the present study have both indefinite and definite articles, but the definite articles in Portuguese and Spanish have a much wider distribution than those in Danish and Swedish (which are more similar to English). These facts about the learners' L1s account well for the patterns seen in their use of L2 English *the*: the Finnish speakers use *the* significantly less frequently than the Swedish and Danish speakers, who in turn use this word significantly less frequently than the Portuguese and Spanish speakers.

Other words in our model whose L1 effects are quite transparent include *away* and *come*, which were used significantly less frequently by the Portuguese and Spanish speakers than by the Danish, Finnish and Swedish speakers. Concerning *away*, this word occurs most frequently in our data in the collocation *run away*, which is used in reference to several scenes, such as the following:

(1) Bread theft scene: *Girl stole a bread and run away.* (f5-62, Finn, Grade 5).
(2) Paddy wagon wreck scene: The policeman, lady and the man fell out of the car. The lady and the man run away. (d6-07, Dane, Grade 6).
(3) Closing scene: Then a policeman comes and they runs away from the place they sat on. (s7-48, Swede, Grade 7).

The use of the phrasal verb *run away* is common in all these contexts in the narratives written by the Danes, Finns and Swedes. Its connection with the L1 is particularly salient in the case of the Danes and Swedes, whose L1 has a direct counterpart (Danish=*løbe væk*; Swedish=*springa iväg*). The connection with Finnish is a little less clear because Finnish offers so many competing options for expressing the notion of running away. While collecting the L2 data from Finnish and Swedish speakers in Finland, we recruited a number of participants to perform the same writing task in their L1 (see Jarvis, 2000). The narratives written by the Swedish speakers confirm the overwhelming preference for *springa iväg* (=run away) in the relevant contexts, whereas the narratives written by the Finnish speakers show three highly common patterns: *karata* (=flee), *lähteä karkuun* (lit., leave into fleeing/flight), and *lähteä pois* (=leave away). The third of these options is closest to *run away*, and the literal counterpart of run away (*juosta pois*) was also used by a few Finns who performed the task in their L1 (e.g. *Mies lähtee ja he juoksevat pois*='The man leaves and they run away'; produced by fw-14, a Finnish 5th grader). Evidence that this L1 expression had an influence on the Finnish speakers' choice of *away* in English can be seen in the sentence *Then she run **pois**, but she hit to Charlie Chaplin*, produced by a Finnish-speaking fifth grader (f5-43) who evidently did not know the word *away*, and substituted it with the L1 equivalent *pois* (=away).

While examining the narratives produced by Portuguese and Spanish speakers, we noted that *run away* was used relatively rarely, and that the singleton verbs *run* and *escape* were frequently used in the same contexts where the Danes, Finns and Swedes used *run away*. The high occurrence of *escape* was particularly striking, and was most likely motivated by the cognate *escapar* (=escape), which exists in both Portuguese and Spanish. Indeed, in L1 Spanish narratives we collected in Mexico, we noted an overwhelming preference for *escapar* in precisely the same contexts.

In the case of *come*, the participants' use and nonuse of this verb also seem to reflect straightforward influence from their L1s. Finns' and Swedes' high use of *come* in their English narratives was directly paralleled by a high use of the corresponding verbs (Finnish = *tulla*; Swedish = *komma*) in the same contexts in the L1 Finnish and L1 Swedish samples. The Spanish and Portuguese speakers showed a low use of *come* but a high use of *arrive* in the same contexts, which was paralleled by a high use of *llegar* (arrive) in these contexts in the L1 Spanish samples. Although a full, detailed comparison-based examination of the effects of L1 influence on the participants' use of each of the 36 words in our L1 classification model will require a separate study, the evidence we have discussed so far leaves little doubt in our minds that the successful L1 classification accuracy achieved by the DA classifier in this study was indeed largely due to its detection of L1 influence.

Finally, returning to questions raised earlier about patterns of misclassification, we pointed out in our Results section that when texts were misclassified, they were misclassified primarily as having been written by speakers of closely related L1s (see Table 2.5). However, we also noted that a surprisingly high proportion (11.7%) of the texts written by Danes were misclassified as having been written by Finns, and an even higher proportion (20.0%) of the texts written by Finns were misclassified as having been written by Swedes. In order to understand these results better, we have provided a finer-grained breakdown of the classification results for Danes in Table 2.8, and

Table 2.8 Breakdown of the classification of texts written by Danes (percentages)

Actual group	Predicted L1				
	Danish	Finnish	Portug.	Spanish	Swedish
Danish, Grade 6, Eng 3 years	**69.2**	3.8	3.8	3.8	19.2
Danish, Grade 8, Eng 5 years	**58.8**	17.6	0.0	0.0	23.5

Table 2.9 Breakdown of the classification of texts written by Finns (percentages)

	Predicted L1				
Actual group	Danish	Finnish	Portug.	Spanish	Swedish
Finnish, Grade 5, Eng 2 years, Sw 0 years	5.7	**77.1**	2.9	8.6	5.7
Finnish, Grade 7, Eng 4 years, Sw <1 year	2.9	**68.6**	0.0	11.4	17.1
Finnish, Grade 9, Eng 6 years, Sw 2 years	5.7	**71.4**	0.0	2.9	20.0
Finnish, Grade 9, Eng 2 years, Sw 6 years	8.6	**48.6**	0.0	5.7	37.1

for Finns in Table 2.9. In these tables, the participants are divided into subgroups according to their grade levels and years of English instruction. Table 2.9 also shows the number of years each subgroup of Finnish speakers had studied Swedish, if at all. The percentages of texts classified correctly by L1 background are highlighted in bold.

The main point of interest regarding the misclassification of texts written by Danish speakers is that the vast majority of the texts incorrectly predicted to have been written by Finns were produced by eighth graders. While examining the eight specific texts written by eighth-grade Danes that were incorrectly associated with Finns, we found that two of these were simply lists rather than prose, such as the following text produced by participant d0-24.

girl
man
policeman
car
food
bread
house
policeman
cow
man
girl
milk
girl is hungry

Two other texts written by Danish eighth graders that were misclassified as having been written by Finns were exceedingly short (<62 words), and yet another was largely a critique of the film rather than a description of it. It appears that these texts were misclassified as having been written by Finns either because of their low use of articles, such as in the texts that were written as lists, or because of the relatively low use and small range of function words found therein. These factors do not seem to have much to do with the effects of L1, culture or education, but rather seem to indicate that the Danish participants who produced these texts either did not understand the task correctly or did not have the required L2 proficiency to complete it successfully. Concerning the latter possibility, the Danish eighth graders' teacher in fact reported to us that he had a couple of students with very low proficiency whom he instructed simply to write down individual words so that they could still participate in the task even if they could not write a coherent English narrative.

The misclassification of texts written by Finnish speakers as having been written by Swedish speakers, on the other hand, seems to have a different explanation. In Table 2.9, we see that the percentage of texts misclassified as having been written by Swedes increases steadily in accordance with the number of years the Finns have studied Swedish. While examining the English narratives produced by Finnish speakers, we noted that certain words, such as *a, into* and *the* – which are significantly more frequently used by Swedes than by Finns – become steadily more frequent in accordance with years of Swedish instruction and less so in accordance with years of English instruction. Similar findings have been reported by Jarvis (2002), Odlin and Jarvis (2004) and especially Ringbom (1987, 2007), which strongly suggests that our classification results have been affected not just by L1 influence, but also by L2 influence. L1 influence enhanced our L1 classification accuracy, of course, whereas L2 influence appears to have degraded it. Interestingly, L2 influence appears to play a major role only when the L2 is closely related to the target language (see Ringbom, 1987, 2007), as can be seen in the fact that the texts written by Swedish speakers in the present study – all of whom had studied Finnish longer than English – were relatively rarely misclassified as having been written by Finns (see Table 2.5).

Conclusion

The present study has shown that a machine-learning algorithm is capable of learning to predict the L1 associations of L2 texts with high levels of accuracy on the basis of the lexical styles found therein. Our study has furthermore shown that high levels of L1 classification accuracy are achievable even when (1) lexical styles are characterized in relation to only a few dozen highly frequent words; (2) there are five L1 backgrounds to choose from; (3) some of the L1s are very closely related to each other; and (4) the levels of L2 proficiency vary widely within each L1 group. These results suggest that learners'

L2 word choice tendencies contain constellations of several, relatively frequent and functionally complementary words – both function words and content words – whose patterns of use are predictably L1-related. In the present study, we operationalized learners' lexical styles as consisting of 53 words, and we interpreted the results as showing that 36 of these words are predictably L1 related, not just individually, but more importantly, collectively. In our discussion on the results, we presented evidence that strongly suggests that the differences in the use of a number of these words are indeed due to direct L1 influence. Although we also presented evidence that suggests that L2 influence is at play, and additionally pointed out some effects that are presumably not the result of crosslinguistic influence at all, our overall conclusion is that, in the L1 classification task we focused on in the present study, the high levels of L1 classification success we achieved are most likely mainly due to the successful detection of L1 influence. Even though in some ways this is only the beginning of the story regarding the quality and quantity of L1 influence in our data, we find that the detection-based approach has led us to a very clear, well-structured and well-delimited set of features whose crosslinguistic effects can be examined at a finer level of scrutiny in follow-up work relying on comparison-based analyses.

Possibilities for fruitful future research in this area are manifold. Here, we will mention just a few of the more crucial issues that need to be resolved. One has to do with the potential for classifiers to learn to discriminate among more than five L1 backgrounds. In light of the existence of hundreds and even thousands of L1s on the planet, one wonders how far this methodology can be taken while still achieving high levels of L1 classification accuracy. It seems doubtful that a set of just 36 words would be predictive enough to distinguish among, say, 100 L1 backgrounds with satisfactory results. But, are high levels of L1 classification accuracy achievable at all with so many L1 backgrounds, and if so, what is the optimal number of features? Similarly, what is the optimal set of features regardless of how many L1 backgrounds are involved? In the present study, we relied on the stepwise procedure to determine the optimal set of features in each fold of our cross-validation. One problem with the stepwise procedure, however, is that the results depend heavily on which feature is selected first. It would be useful in future studies to compare all possible combinations of features, and if this is not possible, to force the stepwise procedure to allow each feature its own turn to be selected first and to see what types of models ensue. It would also be valuable in future research to look more closely at how words work in combination with one another, and how these combinations might reflect crosslinguistic influence. There is of course also a need for L1 classification studies that examine the usefulness of other types of features – including word n-grams, error categories and various types of textual indices – not only in narratives, but also in other types of writing tasks, as well. Fortunately, the remaining chapters of this book do just this.

References

Alpaydin, E. (2004) *Introduction to Machine Learning*. Cambridge, MA: MIT Press.
Baayen, R.H. (2008) *Analyzing Linguistic Data: A Practical Introduction to Statistics Using R*. Cambridge: Cambridge University Press.
Burns, R.B. and Burns, R.A. (2008) *Business Research Methods and Statistics Using SPSS*. London: Sage.
Crossley, S.A., Salsbury, T. and McNamara, D.S. (2009) Measuring L2 lexical growth using hypernymic relationships. *Language Learning* 59, 307–334.
Dagut, M. and Laufer, B. (1985) Avoidance of phrasal verbs – A case for contrastive analysis. *Studies in Second Language Acquisition* 7, 73–79.
De Bot, K. (2004) The multilingual lexicon: Modelling selection and control. *The International Journal of Multilingualism* 1, 17–32.
Dewaele, J-M. (1998) Lexical inventions: French interlanguage as L2 versus L3. *Applied Linguistics* 19, 471–490.
Downing, P. (1980) Factors influencing lexical choice in narrative. In W.L. Chafe (ed.) *The Pear Stories: Cognitive, Cultural, and Linguistic Aspects of Narrative Production* (pp. 89–126). Norwood, NJ: Ablex.
Ecke, P. (2001) Lexical retrieval in a third language: Evidence from errors and tip-of-the-tongue states. In J. Cenoz, B. Hufeisen and U. Jessner (eds) *Cross-Linguistic Influence in Third Language Acquisition: Psycholinguistic Perspectives* (pp. 90–114). Clevedon: Multilingual Matters.
Ellis, N.C. (2002) Frequency effects in language processing. *Studies in Second Language Acquisition* 24, 143–188.
Ellis, N.C. (2004) Frequency and the emergence of linguistic structure (Book review). *Studies in Second Language Acquisition* 26, 618–621.
Ellis, N.C. (2006) Selective attention and transfer phenomena in L2 acquisition: Contingency, cue competition, salience, interference, overshadowing, blocking, and perceptual learning. *Applied Linguistics* 27, 164–194.
Estival, D., Gaustad, T., Pham, S.B., Radford, W. and Hutchinson, B. (2007) Author profiling for English emails. *Proceedings of the 10th Conference of the Pacific Association for Computational Linguistics (PACLING 2007)* (pp. 31–39). Melbourne, Australia.
Field, A. (2005) *Discovering Statistics Using SPSS*. London: Sage Publications.
Graham, R. and Belnap, K. (1986) The acquisition of lexical boundaries in English by native speakers of Spanish. *International Review of Applied Linguistics in Language Teaching* 24, 275–286.
Green, D. (1998) Mental control of the bilingual lexico-semantic system. *Bilingualism: Language and Cognition* 1, 67–81.
Hasselgren, A. (1994) Lexical teddy bears and advanced learners: A study into the ways Norwegian students cope with English vocabulary. *International Journal of Applied Linguistics* 4, 237–260.
Helms-Park, R. (2001) Evidence of lexical transfer in learner syntax: The acquisition of English causatives by speakers of Hindi–Urdu and Vietnamese. *Studies in Second Language Acquisition* 23, 71–102.
Hiki, K. (1995) An exploratory study into second language learner knowledge of semantically similar lexical items: The case of verbs of perception. PhD thesis, Indiana University.
Hohenstein, J., Eisenberg, A. and Naigles, L. (2006) Is he floating across or crossing afloat? Cross-influence of L1 and L2 in Spanish–English bilingual adults. *Bilingualism: Language and Cognition* 9, 249–261.
Holmes, D.I. (1994) Authorship attribution. *Computers and the Humanities* 28, 87–106.
Holmes, D.I. (1998) The evolution of stylometry in humanities scholarship. *Literary and Linguistic Computing* 13, 111–117.

Holmes, D.I., Gordon, L.J. and Wilson, C. (2001) A widow and her soldier: Stylometry and the American Civil War. *Literary and Linguistic Computing* 16, 403–420.
Hoover, D.L. (2003) Another perspective on vocabulary richness. *Computers and the Humanities* 37, 151–178.
Ijaz, I.H. (1986) Linguistic and cognitive determinants of lexical acquisition in a second language. *Language Learning* 36, 401–451.
Ioup, G. (1984) Is there a structural foreign accent? A comparison of syntactic and phonological errors in second language acquisition. *Language Learning* 34, 1–17.
Jarvis, S. (1998) *Conceptual Transfer in the Interlingual Lexicon*. Bloomington, IN: Indiana University Linguistics Club Publications.
Jarvis, S. (2000) Methodological rigor in the study of transfer: Identifying L1 influence in the interlanguage lexicon. *Language Learning* 50, 245–309.
Jarvis, S. (2002) Topic continuity in L2 English article use. *Studies in Second Language Acquisition* 24, 387–418.
Jarvis, S. and Odlin, T. (2000) Morphological type, spatial reference, and language transfer. *Studies in Second Language Acquisition* 22, 535–556.
Jarvis, S., Castañeda-Jiménez, G. and Nielsen, R. (2004) Investigating L1 lexical transfer through learners' wordprints. Paper presented at the Second Language Research Forum (SLRF) 2004, State College, PA.
Jarvis, S. (2010) Comparison-based and detection-based approaches to transfer research. In L. Roberts, M. Howard, M. Ó Laoire and D. Singleton (eds) *EUROSLA Yearbook 10* (pp. 169–192). Amsterdam: John Benjamins.
Jarvis, S. (2011a) Conceptual transfer: Crosslinguistic effects in categorization and construal. *Bilingualism: Language and Cognition* 14, 1–8.
Jarvis, S. (2011b) Data mining with learner corpora: Choosing classifiers for L1 detection. In F. Meunier, S. De Cock, G. Gilquinand, M. Paquot (eds) *A Taste for Corpora. Honour of Sylviane Granger* (pp. 131–158). Amsterdam: John Benjamins.
Koppel, M., Schler, J. and Zigdon, K. (2005) Determining an author's native language by mining a text for errors. In *Proceedings of the Eleventh ACM SIGKDD International Conference on Knowledge Discovery in Data Mining* (pp. 624–628). Chicago: Association for Computing Machinery.
Kotsiantis, S. (2007) Supervised machine learning: A review of classification techniques. *Informatica Journal* 31, 249–268.
Lecocke, M. and Hess, K. (2006) An empirical study of univariate and genetic algorithm-based feature selection in binary classification with microarray data. *Cancer Informatics* 2, 313–327.
Lado, R. (1957) *Linguistics Across Cultures*. Ann Arbor, MI: University of Michigan Press.
Lakoff, G. (1987) *Women, Fire, and Dangerous Things: What Categories Reveal about the Mind*. Chicago: University of Chicago Press.
Laufer, B. and Eliasson, S. (1993) What causes avoidance in L2 learning: L1-L2 differences, L1-L2 similarity, or L2 complexity? *Studies in Second Language Acquisition* 15, 35–48.
Liu, J.Y., Zhuang, D.F., Luo, D. and Xiao, X. (2003) Land-cover classification of China: Integrated analysis of AVHRR imagery and geophysical data. *International Journal of Remote Sensing* 24, 2485–2500.
Master, P. (1997) The English article system: Acquisition, function, and pedagogy. *System* 25, 215–232.
Mayfield Tomokiyo, L. and Jones, R. (2001) You're not from 'round here, are you? Naive Bayes detection of non-native utterance text. In *Proceedings of the Second Meeting of the North American Chapter of the Association for Computational Linguistics (NAACL '01)*, unpaginated electronic document. Cambridge, MA: The Association for Computational Linguistics.
McLachlan, G.J. (2004) *Discriminant Analysis and Statistical Pattern Recognition*. Hoboken, NJ: Wiley.

Molinaro, A.M., Simon, R. and Pfeiffer, R.M. (2005) Prediction error estimation: A comparison of resampling methods. *Bioinformatics* 21, 3301–3307.

Nilsson, P.-O. (2006) A multidimensional perspective on collocational patterning in Swedish fiction texts translated from English. *Literary and Linguistic Computing* 21, 113–126.

Odlin, T. (1996) On the recognition of transfer errors. *Language Awareness* 5, 166–178.

Odlin, T. and Jarvis, S. (2004) Same source, different outcomes: A study of Swedish influence on the acquisition of English in Finland. *International Journal of Multilingualism* 1, 123–140.

Paquot, M. (2007) EAP vocabulary in EFL learner writing: From extraction to analysis: A phraseology-oriented approach. PhD thesis, Université catholique de Louvain, Centre for English Corpus Linguistics.

Paquot, M. (2008) Exemplification in learner writing: A cross-linguistic perspective. In F. Meunier and S. Granger (eds) *Phraseology in Foreign Language Learning and Teaching* (pp. 101–119). Amsterdam: Benjamins.

Pavlenko, A. (1997) Bilingualism and cognition. PhD thesis, Cornell University.

Pavlenko, A. and Driagina, V. (2007) Russian emotion vocabulary in American learners' narratives. *Modern Language Journal* 91, 213–234.

Pavlenko, A. and Malt, B.C. (2011) Kitchen Russian: Cross-linguistic differences and first-language object naming by Russian–English bilinguals. *Bilingualism: Language and Cognition* 14, 19–46.

Poulisse, N. (1999) *Slips of the Tongue: Speech Errors in First and Second Language Production*. Amsterdam: Benjamins.

Ringbom, H. (1987) *The Role of the First Language in Foreign Language Learning*. Clevedon: Multilingual Matters.

Ringbom, H. (1998) Vocabulary frequencies in advanced learner English: A crosslinguistic approach. In S. Granger (ed.) *Learner English on Computer* (pp. 41–52). London: Longman.

Ringbom, H. (2001) Lexical transfer in L3 production. In J. Cenoz, B. Hufeisen and U. Jessner (eds) *Cross-Linguistic Influence in Third Language Acquisition: Psycholinguistic Perspectives* (pp. 59–68). Clevedon: Multilingual Matters.

Ringbom, H. (2007) *Cross-Linguistic Similarity in Foreign Language Learning*. Clevedon: Multilingual Matters.

Schachter, J. (1974) An error in error analysis. *Language Learning* 24, 205–214.

Schulerud, H. and Albregtsen, F. (2004) Many are called, but few are chosen: Feature selection and error estimation in high dimensional spaces. *Computer Methods and Programs in Biomedicine* 73, 91–99.

Schumann, J. (1986) Locative and directional expressions in basilang speech. *Language Learning* 36, 277–294.

Sebastiani, F. (2002) Machine learning in automated text categorization. *ACM Computing Surveys* 34, 1–47.

Shen, C., Breen, T.E., Dobrolecki, L.E., Schmidt, C.M., Sledge, G.W., Miller, K.D. and Hickey, R.J. (2007) Comparison of computational algorithms for the classification of liver cancer using SELDI mass spectrometry: A case study. *Cancer Informatics* 3, 329–339.

Sjöholm, K. (1995) *The Influence of Crosslinguistic, Semantic, and Input Factors on the Acquisition of English Phrasal Verbs: A Comparison between Finnish and Swedish Learners at an Intermediate and Advanced Level*. Åbo, Finland: Åbo Akademi University Press.

Slobin, D. (1996) From 'thought and language' to 'thinking for speaking'. In J. Gumperz and S. Levinson (eds) *Rethinking Linguistic Relativity* (pp. 70–96). Cambridge: Cambridge University Press.

Stamatatos, E., Fakotakis, N. and Kokkinakis, G. (2000) Automatic text categorization in terms of genre and author. *Computational Linguistics* 26, 461–485.

Stamatatos, E., Fakotakis, N. and Kokkinakis, G. (2001) Computer-based authorship attribution without lexical measures. *Computers and Humanities* 35, 193–214.
Strick, G.J. (1980) A hypothesis for semantic development in a second language. *Language Learning* 30, 155–176.
Tsur, O. and Rappoport, A. (2007) Using classifier features for studying the effect of native language on the choice of written second language words. In *Proceedings of the Workshop on Cognitive Aspects of Computational Language Acquisition* (pp. 9–16). Cambridge, MA: The Association for Computational Linguistics.
von Stutterheim, C. and Nüse, R. (2003) Processes of conceptualization in language production: Language specific perspectives and event construal. *Linguistics* 41, 851–881.
Williams, S. and Hammarberg, B. (1998) Language switches in L3 production: Implications for a polyglot speaking model. *Applied Linguistics* 19, 295–333.
Wong, S-M.J. and Dras, M. (2009) Contrastive analysis and native language identification. In *Proceedings of the Australasian Language Technology Association* (pp. 53–61). Cambridge, MA: The Association for Computational Linguistics.
Youmans, G. (1990) Measuring lexical style and competence: The type-token vocabulary curve. *Style* 24, 584–599.
Young, R. (1996) Form–function relations in articles in English interlanguage. In R. Bayley and D. Preston (eds) *Second Language Acquisition and Linguistic Variation* (pp. 135–175). Amsterdam: Benjamins.

Appendix

Sample texts

Text written by a Danish-speaking 6th grader (D621) with three years of English instruction

It begins with a woman that steals a bread and runs into a man. The baker comes with some policemen. The man gets into a restaurant, gets food, eats it and ends in a police car. The man and the woman gets out and the movie has a happy ending. The man and the woman sits on some grass. Then they talk a little bit. Then there a little cut-in where they live in a house with a cow. Then there comes a policeman.

Text written by a Finnish-speaking 7th grader (FB09) with four years of English instruction

The girl stole a bread, but police caught her. Chaplin said that he is stole a bread. They believe first, but then the woman said 'It was the girl not the man.' And then they caugh the girl. Chaplin went to eat and taked two foods and didn't pay. The policeman took he to the car. The girl came too to the car. They both escaped. They went to sit under the tree. And imagine their own home. The policeman came and they left.

Text written by a Swedish-speaking 7th grader (SA28) with two years of English instruction

It was outside the bakery and a women steal a bread from the car. She run along the street and craschked with a man. Another women saw when he took it and tell it. They run after her and a policeman come. They took the man and went away. The second women tell at it was the women it was not the man. They run after the policeman and the second man and tell it. They took the women and the man in a policecar with some other people. The car crashing with another and the man and the women run away together along the street. A man and a girl sitting under a tree and the girl tell to him at she have not a home. She live everywhere. They went into a house and the girl make something to eat.

Text written by a Spanish-speaking 7th grader (S709MA) with three years of English instruction

The story starts when a girl see a bread's store and stole a bread, a woman see this and she said to the man. The girl run and crash with a man and the police goes but the mans said that he stole the bread but next the woman and the man went to the police and said that the girl stole the bread. When the man learn he goes to the caffetery and bougth much food but not give money and the police take her, when was in the police's car the girl too was here and the two jumped with the police out of the car and they runs. They sit in the grass and the mand question that if she can live in a house because she was a poor women and said yes next they goes because the police was here.

Text written by a Portuguese-speaking 8th grader (P710) with five years of English instruction

Charles is a man without a family and one day he's walking at the street and a woman fall on him cause se's running because she steal a bread from the car of the bakery, and a oldwoman see it and call the bakeryman and he and the policeman catch the woman that is with Charles, and say it was him who stole the bread, but the old woman say it wasn't him and that it was the woman, so the police take the woman. After it, Charles get in a cafeteria, eat a lot of thinks, call the policeman that is passing on the street and say that he's not going to pay the woman of the cafeteria, so the police man take him, and while the policeman is calling, Charles give many thinks to a kid and don't pay for him. When he get in the police car he sit and suddenly the woman of the bread get in there and they run away of the police and sit in the garden of house and stay there, talking and imaging how would be their future together, and he say he's going to buy them a house, even if he have to work for it, then a policeman appeared and they just go walking together by the street.

3 Exploring the Role of *n*-Grams in L1 Identification

Scott Jarvis and Magali Paquot

Introduction

Chapter 2 showed that relatively high levels of L1 classification accuracy can be achieved under the following conditions:

(1) Five L1 groups, some of which are closely related to each other.
(2) The learners within each group vary widely in terms of L2 proficiency.
(3) The texts are all written narrative descriptions of a silent film.
(4) The features (i.e. variables) used by the classifier include a few dozen highly frequent words.

Conditions (1) and (2) were intended to make the detection task challenging for the classifier in order to investigate how sensitive the classifier is to even subtle between-group differences in learners' language-use patterns, and simultaneously to gather possible evidence of L1 effects that may tend to evade conscious awareness but are nevertheless reliable enough – even across proficiency levels – to be detected by a computer-based classifier. Condition (3) represented a control variable whose purpose was to limit the range of variation in the data to that which could be attributed to proficiency differences (within-group) and L1 differences (between-group). This was done to enhance the clarity of interpretations that could be made on the basis of the results – to show whether certain L1-related tendencies are reliable enough such that they are detectable even when proficiency differences within L1 groups are greater than differences between groups. Finally, condition (4) represented the wealth of resources that were made available to the classifier. In order to test the reliability of L1 lexical effects as well as the strength, sensitivity, and practicality of the classifier, the pool of features made available to the classifier was intentionally restricted to just 53 of the most frequent words in the data. The stepwise feature-selection parameters were further set in such a way as to allow the classifier to build its L1 prediction model using no more than 40 of the 53 features that were made available to it. This was done for purposes of adhering to the convention of restricting the number of variables to no more than 10% of the number of cases.

The purpose of the present study is to vary these conditions in a way that will allow us to gain further insights into the usefulness of the classifier and the nature and reliability of L1-related lexical patterns that might be found in the data. We do this, first, by increasing the difficulty of the detection task in relation to conditions (1) and (3) – by increasing the number of L1 groups to 12 and by using essays with a greater range of content variation (argumentative essays written in response to a variety of open-ended prompts). At the same time, for reasons of interpretational clarity, we reduce the amount of variation related to condition (2) by choosing texts that were written by learners at an overall more advanced level of English proficiency, and which all meet a certain length criterion (i.e. 500–1000 words). Because the increased difficulty of the detection task can be expected to greatly reduce the L1 classification accuracy of the classifier, we attempt to compensate for this by bolstering condition (4) through the use of a larger pool of features (which also requires a larger number of cases)[1] and by expanding the features to include not just individual words (i.e. unigrams or 1-grams) but also multi-word sequences (i.e. *n*-grams). Our purpose in this study, in other words, is to make the detection task more difficult while simultaneously attempting to make the classifier more powerful, or more sensitive to subtle L1-related patterns. The main focus of the present chapter is the potential benefit of *n*-grams in combination with 1-grams in the detection of learners' L1 backgrounds.

The research questions that guide the present study are:

(1) Do 1-grams remain effective discriminators of learners' L1 backgrounds even when (a) the number of L1 groups is increased substantially beyond five, (b) the texts are longer and reflect somewhat higher levels of proficiency and (c) the texts represent a range of open-ended argumentative topics rather than involving controlled narratives?
(2) Are *n*-grams of other lengths (i.e. 2-, 3- and 4-grams) equally or even more effective discriminators of learners' L1 backgrounds than 1-grams are?
(3) Is L1 classification most effective through the use of a combination of *n*-grams of differing lengths (from 1- to 4-grams)?

Background

One way of characterizing a language variety, such as a dialect or register, is to create a profile of the relative frequencies with which specific words and word categories (e.g. nouns, verbs) are used within that variety. This method has been used in previous studies to identify the distinctive features of spoken English (Leech *et al.*, 2001), academic English (Coxhead, 2000), and American English (Davies & Gardner, 2010). Recent studies have shown that text types and genres can also be characterized by their use of more intricate lexical and grammatical patterns, which are often captured through *n*-gram analyses. Crossley and Louwerse (2007), for example, found that certain sets of 2-grams (e.g. *don't know, you know, I don't, I know, to do, that I, I mean, but I, that was, and I, a lot*) are useful for distinguishing between scripted versus unscripted, deliberate versus unplanned, spatial versus nonspatial and directional versus nondirectional discourse. Stubbs and Barth (2003) similarly found that *n*-grams are useful for distinguishing fiction from nonfiction writing, and they reported more specifically that over half of the 2-grams that are distinctive of fiction writing contain a personal pronoun while over a quarter of the 3-grams are time and place expressions (e.g. *a long time, for a moment, at the end*). Biber *et al.* (2004) made use of lexical bundles (or 4-grams, in their case) to investigate the language found in classroom teaching and textbooks. They found that classroom teaching shows a more extensive use of stance lexical bundles (e.g. *if you want to, I want you to, we're going to do*) and discourse-organizing lexical bundles (e.g. *if you look at, has to do with, on the other hand*) than is found in conversation. The authors also reported a more widespread use of referential bundles (e.g. *one of the things, and things like that, in terms of the*) in classroom teaching than in academic prose. These studies and many others (e.g. Biber, 2009; Biber & Conrad, 1999; Biber *et al.*, 1999) confirm that *n*-grams are useful discriminators of text types and genres.

Additional studies have investigated *n*-grams in learner corpora, particularly for the purpose of examining whether learners' use of *n*-grams distinguishes them from native speakers of the target language. The results of these studies have shown that there are indeed clear differences. For learners at lower proficiency levels, such differences often involve errors, but 'at an advanced level are as much (if not more) a question of over- and under-use of linguistic items or structures as a question of downright errors' (Granger *et al.*, 2009: 41). Crucially, learners' patterns of over- and under-use are highly complex phenomena and are subject to multiple effects, as shown in a study by De Cock *et al.* (1998). The data in this study were collected through informal interviews with advanced French-speaking learners of English as a foreign language, as well as with native speakers of British English. In an examination of both groups' use of 3-grams, the researchers found that advanced learners use what they refer to as *prefabs* (i.e. prefabricated chunks, or memorized sequences of words), but the chunks they use 'are (1) not necessarily the same as those used by NSs [native speakers]; (2) are not used with the same frequency; (3) have different syntactic uses; and (4) fulfil different pragmatic functions' (De Cock *et al.*, 1998: 78; see also De Cock, 2004).

There are very few studies that compare different varieties of learner language in relation to their use of *n*-grams. However, the analyses that do exist appear to hold a good deal of promise for L1 identification research. Paquot (2007), for example, compared the use of 2- to 5-grams in three sub-corpora of the *International Corpus of Learner English* (or ICLE; Granger et al., 2009). The sub-corpora in question were essays written in L2 English by native speakers of Dutch, French and Spanish. Paquot found that these three learner groups exhibit strikingly different patterns of *n*-gram use in their essays. For example, the 3-gram *as far as* is overused in the French sub-corpus but is underused in the Spanish and Dutch sub-corpora; the 4-gram *that is to say* is more frequently used by French- and Spanish-speaking learners than by Dutch-speaking learners; there is a marked preference for *a lot of* in the Dutch and Spanish sub-corpora, but this 3-gram is less often used by French-speaking learners. More interestingly, overused and underused *n*-grams seem to point to major differences between French- and Spanish-speaking learners versus Dutch-speaking learners in their use of lexical clusters (or *n*-grams) involving the first person plural pronouns *we* and *us*. Unlike French- and Spanish-speaking learners, Dutch-speaking learners do not make heavy use of a wide range of lexical sequences involving *we* and *us*. More specifically, they tend to underuse the *n*-grams *let us, because we, when we, what we, if we, and we, we can, we cannot, we did, we may, we must, we need, we shall, we should, we would, we think, we can not, we can see, we must be, we tend to* and *we will see*. Paquot further showed that, even though French- and Spanish-speaking learners of English behave similarly in the sense that both groups rely heavily on lexical sequences involving *we* and *us*, the two groups of learners do not overuse these pronouns in the same way. Examples of overused *n*-grams in the writing of French-speaking learners include *let us, we may, we might, we (can) notice, we can say, we have to* and *we (can/may) wonder*. In contrast, the *n*-grams overused in the writing of Spanish-speaking learners include the following: *we can, if we, because we, as we, we consider, we can get, we can observe, we can see, we can talk* and *we could say*.

In some studies, *n*-grams are examined as sequences of word classes (parts of speech, or POS) rather than as sequences of specific words. Word-class sequences are often referred to as POS *n*-grams (e.g. Mayfield Tomokiyo & Jones, 2001), such as POS 2-grams (e.g. noun+verb), POS 3-grams (e.g. determiner+adjective+noun) and so forth. A study by Aarts and Granger (1998) compared POS 3-grams in three sub-corpora of the ICLE (Dutch, Finnish and French) and found that, although all three learner groups underuse sentence-initial preposition-headed *–ing* clauses (e.g. preposition+verb-*ing*+X, as in *By arguing that*..., *By using this* ...), French learners stand out in their use of sequences that include a particle. More specifically, they overuse three types of structures: (1) sentence-initial marked infinitives used as adverbials of purpose (as in *To answer that question, it seems necessary to* ...); (2) sentence-initial marked infinitives instead of gerunds in subject position (as in *To live in the same nation also means* ...) and (3) coordinated marked infinitives (as in *a real opportunity to* *develop and to find* new outlets). The abundance of these types of group-specific patterns in the data led the researchers to conclude that 'there are more L1-specific features of advanced interlanguage than "universal" ones' (Aarts & Granger, 1998: 140).

The findings of past studies thus provide compelling evidence of L1 effects in the types of lexical and POS *n*-grams that learners produce in an L2. On this basis, we assume that lexical *n*-grams will also prove useful in analyses involving machine-learning protocols for automatically classifying texts according to the L1s of the learners who produced them. However, the existing literature does not directly indicate whether this will be the case, given that lexical *n*-grams have rarely been used in studies of automated text classification. Instead, the typical features (or variables) used in this area of research are limited mainly to function words, lexical richness measures, POS *n*-grams and letter *n*-grams (cf. Santini, 2004). There are only two studies we are aware of that make use of lexical *n*-grams in automated text classification. These include Baroni and Bernardini (2006) and Mayfield Tomokiyo and Jones (2001). Only the latter deals with L1 identification.

The study by Baroni and Bernardini (2006) reports the results of experiments in which a statistical classifier known as Support Vector Machines (SVMs) was employed to distinguish geopolitical articles originally written in Italian from similar articles translated by experts into Italian from another language. The authors explored multiple ways of representing a text as a feature vector, by varying both the size (1-, 2- and 3-grams) and the type (word-form *n*-grams, word lemma *n*-grams, POS *n*-grams and mixed *n*-grams) of the measured features. The results of their experiments show that most of the feature vectors they used allowed the SVM to classify the texts as original versus translated with accuracy levels substantially above chance (where chance = 50% accuracy). The best-performing sets of features were 1-grams made up of word forms (77.1% classification accuracy) and 2-grams made up of a function-word word form and a content word converted into a part-of-speech tag (e.g. *the N*) (also 77.1% classification accuracy). Word-form 2- and 3-grams also performed well above chance (73.8% and 62.5%, respectively), as did lemma 2- and 3-grams (74.0% and 65.4%, respectively). Besides comparing the effectiveness of analyses based on different types of features, the researchers also showed that when information from all analyses was combined, they were able to achieve a classification accuracy as high as 86.7%. The researchers concluded that the results of this study 'show that high quality translations have enough features in common to be identifiable with precision close to 90% and recall above 80%' (Baroni & Bernardini, 2006: 268). To the extent that the distinguishing features of translated texts reflect language patterns found in the original texts (i.e. the source language) from which they were translated, these findings suggest that similar automated classification procedures relying on combinations of *n*-grams might lead to successful automated detection of L1s (i.e. source languages) in samples of learner speech or writing.

As mentioned, the only study we are aware of that has directly investigated this question is Mayfield Tomokiyo and Jones (2001). The researchers in this study used a simple Bayesian classifier to examine whether lexical n-grams and POS n-grams could be used to distinguish English spoken texts produced by native speakers, Chinese speakers and Japanese speakers. The authors experimented with several different combinations of features, including lexical 1-grams, lexical 2-grams, lexical 3-grams, POS 1-grams, POS 2-grams, POS 3-grams and lexical n-grams in which nouns (and only nouns) were changed to POS tags. The results of the analyses performed on participants' spontaneous speech samples showed that lexical n-grams consistently performed better than POS n-grams. A combination of lexical 1- and 2-grams resulted in 87% accuracy in distinguishing native speakers from nonnative speakers and 93% accuracy in distinguishing between Chinese and Japanese speakers, whereas the corresponding results for a combination of POS 1- and 2-grams were 76% (native versus nonnative) and 86% (Chinese versus Japanese). Including lexical 3-grams along with lexical 1- and 2-grams improved the classification accuracy for natives versus nonnatives (96%), but decreased the accuracy for identifying Chinese versus Japanese speakers (86%). Even though lexical n-grams were more useful than POS n-grams for distinguishing between Chinese and Japanese speakers, the highest level of discrimination between the two nonnative groups was obtained through an analysis that included a combination of lexical 1- and 2-grams in which nouns were changed to POS tags. Using this combination of features, the researchers achieved 100% classification accuracy. Such a high level of classification accuracy is very rare in classification research, and the low number and uneven distribution of participants in the study (eight native English speakers, six Chinese speakers and 31 Japanese speakers) cast some doubt on the results, as does the possibility that the two learner groups were not at comparable levels of English proficiency. Nevertheless, the results of this study do suggest that automated text classification performed with n-gram variables can achieve high levels of L1 classification accuracy, at least when there are only two L1s to discriminate between.

Although Mayfield Tomokiyo and Jones (2001) appears to be the only prior study that has examined the usefulness of lexical n-grams for automated L1 classification, a few other L1 classification studies have been conducted using other types of predictor variables, such as single words, letter n-grams, POS n-grams and error types. Several of these studies involve analyses of texts extracted from the ICLE. Koppel *et al.* (2005), for example, used an SVM classifier with a pool of 1035 features (400 function words, 200 frequent letter n-grams, 185 error types and 250 rare part-of-speech bigrams) to identify the L1 backgrounds of English texts written by speakers of five different L1s: Bulgarian, Czech, French, Russian and Spanish. With all 1035 features, the classifier achieved an L1 classification accuracy of 80%. Running separate analyses on subsets of these features, the researchers showed that a classification accuracy of 75% could be achieved with the 400 function words alone, and 71% accuracy could be reached with just the 200 letter *n*-grams. Like the study by Mayfield Tomokiyo and Jones (2001), these results suggest that single words might be the most useful predictor variable for L1 classification, but the highest levels of classification accuracy are achieved through a combination of single words and other types of linguistic features. A confirmation of these findings can be found in studies by Tsur and Rappoport (2007) and Wong and Dras (2009), which use similar sets of variables in L1 classification analyses of similar sub-corpora of the ICLE. The study by Wong and Dras is noteworthy in its achievement of an L1 classification accuracy of 74% in a classification task involving seven L1 backgrounds (i.e. Chinese and Japanese in addition to the five used in the study by Koppel *et al.*, 2005). This is the highest number of L1s we are aware of in any previous L1 classification study. Wong and Dras achieved 74% L1 classification accuracy using an SVM classifier with a set of features made up of function-word 1-grams and POS *n*-grams. Function-word 1-grams alone led to a classification accuracy of 65%, which was the highest level of classification accuracy achieved by any individual feature type by itself.

Regarding the first research question we introduced earlier, the results of past studies suggest that lexical 1-grams are indeed effective discriminators of learners' L1 backgrounds even when the number of L1s is extended beyond five and when the texts are relatively long and represent open-ended topics. However, the only study that has addressed this particular question is Wong and Dras (2009), but it did so only with function-word 1-grams. We do not yet know how effective content-word 1-grams are for this purpose, or how effective a combination of content- and function-word 1-grams are in discriminating among even larger numbers of L1s.

Concerning our second question, the results of previous research suggest that lexical *n*-grams of other lengths (e.g. 2-, 3- and 4-grams) are not as effective as 1-grams in identifying learners' L1s. However, the only study that has addressed this question even partially is Mayfield Tomokiyo and Jones (2001), which was not optimally designed for comparing lexical *n*-grams of differing lengths. As the authors admit, the speech samples in the study were too short for proper 3-gram modelling (Mayfield Tomokiyo & Jones, 2001: 6). This apparently was not a problem for 2-grams, which were used in a number of the study's analyses, but unfortunately the authors do not provide a direct comparison of the effectiveness of lexical 1- versus 2-grams.

As regards our third and final question, Mayfield Tomokiyo and Jones (2001) is also the only study that has looked at the effectiveness of a pool of features that includes lexical *n*-grams of differing lengths. Although they did not compare the effectiveness of 1-grams versus 2-grams, they did compare the effectiveness of a combined pool of 1-grams and 2-grams with the effectiveness of a pool that includes 1-, 2- and 3-grams. As mentioned, the former was found to be more effective for identifying learners' L1 backgrounds, whereas the latter was found to be more effective for discriminating between native and nonnative speakers. Based on the limitations already noted for the study by Mayfield Tomokiyo and Jones, we are not sure whether a combination of 1- and 2-grams is more effective than 1-grams alone for L1 classification, nor are we sure that a combination of 1-, 2- and 3-grams will be less effective than a combination of 1- and 2-grams. The study by Koppel *et al.* (2005) suggests that a combination of all available features is advantageous for L1 detection, whereas the findings of Mayfield Tomokiyo and Jones (2001) as well as Wong and Dras (2009) indicate that the optimal solution often lies in a combination of some but not all types of features. The purpose of the present study is to determine what the optimal set of lexical *n*-grams is for the L1 classification of ICLE texts representing 12 L1 backgrounds.

Method

Learner Corpus

The texts used in the present study were extracted from the second edition of the *International Corpus of Learner English* (ICLE), which, as mentioned in Chapter 1, is a corpus made up of argumentative and literary essays written in English by learners from 16 different mother-tongue (L1) backgrounds (cf. Granger *et al.*, 2009). The learners who produced the essays in the ICLE represent a variety of learner profiles in terms of proficiency (from B1 to C2 level of the *Common European Framework of Reference for Languages*). The texts also reflect a range of topics and task conditions.

In order to arrive at a sample that would be sufficiently large and also sufficiently balanced across L1 groups in relation to proficiency and text type, we selected argumentative essays written by learners from only 12 of the 16 L1 backgrounds represented in the ICLE. We did not include essays written by Chinese, Japanese, Turkish or Tswana speakers as these four groups consist of a high proportion of lower proficiency texts (cf. Granger *et al.*, 2009: 11–12). In a further attempt to increase the comparability of texts across L1 groups, we also selected only essays that were between 500 and 1000 words in length based on the assumption that essays outside of this range may be outliers in relation to the L2 ability levels of the learners who wrote them (cf. Jarvis *et al.*, 2003). A breakdown of the 2033 texts from the ICLE that met our criteria for inclusion in the present study is given in Table 3.1.

Table 3.1 Texts included in the present study

L1	Number of texts
Bulgarian	140
Czech	116
Dutch	125
Finnish	121
French	200
German	182
Italian	86
Norwegian	270
Polish	288
Russian	144
Spanish	144
Swedish	217
TOTAL	**2033**

Classifier

The approach to classification that we chose for this study, and which is also used in all the studies in this book, is Multivariate Linear Discriminant Function Analysis, or simply Discriminant Analysis (DA). Several different forms of DA exist (e.g. McLachlan, 2004), and the one we used in the present study is the one available in the SPSS statistical software application (we used SPSS 17.0 in the present study). We chose DA instead of Support Vector Machines (SVM) because of the relatively higher clarity of interpretation offered by the former in relation to how features cluster together within the model, and how they relate to the model's ability to distinguish groups from one another (Baayen, 2008: 163). Additionally, as shown in a companion article by Jarvis (2011), DA achieves the highest L1 classification accuracy in a comparison of 20 classifiers (including SVM) that were used to classify the same data that are the focus of the present study.

As described in Chapter 1, DA uses the features that are fed into it to create a multidimensional statistical model where each case (=text) is treated as a feature vector that is converted into a multidimensional coordinate within the model's space. The model also determines a central coordinate, or centroid, for each group (=L1). The number of dimensions in a DA is equal to the number of groups minus one, which in the present study means 11 dimensions. These dimensions are referred to as discriminant functions, and the multidimensional coordinate for any given text will be the text's score in relation to each of the 11 functions. The text's score for each function is calculated as follows: $b_1x_1 + b_2x_2 + \cdots + b_nx_n + c$, where the bs are discriminant coefficients (or weights), the x's are discriminating features (i.e. the relative frequencies of the selected n-grams) and c is a constant. DA sets the discriminant coefficients and the constant to values that result in the smallest distances between cases representing the same group (i.e. texts representing the same L1) and the greatest distances between groups. Different coefficients and constants are determined for each discriminant function in such a way that they are orthogonal to one another. The first function always results in the greatest distinction among groups, but the use of multiple functions adds depth to the model that often allows the classifier to separate groups on one dimension where they may overlap on another.

DA can be conducted either through the so-called *enter* procedure, where all the features fed into the DA are used to construct the model, or through the so-called *stepwise* procedure, where the features fed into the DA are selectively chosen, one at a time, according to which successive feature will contribute the most to the model's ability to distinguish among the groups (i.e. L1s). The enter procedure is used when the researcher's selection of features for the DA is theoretically motivated or at least determined by data-external and/or pre-existing criteria, whereas the stepwise procedure takes advantage of data-internal relationships in order to find an optimal set of features for classifying the data set under investigation. In the present study, we used the enter procedure for addressing Research Questions 1 and 2, and we used the stepwise procedure for addressing Research Question 3.

The stepwise procedure in SPSS uses a forward–backward or fully stepwise procedure (cf. McLachlan, 2004: 412), which, at each step, evaluates features for both entry into and removal from the model. It is guided in this process by criteria set by the user. The most commonly used criterion appears to be the probability of F, which reflects whether the entry or removal of a particular feature will result in a significant improvement in the classifier's ability to distinguish among the groups. The stepwise procedure ends when no more features meet the entry or removal criteria, or when the procedure reaches the maximum number of iterations set by the researcher. These criteria can be adjusted to increase or decrease the number of features that will be selected. In the present study, we used the fairly strict feature-selection criteria of $p < 0.01$ for entry and $p > 0.05$ for removal. We did this in order to avoid excessive feature selection, as we will describe in more detail shortly.

The results of a DA analysis include information about how accurately the classifier is able to classify the cases that were used to construct the L1 classification model, but this will almost always be an overestimation of how accurately the model will be able to predict the group membership of cases it has not yet encountered. An estimate of the classifier's predictive power is accomplished through the use of cross-validation (CV). As described in Chapter 1, CV involves partitioning the data into training and testing sets, using a training set to set the parameters of the model, and then applying those parameters to a testing set to see how well the model can classify texts that were not used to set the parameters.

The preferred methods of CV are often referred to with the term *k-fold CV*. This type of CV involves the use of several partitions of the data. For example, in 10-fold CV, the data are divided into 10 equal partitions, and in each stage of the CV, one partition is held back as the testing set while the other nine partitions are combined and used as the training set. The overall accuracy of the 10-fold CV is then the total percentage of testing-set cases classified correctly across all 10 folds of the CV. Another common form of *k*-fold CV is leave-one-out CV (LOOCV), which — as the term implies — involves treating each individual text as its own partition, and then in each stage of the CV, holding back just one text as the testing set while using all others as the training set. The overall accuracy of the LOOCV is, as before, the total percentage of testing-set cases classified correctly across all stages of CV. Both 10-fold and LOOCV have been shown to give similar, essentially unbiased and stable estimates of the classifier's ability to correctly classify cases that it has not yet encountered. However, because LOOCV is less computationally efficient, 10-fold CV has become 'the procedure of choice for assessing predictive accuracy' for many researchers (Lecocke & Hess, 2006: 315). This is the form of CV we chose for all of the DA analyses used in the present study.

It should be noted, however, that the recommended forms of cross-validation for stepwise DA (where feature selection occurs during the DA) are somewhat different and more complicated than CV used for entry-procedure DA (where feature selection takes place prior to the DA). In entry-procedure DA, the same features that are used in the initial analysis of the entire data set are also used in all stages of the CV. For convenience, we will refer to this form of CV as *CV after feature selection*. In stepwise DA, on the other hand, feature selection takes place during the model construction process and takes advantage of randomly occurring strong statistical relationships in the data. Those features may account well for the particular set of data under investigation, but if some of their internal relationships are strong simply by chance, then any CV that makes use of precisely those features with any partitions of the original data set will result in overly optimistic classification accuracy rates that do not reflect the actual generalizable predictive power of the classifier. To prevent this type of selection bias from affecting one's CV results, it is best to follow stepwise DA with a form of CV that can be referred to as *CV with embedded feature selection*, and which has alternatively been referred to as honest, or complete CV (Lecocke & Hess, 2006: 316; Molinaro *et al.*, 2005: 3303). This type of CV involves conducting the CV in such a way that stepwise feature selection occurs within each fold of the CV. This means that the set of features selected through the stepwise procedure will likely vary somewhat from one fold to the next fold of the CV. However, the features that are selected most often across the folds of the CV give a good indication of which features are reliably indicative of group-membership (e.g. Schulerud & Albregtsen, 2004), and the overall accuracy rate of this type of CV is also a reliable, essentially unbiased estimate of the generalizable accuracy of the model (e.g. Molinaro et al., 2005).

Given these considerations, we used 10-fold *CV after feature selection* for our DA analyses involving the enter procedure, and used 10-fold *CV with embedded feature selection* for our DA analyses involving the stepwise procedure. In each fold of every CV, we set the classifier's parameters (i.e. the discriminant coefficients and group centroids) using a training set consisting of 90% of the texts from the entire data set, and then used those parameters to calculate discriminant function scores for each of the texts in the remaining 10% of cases that were held back as the testing set. The resulting scores represent coordinates in multidimensional space for each text in the testing set. In order to classify them by L1, we measured their distance to each L1 centroid, and classified a text as belonging to the L1 whose centroid it was nearest to. We followed the same procedures for each of the 10 nonoverlapping testing sets, and used the overall percentage of texts classified correctly across all 10 folds of the CV as the cross-validated classification accuracy for that particular analysis.

Features

The features used in the present study include 1-, 2-, 3- and 4-grams found in the data. Scripts written in the programming language *Perl* were used to extract all four classes of *n*-grams from our database of 2033 texts. The initial output showed raw frequencies of occurrence per text for 1-, 2-grams and so forth. We used the number of word tokens per text to convert each of these raw frequencies into relative frequencies, which reflected the rate of occurrence for each *n*-gram per 1000 words of text.

Mindful of the convention of using at least 10 cases per variable in parametric multivariate analyses, we limited the number of features per analysis to roughly one-tenth the number of texts in the training set. Each training set consisted of either 1829 or 1830 texts (i.e. 90% of the 2033 texts in the overall database), and we limited the number of features that could be included in any model of the classifier to no more than 200 (note: $200/1829 = 10.9\%$), a value we deemed to be optimal in relation to considerations of convenience, predictive power and statistical reliability. Our first analysis involved 1-grams (see Research Question 1), and for this analysis we selected the 200 most frequent 1-grams in the data that were not prompt-induced (e.g. *the, to, of, and, a, is, in, that, it, are, for, be, not, they, have, we*). We operationalized prompt-induced words as all content words (and their families) that appeared in any of the essay prompts and were used by more than 35 learners. The use of such words in more than 35 essays could skew our analysis as some prompts are statistically biased toward certain L1 backgrounds. Some of the disqualified 1-grams include *society, prison, science, technology, television, religion, imagination* and *dream*, which appear in essay prompts such as the following:

- 'The **prison** system is outdated. No civilized **society** should punish its criminals: it should rehabilitate them'
- 'Some people say that in our modern world, dominated by **science** and **technology** and industrialisation, there is no longer a place for **dreaming** and **imagination**. What is your opinion?'
- 'Marx once said that **religion** was the opium of the masses. If he was alive at the end of the 20th century, he would replace **religion** with **television**'

We manually disqualified such words from our analyses in order to reduce the possible confound between prompt effects and L1 effects because some prompts were chosen more by some L1 groups than by others. We recognize that 35 is a somewhat arbitrary number for a cut-off criterion, but we found that this number provided us with an objective criterion that best matched our own intuitions about which words were potentially prompt-induced (and topic dependent).

Our selection of 200 2-grams (e.g. *of the, on the, there is, I think, we are*) and 200 3-grams (e.g. *a lot of, in order to, the fact that, one of the, on the other, in my opinion*) proceeded in exactly the same manner as with 1-grams. Our selection of 4-grams also followed the same procedures except that the relatively lower frequencies of 4-grams in the data meant that there were only 122 nonprompt-induced 4-grams that occurred at least 35 times in the data (e.g. *on the other hand, at the same time, I would like to, to be able to, is one of the*). We selected these 122 items for our 4-gram analysis. We originally intended to investigate 5-grams, too, but there were only 11 5-grams that met our criteria for inclusion, and we found this number to be too low for our statistical analyses.

The present study involves separate enter-procedure DA analyses for 1-, 2-, 3- and 4-grams (cf. Research Questions 1 and 2), and a final set of DA analyses involving stepwise feature selection from the previously mentioned 200 1-grams, then stepwise feature selection from the combined set of 400 1- and 2-grams, then stepwise feature selection from the combined set of 600 1-, 2- and 3-grams, and finally stepwise feature selection from the combined set of 722 1-, 2-, 3- and 4-grams . The purpose of the stepwise analyses is to determine the degree to which L1 detection through lexical features can be enhanced through the use of *n*-grams of varying lengths (cf. Research Question 3).

Results

Comparing Different Sizes of *n*-Grams (CV after Feature Selection)

Using 10-fold *CV after feature selection*, our analyses showed that a DA model built on 200 highly frequent 1-grams was able to correctly identify 1077 (or 53.0%) of the 2033 texts in our database. This is significantly and substantially higher than the chance level of 8.3% (df = 121, $n = 2033$, $X^2 = 5138.26$, $p < 0.001$; Cohen's Kappa = 0.482), and is also significantly and substantially higher than the baseline accuracy of 14.2% ($t[2032] = 30.28$, $p < 0.001$), which is the accuracy level that would be attained if all texts were classified as belonging to the largest L1 group (i.e. Polish = 288 texts; 288/2033 = 14.2%). The results of the 1-gram analysis are shown in more detail in Table 3.2 in the form of a classification matrix (alternatively referred to as a confusion matrix), which indicates the percentage of texts from each L1 group that were predicted to belong to any of the 12 groups. The percentages of texts that were classified as belonging to the correct L1 groups are highlighted in bold text.

From the various values shown in Table 3.2, it is clear that some L1s were identified more accurately than others, with texts written by Polish speakers classified most accurately (66.0%), and texts written by Italian speakers classified least accurately (41.9%). The results also show interesting patterns

Table 3.2 L1 classification matrix for the 1-gram analysis (values represent percentages)

Actual L1	Predicted L1											
	Bul	Cze	Dut	Fin	Fre	Ger	Ita	Nor	Pol	Rus	Spa	Swe
Bulgarian	**55.0**	4.3	2.9	3.6	3.6	7.1	3.6	4.3	4.3	5.7	1.4	4.3
Czech	8.6	**53.4**	2.6	5.2	1.7	2.6	0.9	4.3	7.8	6.9	3.4	2.6
Dutch	3.2	3.2	**52.0**	4.8	7.2	5.6	1.6	7.2	2.4	1.6	2.4	8.8
Finnish	3.3	2.5	7.4	**49.6**	3.3	3.3	0.8	9.1	5.0	3.3	3.3	9.1
French	2.5	3.0	7.0	2.0	**48.0**	3.5	6.0	1.5	8.5	4.5	6.0	7.5
German	4.9	6.0	8.2	4.9	2.7	**47.8**	3.8	4.4	6.0	2.7	1.6	6.6
Italian	4.7	3.5	7.0	4.7	5.8	10.5	**41.9**	2.3	3.5	7.0	8.1	1.2
Norwegian	2.6	2.2	3.3	5.9	1.9	5.9	0.4	**59.6**	1.5	0.7	3.0	13.0
Polish	5.9	4.2	1.0	3.5	3.8	3.5	1.7	1.0	**66.0**	3.1	3.5	2.8
Russian	8.3	10.4	4.2	7.6	2.8	4.2	4.2	0.7	6.9	**45.8**	2.1	2.8
Spanish	4.9	2.8	3.5	2.8	4.9	2.1	8.3	2.1	8.3	2.1	**52.1**	6.3
Swedish	5.1	2.3	3.2	9.7	4.6	6.5	0.9	11.5	2.8	2.3	4.1	**47.0**

regarding misclassification. For example, Norwegian and Swedish are closely related languages, and this is reflected in the fact that texts written by Norwegians that are misclassified, are misclassified most often as having been written by Swedes, and vice versa. Less expected is the fact that texts written by Finns that are misclassified, are also most often misclassified as having been written by either Norwegians or Swedes, despite the fact that Finnish is a non-Indo-European language that is not typologically related to either Norwegian or Swedish.

The corresponding results for the DA analyses based on 2-, 3- and 4-grams, respectively, are shown in Tables 3.3 through 3.5. The overall L1 classification accuracy for the 2-gram analysis is 39.5% (803 out of 2033 texts correctly classified), for the 3-gram analysis is 31.2% (635 out of 2033 texts correctly classified), and for the 4-gram analysis is 22.0% (447 out of 2033 texts correctly classified). These accuracy rates are all significant: Even the 4-gram results are significantly higher than the baseline of 14.2% ($t[2032] = 6.39, p < 0.001$). However, it is also true that the accuracy rates decrease significantly with each consecutive analysis (from 1- to 2-grams: $t[2032] = 10.32, p < 0.001$; from 2- to 3-grams: $t[2032] = 6.38, p < 0.001$; from 3- to 4-grams: $t[2032] = 7.34, p < 0.001$). This decrease in classification accuracy with increasing sizes of n-grams does not affect all L1 groups equally, though. For example, the decrease in accuracy from the 1-gram analysis to the 2-gram analysis is relatively small for texts written by speakers of Czech, French, German and Russian, but is considerable for most other groups

Table 3.3 L1 classification matrix for the 2-gram analysis (values represent percentages)

Actual L1	Predicted L1										
	Bul	Cze	Dut	Fin	Fre	Ger	Ita	Nor	Pol	Rus	Spa	Swe
Bulgarian	**31.4**	5.7	7.9	5.7	5.7	7.1	8.6	5.0	7.9	6.4	3.6	5.0
Czech	9.5	**50.9**	5.2	5.2	3.4	2.6	3.4	2.6	14.7	1.7	0.0	.9
Dutch	3.2	4.8	**27.2**	7.2	6.4	9.6	4.8	9.6	5.6	4.0	6.4	11.2
Finnish	4.1	3.3	5.8	**38.0**	1.7	11.6	5.0	6.6	6.6	6.6	6.6	4.1
French	5.0	1.0	1.5	5.0	**43.0**	8.0	5.5	2.5	7.5	8.0	9.5	3.5
German	7.1	4.4	6.6	6.0	8.2	**40.1**	3.8	6.6	7.7	3.3	2.2	3.8
Italian	7.0	3.5	4.7	5.8	10.5	1.2	**30.2**	4.7	4.7	5.8	17.4	4.7
Norwegian	6.7	3.3	7.0	7.4	1.5	9.6	2.6	**35.2**	3.0	3.7	3.7	16.3
Polish	7.3	4.9	4.2	4.5	6.6	5.2	2.4	3.1	**49.3**	5.9	2.4	4.2
Russian	7.6	4.9	2.1	4.2	3.5	5.6	3.5	5.6	13.2	**41.7**	3.5	4.9
Spanish	4.9	3.5	4.9	4.9	9.0	2.1	7.6	3.5	7.6	2.1	**44.4**	5.6
Swedish	10.1	1.8	6.9	4.1	3.2	7.8	3.7	17.1	2.8	4.6	3.7	**34.1**

(cf. Tables 3.2 and 3.3). This pattern changes somewhat when comparing the 2-gram results with the 3-gram results, however, and also the 3-gram results with the 4-gram results. One pattern that is nearly perfectly consistent is that the L1 classification accuracies for each L1 group decrease as larger n-grams are used. The only exception to this observation concerns the German-speaking writers, whose texts are identified more accurately with 4-grams than with 3-grams (35.2% vs. 30.8%; cf. Tables 3.4 and 3.5).

Another notable effect of using differently sized n-grams for L1 identification is that the patterns of misclassification change from one analysis to the next. For example, whereas in the 1-gram analysis, Finns are misclassified primarily as Norwegians and Swedes, in the 2-, 3- and 4-gram analyses, they are misclassified mainly as Germans. An additional, interesting example is the French group, whose most frequently misclassified L1 in the 1-gram analysis is Polish, and then in the 2-gram analysis is Spanish, in the 3-gram analysis is Dutch, and in the 4-gram analysis is Italian. This suggests that the degree of similarity between the L2 lexical patterns of various L1 groups depends on the size of the n-grams being examined.

The main characteristics and results of the four L1 classification analyses just described are summarized in Table 3.6. These results show, again, that 1-grams provide the best model of L1 classification with the present data, and that the L1 classification models become progressively worse as larger n-grams are used. By the time we reach 4-grams, the disadvantage of larger n-grams is compounded by the fact that there are fewer items available to

Table 3.4 L1 classification matrix for the 3-gram analysis (values represent percentages)

Actual L1	Bul	Cze	Dut	Fin	Fre	Ger	Ita	Nor	Pol	Rus	Spa	Swe
Bulgarian	**27.9**	5.0	2.1	5.0	6.4	8.6	7.1	7.1	7.9	8.6	7.1	7.1
Czech	9.5	**39.7**	5.2	7.8	2.6	6.0	3.4	5.2	9.5	3.4	3.4	4.3
Dutch	6.4	4.0	**24.8**	4.8	9.6	12.8	4.8	8.0	9.6	4.8	4.8	5.6
Finnish	7.4	4.1	6.6	**24.8**	2.5	17.4	3.3	6.6	9.1	4.1	5.8	8.3
French	6.0	2.5	9.0	5.0	**36.5**	5.5	6.0	4.5	8.5	7.0	6.5	3.0
German	6.0	4.9	8.8	9.3	2.2	**30.8**	6.0	5.5	9.3	5.5	4.9	6.6
Italian	5.8	4.7	5.8	5.8	11.6	5.8	**23.3**	7.0	7.0	5.8	11.6	5.8
Norwegian	5.2	3.3	9.3	7.0	3.3	10.0	4.1	**29.3**	5.2	1.9	4.4	17.0
Polish	6.6	5.9	4.5	8.3	6.3	11.8	3.1	3.8	**33.0**	8.7	6.6	1.4
Russian	10.4	2.8	7.6	3.5	2.1	11.8	3.5	4.9	6.3	**40.3**	2.8	4.2
Spanish	10.4	6.9	3.5	4.9	7.6	9.7	5.6	4.2	4.2	6.9	**30.6**	5.6
Swedish	6.5	3.7	7.4	6.9	3.7	8.8	2.8	18.9	5.5	4.1	2.3	**29.5**

Table 3.5 L1 classification matrix for the 4-gram analysis (values represent percentages)

Actual L1	Predicted L1										
	Bul	Cze	Dut	Fin	Fre	Ger	Ita	Nor	Pol	Rus	Spa	Swe
Bulgarian	**21.4**	3.6	7.1	10.0	2.9	14.3	7.1	9.3	7.1	2.9	10.0	4.3
Czech	3.4	**35.3**	4.3	4.3	3.4	10.3	7.8	5.2	6.9	5.2	7.8	6.0
Dutch	4.0	3.2	**16.0**	7.2	10.4	18.4	4.0	4.0	10.4	7.2	4.8	10.4
Finnish	11.6	5.8	6.6	**10.7**	1.7	14.9	5.8	11.6	12.4	4.1	8.3	6.6
French	6.0	4.5	6.5	5.0	**20.5**	11.5	14.5	7.5	5.5	4.5	8.0	6.0
German	4.9	4.9	8.2	3.8	3.8	**35.2**	5.5	5.5	6.0	7.1	8.2	6.6
Italian	7.0	12.8	7.0	5.8	10.5	14.0	**14.0**	4.7	5.8	3.5	10.5	4.7
Norwegian	4.1	4.4	8.1	7.0	2.2	14.4	3.0	**23.0**	8.1	4.4	5.6	15.6
Polish	5.2	10.1	5.2	11.5	6.6	18.4	5.6	5.2	**18.1**	3.5	5.9	4.9
Russian	8.3	6.9	6.3	4.2	10.4	12.5	3.5	7.6	6.3	**24.3**	8.3	1.4
Spanish	7.6	6.3	6.3	7.6	9.0	11.1	4.2	4.9	8.3	11.1	**18.8**	4.9
Swedish	4.6	4.1	4.1	6.9	5.1	16.1	4.1	17.5	7.8	3.7	2.8	**23.0**

Table 3.6 Summary of classification accuracies for different sizes of *n*-grams

Type of features used	Number of features	Cross-validation	L1 classification accuracy (%)
1-grams	200	10-fold CV after feature selection	53.0
2-grams	200	10-fold CV after feature selection	39.5
3-grams	200	10-fold CV after feature selection	31.2
4-grams	122	10-fold CV after feature selection	22.0

include in the model (i.e. only 122 instead of 200). The two facts actually appear to be closely linked to each other: larger *n*-grams have lower frequencies and less even distributions in the data, thus making them less reliable indicators of L1 group membership. This, of course, does not mean that *n*-grams larger than 1-grams are of no value to L1 detection. *n*-grams of various sizes that have sufficiently high frequencies and sufficiently reliable distributions (i.e. no floor effect) have the potential, at least theoretically, to function as well as 1-grams for L1 classification. In the following section, we examine whether the optimal model for L1 classification involves a mix of *n*-grams of various sizes.

Combined Analyses (CV with Embedded Feature Selection)

For our combined analyses involving *n*-grams of different sizes, we needed to use the stepwise feature-selection procedure in order to reduce the overall pool of *n*-grams from 722 to no more than 200 in order to maintain an acceptable balance of cases to features. Limiting features to a particular number can be achieved in various ways, such as simply by restricting the number of steps the procedure runs through to a specific value (see Chapters 5 and 6). The method we chose for limiting the number of features to 200 was to adopt a strict set of criteria for feature entry (into the model) and feature removal (from the model). We set the *p* value for entry to $p < 0.01$, and the *p* value for removal to $p > 0.05$. This meant that an *n*-gram had to make a very strong unique contribution to the model's ability to discriminate among the L1s in order to be selected for inclusion in the model, and its unique contribution had to remain strong as the model grew larger (i.e. included more features) in order to be retained by the model. These particular criteria turned out to be optimal, allowing a good number but consistently fewer than 200 *n*-grams to be included in any given model.

As mentioned previously, the proper type of cross-validation for classification analyses that include feature selection involves embedding the feature-selection procedures within each fold of the cross-validation. We referred to this method earlier as *CV with embedded feature selection*. For our combined analyses, we used 10-fold CV with embedded feature selection. In order to examine the effects of using *n*-grams of different sizes, we conducted four analyses using this type of CV. In the first analysis, we made available to the DA classifier only the 200 1-grams used in the section 'Comparing Different Sizes of *n*-Grams (CV after Feature Selection)'. The difference was that in the previous analysis, all 200 1-grams were entered into the L1 classification model, whereas in the present analysis, the stepwise procedure selected only those 1-grams that met its entry and removal criteria. As it turned out, the number of 1-grams selected in each fold of the CV ranged from 104 to 118 (mean = 110.7). The overall L1 classification accuracy for the 1-gram analysis (using CV with embedded feature selection) was 49.9%.

In our second analysis, we made available to the DA classifier a pool of 400 *n*-grams made up of the 200 1-grams and 200 2-grams used in the section 'Comparing Different Sizes of *n*-Grams (CV after Feature Selection)'. The number of *n*-grams actually selected in each fold of the CV ranged from 145 to 160 (mean = 152.5). The overall accuracy for the combined analysis involving both 1-grams and 2-grams was 52.8%, which represented a significant improvement over the classification accuracy of the analysis involving 1-grams alone ($t[2032] = 2.97, p = 0.003$).

Our third analysis used a combined pool of 600 *n*-grams made up of the 200 1-grams, 200 2-grams and 200 3-grams used in the section 'Comparing Different Sizes of *n*-Grams (CV after Feature Selection)'. In the present analysis, the number of *n*-grams selected in each fold of the CV ranged from 165 to 181 (mean = 171.8). The overall L1 classification accuracy for this analysis rose slightly from the previous analysis to 53.2%. The improvement in classification accuracy was not significant, however ($t[2032] = 0.43, p = 0.671$).

Our fourth and final analysis used a combined pool of all 722 *n*-grams described earlier: 200 1-grams, 200 2-grams, 200 3-grams and 122 4-grams. The number of *n*-grams selected in each fold of the CV ranged from 169 to 191 (mean = 177.5), and the overall L1 classification accuracy was 53.6%, which is not significantly higher than the accuracies obtained in the analyses involving a combination of either 1-, 2- and 3-grams ($t[2032] = 0.42, p = 0.674$) or even just 1- and 2-grams ($t[2032] = 0.76, p = 0.45$). A classification matrix for this final combined analysis is shown in Table 3.7, and a summary of the characteristics and results of all four of the analyses in this section is given in Table 3.8.

One of the weaknesses of CV with embedded feature selection is that it leaves a certain degree of ambiguity about which features are to be included in the optimal model. This is because not all the same features are chosen in each fold of the CV. In order to clear up some of this ambiguity, we next examine the number of folds in which various *n*-grams were selected. This

Table 3.7 L1 classification matrix for the combined stepwise analysis of 1-, 2-, 3- and 4-grams (values represent percentages)

Actual L1	Predicted L1											
	Bul	Cze	Dut	Fin	Fre	Ger	Ita	Nor	Pol	Rus	Spa	Swe
Bulgarian	**47.9**	3.6	2.9	5.7	3.6	5.7	5.0	5.0	5.7	5.7	4.3	5.0
Czech	4.3	**52.6**	3.4	8.6	1.7	5.2	1.7	2.6	8.6	6.0	3.4	1.7
Dutch	3.2	1.6	**45.6**	7.2	4.8	10.4	0.0	5.6	0.8	3.2	8.0	9.6
Finnish	4.1	2.5	6.6	**47.9**	3.3	5.8	0.0	6.6	6.6	4.1	4.1	8.3
French	4.0	2.0	5.5	3.0	**51.0**	5.5	8.5	1.0	8.0	1.5	7.0	3.0
German	3.3	3.3	7.7	2.2	2.7	**51.6**	4.9	3.8	8.8	3.8	3.3	4.4
Italian	7.0	4.7	3.5	3.5	15.1	3.5	**41.9**	3.5	3.5	1.2	11.6	1.2
Norwegian	4.4	3.0	5.9	4.8	1.9	2.6	0.0	**59.3**	1.9	1.1	1.1	14.1
Polish	3.8	5.2	1.0	3.8	2.1	4.5	1.7	1.0	**68.1**	4.2	1.7	2.8
Russian	11.1	3.5	4.2	4.9	2.8	4.2	2.1	0.7	5.6	**53.5**	3.5	4.2
Spanish	3.5	3.5	3.5	5.6	7.6	5.6	4.2	3.5	5.6	4.2	**51.4**	2.1
Swedish	6.0	1.8	6.9	6.0	2.8	6.5	1.8	11.5	1.8	2.8	2.8	**49.3**

Table 3.8 Summary of classification accuracies for the stepwise analyses

Types of features used	Features submitted	Features selected (mean)	Cross-validation	L1 classification accuracy (%)
1-grams	200	110.7	10-fold CV with embedded feature selection	49.9
1- and 2-grams	400	152.5	10-fold CV with embedded feature selection	52.8
1-, 2- and 3-grams	600	171.8	10-fold CV with embedded feature selection	53.2
1-, 2-, 3- and 4-grams	722	177.5	10-fold CV with embedded feature selection	53.6

information is summarized in Table 3.9. This table shows, for example, that of the 200 1-grams submitted to the stepwise DA, 51 were selected in all 10 folds of the CV, 10 were selected in nine folds and so on, and 67 were not selected at all for inclusion in the DA model of L1 group membership. Corresponding numbers are given for 2-, 3- and 4-grams, and the total

Table 3.9 Number of *n*-grams selected in various numbers of folds of the CV

	1-grams	2-grams	3-grams	4-grams	Total
10 folds	51	14	13	5	83
9 folds	10	10	5	3	28
8 folds	6	7	2	1	16
7 folds	8	5	5	1	19
6 folds	9	4	2	0	15
5 folds	10	2	1	0	13
4 folds	10	5	4	1	20
3 folds	10	8	4	5	27
2 folds	10	12	4	3	29
1 folds	9	21	21	7	58
0 folds	67	112	139	96	414

column shows the total number of *n*-grams of any size that were selected in all 10 folds, in nine folds and so forth. Some of the more noteworthy results shown in Table 3.9 include the fact that 83 *n*-grams were selected in all 10 folds of the CV, and that 414 (i.e. the majority of) *n*-grams were not selected in any of the folds. Following the same assumptions adhered to in Chapter 5, we assume that *n*-grams that are selected in more than half of the folds of a CV are particularly useful for a classification model. Thus, the 161 *n*-grams selected in at least six folds of the CV are the *n*-grams we put forward as representing the optimal L1 classification model for our combined analysis. These 161 *n*-grams are listed in the appendix. In the following section, we look more closely at how individual *n*-grams contribute to the identification of learners' L1 backgrounds.

In the meantime, two additional observations are worth noting. The first is that the L1 classification accuracies achieved in the combined analyses reported in this section are very similar to the L1 classification accuracy achieved in the 1-gram analysis reported in the section 'Comparing Different Sizes of *n*-Grams (CV after Feature Selection)' (cf. Table 3.6 with Table 3.8). The highest L1 classification accuracy (53.6%) was obtained in the stepwise analysis involving a combination of all four types of *n*-grams, but this is not significantly higher than the L1 classification accuracy achieved in the 1-gram analysis reported in the section 'Comparing Different Sizes of *n*-Grams (CV after Feature Selection)' (53.0%) ($t[2032] = 0.52$, $p = 0.602$). On the other hand, the two analyses are probably not directly comparable given that they involve somewhat different assumptions as well as different procedures for feature selection and cross-validation. When 1-grams and a combination of *n*-grams of different sizes are both submitted to the same feature-selection and cross-validation procedures, the accuracy of the combined analysis is significantly higher than that of the 1-gram analysis, as mentioned earlier in this section (see also Table 3.8).

The second noteworthy observation is that the combined analysis shows that *n*-grams beyond 1-grams do indeed contribute to the strength of the L1 classification model. This can be seen quite clearly in Table 3.8, where the addition of 2-, 3- and 4-grams to the pool of features available to the model improves the accuracy of the model. Table 3.9 additionally shows that, in the combined analysis involving *n*-grams of all sizes, 2-, 3- and 4-grams are well represented among the *n*-grams that were selected in all 10 folds of the CV. Furthermore, of the 161 *n*-grams we put forward as representing the optimal combined model (see the appendix), 40 are 2-grams, 27 are 3-grams and 10 are 4-grams. While scrutinizing the results further, we have observed that *n*-grams such as *as far as*, *a lot* and *order to* are among the top 30 *n*-grams in terms of their *F* values for discriminating among the 12 L1 groups, and these *n*-grams as well as various other 2-, 3- and 4-grams were selected earlier than a number of 1-grams during the stepwise feature-selection process.

Discussion

The results suggest the following answers to our three research questions. First, regarding the question of whether 1-grams are effective discriminators of a sizable number of L1 backgrounds (12, in this case), the results of both the 1-gram analysis using the enter method (53.0% accuracy) and the 1-gram analysis using the stepwise method (49.9% accuracy) show that the individual words that learners use are powerful indicators of their L1 backgrounds, and are capable even of discriminating among learners with closely related cultures and L1s with moderate levels of success. Although the levels of L1 classification accuracy achieved with 1-grams in the present chapter are lower than that achieved in Chapter 2 (76.9%), this is to be expected given that the level of chance for the classification task in Chapter 2 was 20%, whereas it is less than 9% for the classification tasks performed in the present chapter. The fact that the L1 backgrounds of over 50% of the 2033 texts in the present study could be identified on the basis of 1-grams alone (in the enter-method analysis in the section 'Comparing Different Sizes of n-Grams (CV after Feature Selection)') is in fact quite remarkable from a theoretical point of view, as it suggests that the L2 word-choice tendencies of the majority of learners are indeed quite consistent and also quite distinctive of their L1 backgrounds. The degree to which those L2 word-choice tendencies reflect characteristics of the learners' L1s is a question we will address later in this section.

Our second research question concerns whether equally high or even higher levels of L1 classification accuracy might be achieved through the use of n-grams beyond 1-grams. The results of our entry-method analyses in the section 'Comparing Different Sizes of n-Grams (CV after Feature Selection)' show that the answer to this question is negative. L1 classification accuracies become progressively and significantly lower when replacing 1-grams with 2-grams, 2-grams with 3-grams and 3-grams with 4-grams. As we have noted, however, this is not always true in relation to the identification of individual L1 groups: specifically, texts written by German speakers are more accurately identified through the use of 4-grams than by means of 3-grams (cf. Tables 3.4 and 3.5).

There are two probable explanations for why 1-grams, as a class, tend to be better discriminators of learners' L1s than n-grams of larger sizes. The first reason can be understood in relation to the observation by Stubbs and Barth (2003: 71) that 'frequent words are often frequent, not in their own right, but because they occur as part of frequent phrases.' Because n-grams are made up of 1-grams, the distribution of a given n-gram larger than one will be fully entailed by the distribution of any of the 1-grams contained therein. Yet, 1-grams also tend to occur in multiple n-grams, so the distribution of a 1-gram will almost always be broader than (i.e. a superset of) the distribution of any n-gram in which it occurs. From this perspective, we can say that the distribution of any particular 1-gram likely reflects the merged distributions of multiple *n*-grams. The present results show that such merged distributions, as a class, tend to be more discriminative of particular L1 backgrounds than are the more restricted distributions of larger *n*-grams.

A second reason why 1-grams tend to be better discriminators is because larger *n*-grams tend to create sparse-data problems (cf. Crossley & Louwerse, 2007: 455). This means, on the one hand, that larger *n*-grams are far less frequent than 1-grams. For example, the most frequent 200 1-grams in our data have a mean relative frequency of 2.98 occurrences per 1000 words, whereas the most frequent 200 2-grams have a mean relative frequency of just 0.65, and this number drops to 0.13 for the most frequent 200 3-grams, and to 0.05 for the most frequent 122 4-grams. Perhaps more importantly, the number of texts in which a particular *n*-gram is found at all decreases substantially from 1-grams to 2-grams and beyond. Of the 200 1-grams investigated in this study, 190 occurred in at least 25% of the 2033 texts in the database. However, of the 200 2-grams, only 83 occurred in at least 25% of the texts, and this number dropped to just 2 of the 200 3-grams. None of the 122 4-grams investigated in this study were found in at least 25% of the texts. What this shows is that *n*-grams larger than 1-grams, and especially larger than 2-grams, are not stratified evenly in the data. Among other consequences, the large number of 0 occurrences for 2-grams and especially for 3- and 4-grams appears to have resulted in a statistical floor effect, where the large number of zeroes across L1 groups makes it difficult to distinguish one group from another.

Despite the disappointing performance of *n*-grams larger than 1-grams in the present study, we have seen in our combined analyses that *n*-grams clearly do have a role to play in L1 identification. Our third research question asks whether L1 classification might be most effective through the use of a combination of *n*-grams of differing lengths, and the results of our stepwise analyses in the section 'Combined Analyses (CV with Embedded Feature Selection)' show that this is indeed the case (see Table 3.8). There is an important caveat, however, which is that, even though the L1 classification accuracy of a combined model including both 1- and 2-grams is significantly higher than that of a model made up solely of 1-grams, the further increases in classification accuracy that occur after adding 3- and 4-grams to the model are not significant. On the other hand, this does not mean that 3-grams and 4-grams are not useful predictors of learners' L1s. In fact, as we proceeded to make available to the classifier *n*-grams of greater lengths, we found that the classifier often selected longer *n*-grams in place of shorter ones. It did this when a longer *n*-gram made a stronger unique contribution to the predictive model than did any of the shorter *n*-grams in the available pool of features. As mentioned earlier, we found the optimal model for the present study to be made up of 84 1-grams, 40 2-grams, 27 3-grams and 10 4-grams (see the Appendix).

In the remainder of this section, we delve into a more in-depth discussion of specific *n*-grams that differentiate learners' L1 backgrounds, and we also discuss the degree to which those *n*-grams can be assumed to reflect patterns of the L1 itself. The strength of a classifier such as DA is its ability to identify group-specific patterns in combinations of features rather than in individual features. However, once the optimal combination of features has been determined, it can be enlightening to examine those best features individually to discover why they are so useful for the classification model. In the remainder of this section, we will highlight a number of individual *n*-grams that appear to be particularly useful for separating learners from different L1 backgrounds. We also describe some of the evidence concerning whether those *n*-grams are likely to exhibit direct L1 influence.

In a classification task involving the identification of the group membership of texts representing 12 L1 backgrounds, one might expect that the best possible *n*-gram in the classification model would be one that shows significant differences across all 12 groups. In order to determine whether any of the 161 *n*-grams in our optimal model (see the appendix) shows such a high level of differentiation, we ran each of these *n*-grams through a one-way ANOVA followed by a Tukey post-hoc test. The results of the ANOVA show significant differences across the 12 L1 groups for all but two of the *n*-grams (*all the*, $p = 0.082$; *without*, $p = 0.060$). For seven other *n*-grams, the p values range from 0.05 down to 0.001 (*that there are*, $p = .031$; *when they*, $p = 0.013$; *does*, $p = 0.007$; *those who*, $p = 0.003$; *give*, $p = 0.001$; *most*, $p = 0.001$; *in front of*, $p = 0.001$). The p values for the remaining 152 *n*-grams are all below 0.001, with F values ranging from 3.2 (*against*) to 27.8 (*of*). The two n-grams with the highest F values (*of, however*) were consistently selected first in the 10 folds of the CV, but the *n*-grams selected after these did not follow the order of their F values. Instead, they were selected in accordance with their unique contribution to the model after removing the amount of variance already accounted for by the *n*-grams already included in the model. Thus, *n*-grams that correlated highly with *of* or *however* (or both) were less likely to be selected.

The Tukey post-hoc tests produced tables showing homogeneous subsets, or clusters of L1 groups. If each L1 group constituted its own cluster, then this would mean that all 12 groups would be significantly different from one another, and the number of clusters would be 12. As it turned out, the largest number of group clusters found in any of the Tukey tests was six, which was found for all of the following five *n*-grams: *have, in, in our, this, we can*. Interestingly, an *n*-gram's F value is not a reliable indicator of the number of homogeneous subsets it produces; for example, the *n*-gram with the highest F value (*of*) produced only four homogeneous subsets. Table 3.10 shows the Tukey results for the 2-gram *we can*, which has six homogeneous subsets. Within each subset, the group means do not differ significantly from one L1 group to another. Across subsets, however, at least some groups are significantly different. Thus, this type of information can be useful for narrowing down the likely

Table 3.10 Tukey HSD*,† post-hoc results for the 2-gram *we can*

L1	n	Homogeneous subsets (values represent group means)					
		1	2	3	4	5	6
German	182	0.21037					
Finnish	121	0.40463	0.40463				
Dutch	125	0.51340	0.51340	0.51340			
Bulgarian	140	0.51660	0.51660	0.51660			
Swedish	217	0.53066	0.53066	0.53066			
Norwegian	270	0.54233	0.54233	0.54233	0.54233		
Polish	288	0.55210	0.55210	0.55210	0.55210		
French	200		0.81769	0.81769	0.81769	0.81769	
Russian	144			0.94531	0.94531	0.94531	0.94531
Italian	86				1.02211	1.02211	1.02211
Spanish	144					1.06782	1.06782
Czech	116						1.38103
p within subset		0.479	0.191	0.141	0.058	0.877	0.132

*Uses harmonic mean sample size = 150.332.
†The group sizes are unequal. The harmonic mean of the group sizes is used. Type I error levels are not guaranteed.
‡Means for groups in homogeneous subsets are displayed.

and unlikely L1 backgrounds for a text with a particular relative frequency for *we can*. This is undoubtedly one of the reasons why *we can* and the other *n*-grams with high numbers of homogeneous subsets were selected so consistently by the stepwise DA. The value of including a large number of *n*-grams in the classification model is that they tend to complement one another regarding which are the likely and unlikely L1 backgrounds for a particular text, often to the extent that they can confidently rule out all but one L1.

Regardless of the number of homogeneous subsets it entails, an *n*-gram can be a valuable part of a larger collection of features when it successfully isolates one L1 group from all others. Our Tukey results show that 20 of the *n*-grams in our optimal set of 161 *n*-grams do this. Nine of these are 1-grams (*but, each, I, is, it, may, my, such, will*), three are 2-grams (*do not, going to, of this*), six are 3-grams (*I think that, are able to, the problem of, not able to, all the time, that in our*) and two are 4-grams (*to be able to, but on the other*). Together, these *n*-grams isolate nine of the 12 L1 groups. The only L1 groups that do not exhibit significantly higher or significantly lower use of at least one of these n-grams in comparison with all other groups are the Bulgarian, Dutch and Norwegian groups. In Table 3.11, we show the Tukey results for the 3-gram *all the time*, which separates the Finnish group from all others.

The fact that some *n*-grams make it possible to identify L1 backgrounds does not necessarily mean that they reflect direct L1 influence. Other potential factors include transfer of training and proficiency level. For example, the 3-gram *as far as*, which distinguishes Polish, French and Russian learners, is most often used in the expression *as far as I am concerned* in the French subcorpus of the ICLE. Transfer may play a part here as the expression has a congruent form in French (*en ce qui me concerne*) but it is clearly reinforced by transfer of training: Although it is rare in English academic writing, *as far as I am concerned* is found in English for Academic Purposes pedagogical material targeting French EFL learners (cf. Paquot, 2010: 160).

Measuring the exact role of L1 influence on the 'unique matrix of frequencies of various linguistic forms' (Krzeszowski, 1990: 212) that characterizes every interlanguage is clearly a task that is beyond the scope of this chapter. This would require a thorough analysis of various transfer effects that have been shown to manifest themselves in foreign language use (Jarvis, 2000). However, some results can be interpreted in the light of previous studies. The fact that the 2-gram *we can* was selected consistently by the stepwise DA can be discussed in relation to a number of studies by Neff and her colleagues that focus on EFL learner writing. Neff *et al.* (2003), for example, compare the use of modals and reporting verbs in ICLE texts written by Dutch, French, German, Italian and Spanish EFL learners. They show that *can* is considerably overused in the writing of Spanish and Italian learners. This overuse stems from the fact that Spanish and Italian learners erroneously use the modal *can* in an epistemic sense, which reflects the more hypothetical senses of the Spanish modal *poder* and the Italian modal *potere*. In contrast, Dutch and German EFL learners have fewer occurrences of the modal *can* in their writing and use it correctly to indicate possibility. In a separate study, Neff *et al.* (2002) report that Spanish EFL learners overuse *we can* (especially when followed by verbs denoting mental or verbal processes) to express root possibility (cf. examples 1 and 2) and ascribe this to the fact that formal Spanish writing adopts a *we*-stance as a strategy for creating a sense of solidarity with the reader (cf. examples 3 and 4).

(1) As a consequence, **we can say that** objectivity is not very common on T.V. (ICLE-SP)
(2) Consequently, **we can see** a great dose of manipulation in every religion. (ICLE-SP)
(3) **Podemos imaginar** el gen O como un interruptor que está encendido o apagado.[2]
 [*We can think of the O gene as a switch that is on or off.*]
(4) Hoy **podemos decir que** todas las corrientes actuales están representadas en la Academia.
 [*Today we can say that all the current trends are represented in the Academy.*]

Our results also show that the 3-gram *on the contrary* contributes significantly to the identification of texts written by French and Italian EFL learners. This can be interpreted in light of Paquot's (2010) analysis of L1 influence in French EFL learners' use of *on the contrary*. She made use of Jarvis' (2000) Unified Framework for transfer studies and compared the French component of the *International Corpus of Learner English* to nine other ICLE sub-corpora. The French learner sub-corpus (ICLE-FR) was found to differ significantly from all other learner groups except for the Italian learner sub-corpus. Granger and Tyson (1996) argue that French learners' overuse and misuse of *on the contrary* is probably due to an over-extension of the semantic properties of French *au contraire*, which can be used to express both concessive and antithetic links. To test for congruity between learners' L1 and interlanguage performance, Paquot compared French EFL learners' use of *on the contrary* in the ICLE, British students' use of *on the contrary* in the *Louvain Corpus of Native Student Essays* (LOCNESS), and French-speaking students' use of the French counterpart *au contraire* in the *Corpus de Dissertations Françaises* (CODIF). She found that the relative frequency of occurrence of *on the contrary* in the interlanguage of French-speaking learners is much closer to the relative frequency of *au contraire* in the CODIF than to the relative frequency of *on the contrary* in LOCNESS (see also Paquot, in preparation). Transfer in this case probably results not so much from the fact that a particular *n*-gram exists in the L1 as from the fact that the *n*-gram is very frequent in the L1 and has a specific function and stylistic profile (Paquot, 2008).

A somewhat more intuitive example concerns the 2-gram *going to*, which, in our data, sets the Spanish learner population apart from all others (cf. examples 5 and 6). The Spanish-speaking learners use this 2-gram significantly more frequently than any other group, and their strong tendency to do so probably originates from the very frequent use of the pattern *ir a* + infinitive in L1 Spanish, which is used to indicate future intensions (cf. examples 7 and 8).

(5) In order to support this argument, **we are going to review** the following subjects: Labour discrimination, the right to vote, the fight against male chauvinist behaviours, the representation of women in important political charges and the recognition of the sexuality in woman. (ICLE-SP)

(6) The last part of my essay **is going to be** about my personal opinion of crime in general. (ICLE-SP)

(7) A estas alturas **no vamos a ensalzar** la figura de Mozart.
['*By now, we are not going to praise the figure of Mozart*']

(8) La estabilización del nivel de las emisiones de dióxido de carbono **va a requerir** una considerable voluntad política.

['The stabilization of the level of carbon monoxide emissions is going to require considerable political will']

Similarly, the Finnish-speaking learners' significant overuse of the 3-gram *all the time* (cf. Table 3.11 and examples 9 through 11) is presumably motivated by the common Finnish phrase *koko ajan* (lit. *whole time*), which, in practice, covers a range of meanings from *usually* to *most of the time* and *all of the time*. Interestingly, phrases in Finnish that more literally correspond with *most of the time* (e.g. *suurimman osan ajasta* = *greatest part of the time*) are much less common and less idiomatic. Taking these L1-related considerations into account, it is therefore not surprising that the Finnish speakers in our study show the lowest use of *most of the time* and the highest use of *all the time*.

(9) Another problem is caused by the fact that computers and other devices of the information age get more sophisticated **all the time**. (ICLE-FI)
(10) The reader cannot help laughing at his descriptions of them whereas Huck is quite serious **all the time**. (ICLE-FI)
(11) I'm not this pessimistic **all the time** but ... (ICLE-FI)

Table 3.11 Tukey HSD*,† post-hoc results for the 3-gram *all the time*‡

		Homogeneous subsets (values represent means)	
L1	n	1	2
Italian	86	0.00000	
Swedish	217	0.03550	
Spanish	144	0.04091	
French	200	0.04349	
Russian	144	0.04467	
Dutch	125	0.04823	
Norwegian	270	0.05839	
Polish	288	0.07469	
German	182	0.07960	
Bulgarian	140	0.09594	
Czech	116	0.10972	
Finnish	121		0.27956
p within subset		0.197	1.000

*Uses harmonic mean sample size = 150.332.
†The group sizes are unequal. The harmonic mean of the group sizes is used. Type I error levels are not guaranteed.
‡Means for groups in homogeneous subsets are displayed.

Conclusion

The purpose of the present study has been to probe the limits of L1 classification in relation to lexical patterns found in learners' L2 writing. Using Chapter 2 as a point of reference, we increased the difficulty of our classification task while simultaneously trying to compensate for the increased difficulty by making the DA classifier more powerful. The difficulty of the classification task resulted mainly from two conditions: the relatively high number of L1s (i.e. 12), and the fact that the data contained a high degree of content variability (i.e. open-ended essays written in response to various prompts). Our attempts to increase the power of the DA model included the use of an expanded pool of hundreds of discriminative features (i.e. words) and the fact that we examined not only individual words but also sequences of two, three and four words. Based on prior work that shows that lexical *n*-gram patterns vary across learners from different L1 backgrounds (e.g. Aarts & Granger, 1998; De Cock *et al.*, 1998; Paquot, 2007), we assumed that the inclusion of *n*-grams in an L1 classification model could substantially boost L1 identification beyond the levels achieved through 1-grams alone.

The only previous study we know of that has attempted L1 classification through the use of lexical *n*-grams is Mayfield Tomokiyo and Jones (2001). As we mentioned earlier, their study shows that the highest level of classification accuracy is attained through a model that includes both 1- and 2-grams, but not 3-grams. The results of the present study support these findings in the sense that our L1 classification model that includes both 1- and 2-grams is significantly more accurate than the model that includes only 1-grams, whereas the models that additionally include 3- and 4-grams are not significantly more accurate than the model including only 1- and 2-grams. On the other hand, our results are more nuanced than those of the prior study in that ours show that the optimal model is not limited to 1- and 2-grams, but rather consists of an amalgam of carefully selected 1-, 2-, 3- and 4-grams.

The fact that our combined models were all successful in identifying the correct L1s of over half of the texts, even though the level of chance was less than 9% and the baseline was just over 14%, is quite encouraging. It suggests, first of all, that learners from individual L1 backgrounds do have relatively consistent within-group and also distinctive between-group word-choice tendencies. Second of all, it suggests that a classifier such as DA is quite effective in homing in on those often extremely subtle and interwoven group-specific tendencies, even when the number of groups is fairly high and some of the L1s are very closely related (e.g. Italian and Spanish; Norwegian and Swedish).

We would, of course, expect that a classifier could achieve even higher levels of L1 classification accuracy through a combination of a wider variety of variables, including not only lexical variables but also grammar- and discourse-related variables, as well as error categories (see Chapter 6). Our purpose in the present study, however, has been to investigate the degree to which learners' lexical usage patterns alone might set them apart from one another in terms of their L1 backgrounds. As mentioned, our results do indeed suggest that lexical *n*-gram patterns alone are powerful indicators of learners' L1s, enabling the prediction of a learner's L1 with greater than a 50% chance of success when there are as many as 12 L1s to choose from. Because of the rigor with which we cross-validated our L1 classification models, we assume that the same procedures and pools of *n*-grams we used will produce similar rates of L1 classification accuracy when applied to other data involving argumentative essays written by learners having similar profiles as those in the present study.

Although our results demonstrate that the data contain relatively reliable group-specific word-choice patterns, we have remained cautious in our interpretations of the results as regards the degree to which those patterns derive from the learners' L1s. Whereas it is certainly possible that L1 transfer is at play in most of the *n*-grams selected in our optimal model (cf. Aarts & Granger, 1998: 140), it is also important not to assume that successful L1 classification necessarily entails L1 influence unless all other relevant variables have been controlled (i.e. eliminated, held constant, or equally stratified) across groups. In cases where learners representing different L1 groups differ not only in relation to their L1s, but also in relation to (1) the nature of the writing task they were given; (2) the nature and extent of their training in the target language; (3) the types and amounts of exposure they have had to the target language; and (4) the levels of proficiency they have attained in the target language and any other languages they have learned, we can expect that any or all of these factors may be the reason for the group-specific patterns found in the data.

L1 classification of the type we have conducted in this study is first of all a text classification problem (see Mayfield Tomokiyo & Jones, 2001) rather than a matter of examining transfer processes per se. At the same time, our classification-based analysis of this learner corpus has identified a large number of lexical items and multiword sequences that are – both individually and collectively – predictive of learners' L1 backgrounds, and which are therefore worthy of further scrutiny regarding the possibility that they do indeed reflect direct L1 influence. For this reason, we consider this type of analysis to represent a valuable new impetus for future directions in transfer research. Traditional studies dealing with second language acquisition, including transfer, have often investigated 'bits and pieces of learners' language chosen for analysis because they caught the researcher's eye, seemed to exhibit some systematicity, confirmed some intuition one had about SLA, or had been found interesting in L1 acquisition' (Lightbown, 1984: 245). In transfer research, the objects of investigation have often been selected on the basis of contrastive analysis or error analysis. The detection-based, corpus-driven approach we have followed in this paper expands the scope of transfer inquiry to include items that might otherwise never have attracted the researcher's eye. This is the nature of discovery, and as described in Chapter 1, the detection-based approach is well suited to a program of discovery.

The pursuit of an approach that fosters new discovery has the tendency to raise a number of new questions along the way. This is certainly true of the present study. In addition to questions about which precise set of *n*-grams is most useful for L1 identification and which of those *n*-grams actually reflect direct L1 influence, the present study has also raised a number of additional questions. One of these questions has to do with the possible influences of other languages besides the L1. For example, we mentioned earlier that when texts written by Finnish speakers are misclassified on the basis of 1-gram usage patterns, they are most frequently misclassified as having been written by Norwegians or Swedes. Does this reflect a cultural dimension of language use (e.g. a Nordic variety of English), or does it reflect the fact that the Finnish speakers have all studied Swedish in school and might therefore be exhibiting Swedish influence in their English writing (e.g. Ringbom, 2007), or both? The patterns of misclassification in the results may indeed reflect the effects of several cultural, educational and linguistic variables.

Another question for future research is what the highest possible rate of L1 classification accuracy is for the data we have examined. When attempting to differentiate 12 L1 groups, is it even possible to achieve accuracy rates higher than, say, 60%? Could this be done with a more carefully selected set of *n*-grams? Could it be done with a wider range of linguistic features that extends beyond the lexical realm? Could it be done with a different classifier than the DA classifier we have used in the present study (but see Jarvis, 2011)? These are important avenues for future exploration.

Another recommendation for further inquiry includes the need to examine longer learner texts and texts representing additional tasks (even oral tasks) and genres. It would also be ideal to run an L1 classification analysis on a corpus that has been tightly controlled for a wide range of factors in order to ensure that the participants representing different L1s are equivalent in all relevant respects except their L1s. Such a corpus would be very difficult to compile, but it would make the L1 classification results a more reliable indicator of the direct L1 influence in the data. Finally, regarding the development of new tools, we believe that it would be very beneficial to develop an L1 classifier that takes both L1 and L2 data into consideration when determining the likelihood that a particular text was written by a speaker of one L1 versus another. The output of such a classifier would presumably constitute direct evidence of L1 influence, and might also be useful for detecting influences from other languages the learner has previously acquired.

Notes

(1) The training sets in Chapter 2 included just over 400 cases.
(2) All Spanish examples come from the news and academic components of the Corpus del Español (http://www.corpusdelespanol.org/).

References

Aarts, J. and Granger, S. (1998) Tag sequences in learner corpora: A key to interlanguage grammar and discourse. In S. Granger (ed.) *Learner English on Computer* (pp. 132–141). London: Addison Wesley Longman.

Baroni, M. and Bernardini, S. (2006) A new approach to the study of translationese: Machine-learning the difference between original and translated text. *Literary and Linguistic Computing* 21, 259–274.

Baayen, R.H. (2008) *Analyzing Linguistic Data: A Practical Introduction to Statistics Using R*. Cambridge: Cambridge University Press.

Biber, D. (2009) A corpus-driven approach to formulaic language in English: Multi-word patterns in speech and writing. *International Journal of Corpus Linguistics* 14, 275–311.

Biber, D. and Conrad, S. (1999) Lexical bundles in conversation and academic prose. In H. Hasselgård and S. Oksefjell (eds) *Out of Corpora: Studies in Honour of Stig Johansson* (pp. 181–190). Amsterdam: Rodopi.

Biber, D., Johansson, S., Leech, G., Conrad, S. and Finegan, E. (1999) *Longman Grammar of Spoken and Written English*. Longman: Harlow.

Biber, D., Conrad, S. and Cortes, V. (2004) If you look at . . . : Lexical bundles in university teaching and textbooks. *Applied Linguistics* 25, 371–405.

Coxhead, A. (2000) A new academic word list. *TESOL Quarterly* 34, 213–238.

Crossley, S. and Louwerse, M. (2007) Multi-dimensional register classification using bigrams. *International Journal of Corpus Linguistics* 12, 453–478.

Davies, M. and Gardner, D. (2010) *A Frequency Dictionary of American English: Word Sketches, Collocates, and Thematic Lists*. New York: Routledge.

De Cock, S. (2004) Preferred sequences of words in NS and NNS speech. *Belgian Journal of English Language and Literatures (BELL), New Series* 2, 225–246.

De Cock, S., Granger, S., Leech, G. and McEnery, T. (1998) An automated approach to the phrasicon of EFL learners. In S. Granger (ed.) *Learner English on Computer* (pp. 67–79). London: Addison Wesley Longman.

Granger, S. and Tyson, S. (1996) Connector usage in the English essay writing of native and non-native EFL speakers of English. *World Englishes* 15, 19–29.

Granger, S., Dagneaux, E., Meunier, F. and Paquot, M. (2009) *The International Corpus of Learner English. Handbook and CD-ROM*. Version 2. Louvain-la-Neuve: Presses universitaires de Louvain.

Jarvis, S. (2000) Methodological rigor in the study of transfer: Identifying L1 influence in the interlanguage lexicon. *Language Learning* 50, 245–309.

Jarvis, S., Grant, L., Bikowski, D. and Ferris, D. (2003) Exploring multiple profiles of highly rated learner compositions. *Journal of Second Language Writing* 12, 377–403.

Jarvis, S. (2011) Data mining with learner corpora: Choosing classifiers for L1 detection. In F. Meunier, S. De Cock, G. Gilquin and M. Paquot (eds) *A Taste for Corpora. In Honour of Sylviane Granger* (pp. 131–158). Amsterdam: John Benjamins.

Koppel, M., Schler, J. and Zigdon, K. (2005) Determining an author's native language by mining a text for errors. In *Proceedings of the Eleventh ACM SIGKDD International Conference on Knowledge Discovery in Data Mining* (pp. 624–628). Chicago: Association for Computing Machinery.

Krzeszowski, T. (1990) *Contrasting Languages. The Scope of Contrastive Linguistics.* Berlin: Mouton de Gruyter.

Lecocke, M. and Hess, K. (2006) An empirical study of univariate and genetic algorithm-based feature selection in binary classification with microarray data. *Cancer Informatics* 2, 313–327.

Leech, G., Rayson, P. and Wilson, A. (2001) *Word Frequencies in Written and Spoken English: Based on the British National Corpus.* London: Longman.

Lightbown, P.M. (1984) The relationship between theory and method in second-language-acquisition research. In A. Davies, C. Criper and A. Howatt (eds) *Interlanguage* (pp. 241–252). Edinburgh: Edinburgh University Press.

Mayfield Tomokiyo, L. and Jones, R. (2001) You're not from 'round here, are you? Naive Bayes detection of non-native utterance text. In *Proceedings of the Second Meeting of the North American Chapter of the Association for Computational Linguistics (NAACL '01)*, unpaginated electronic document. Cambridge, MA: The Association for Computational Linguistics.

McLachlan, G.J. (2004) *Discriminant Analysis and Statistical Pattern Recognition.* Hoboken, NJ: Wiley.

Molinaro, A.M., Simon, R. and Pfeiffer, R.M. (2005) Prediction error estimation: A comparison of resampling methods. *Bioinformatics* 21, 3301–3307.

Neff, J., Dafouz, E., Díez, M., Martínez, F. and Prieto, R. (2002) Evidentiality and the construction of writer stance in native and non-native texts. In J. Hladky (ed.) *Language and Function* (pp. 231–243). Amsterdam: John Benjamins.

Neff, J., Dafouz, E., Díez, M., Martínez, F., Rica, J.P., Prieto, R. and Sancho, C. (2003) Contrasting learner corpora: The use of modal and reporting verbs in the expression of writer stance. In S. Granger and S. Petch-Tyson (eds) *Extending the Scope of Corpus-based Research* (pp. 211–230). Amsterdam: Rodopi.

Paquot, M. (2007) EAP vocabulary in EFL learner writing. A phraseology-oriented approach. PhD thesis, Université Catholique de Louvain.

Paquot, M. (2008) Exemplification in learner writing: A cross-linguistic perspective. In F. Meunier and S. Granger (eds) *Phraseology in Language Learning and Teaching* (pp. 101–119). Amsterdam: Benjamins.

Paquot, M. (2010) *Academic Vocabulary in Learner Writing: From Extraction to Analysis.* London: Continuum.

Paquot, M. (in preparation) Unveiling L1-induced effects with the help of learner corpora: Transfer of lexical priming.

Ringbom, H. (2007) *Cross-Linguistic Similarity in Foreign Language Learning.* Clevedon: Multilingual Matters.

Santini, M. (2004) State-of-the-art on automatic genre identification [Technical Report ITRI-04-03, 2004]. Information Technology Research Institute, UK: University of Brighton.

Schulerud, H. and Albregtsen, F. (2004) Many are called, but few are chosen: Feature selection and error estimation in high dimensional spaces. *Computer Methods and Programs in Biomedicine* 73, 91–99.

Stubbs, M. and Barth, I. (2003) Using recurrent phrases as text-type discriminators: A quantitative method and some findings. *Functions of Language* 10, 61–104.

Tsur, O. and Rappoport, A. (2007) Using classifier features for studying the effect of native language on the choice of written second language words. In *Proceedings of the Workshop on Cognitive Aspects of Computational Language Acquisition* (pp. 9–16). Cambridge, MA: The Association for Computational Linguistics.

Wong, S.-M.J. and Dras, M. (2009) Contrastive analysis and native language identification. In *Proceedings of the Australasian Language Technology Association* (pp. 53–61). Cambridge, MA: The Association for Computational Linguistics.

Appendix

The 161 *n*-grams selected in six or more folds of the 10-fold cross-validation using embedded feature selection, ordered first by number of folds and second by alphabetical order

Folds	*n*-Gram	Folds	*n*-Gram	Folds	*n*-Gram	Folds	*n*-Gram
10	a	10	most	10	with	8	on the one
10	a lot	10	most of the time	10	with the help of	8	only
10	a person	10	my	10	years	8	order to
10	according to	10	no	9	between	8	say that
10	all	10	not able to	9	but on the other	8	they
10	all the	10	now	9	cannot	8	we
10	all the time	10	of	9	do not	8	you are
10	also	10	of a	9	even	7	a number of
10	always	10	often	9	give	7	at the end
10	and	10	on the contrary	9	him	7	by
10	and so	10	on the other	9	in front of	7	does
10	and to	10	or	9	in my opinion	7	don't
10	are able to	10	other	9	in our	7	for instance
10	as far as	10	others	9	in which	7	has
10	because	10	out	9	into	7	I
10	become	10	part of	9	is no	7	is true that
10	but	10	since	9	it	7	look at the
10	could	10	some	9	it is	7	must
10	each	10	sometimes	9	not have to	7	not have
10	fact	10	still	9	of course	7	not only
10	first of all	10	such	9	on the basis of	7	of this
10	for	10	such as	9	that in our	7	problem
10	get	10	that	9	there	7	those
10	have	10	that is to say	9	think that	7	those who
10	how	10	the	9	to be able to	7	to make the
10	however	10	the cause of	9	to do	7	when it comes to
10	if	10	the fact is that	9	to do with	6	against
10	in	10	the most	9	try to	6	an

Folds	n-Gram	Folds	n-Gram	Folds	n-Gram	Folds	n-Gram
10	in the past	10	the opportunity to	9	we can	6	can
10	in this	10	the problem of	9	were	6	example
10	in this way	10	these	9	without	6	have to
10	is	10	things	8	and that is why	6	i think that
10	it is important	10	this	8	as	6	in a
10	it seems to me	10	to	8	as long as	6	just
10	its	10	to get	8	every	6	like
10	made	10	very	8	fact that	6	of the
10	many	10	way of	8	going to	6	on
10	may	10	we have	8	has to	6	one
10	might	10	which	8	like to	6	that there are
10	mind	10	will	8	need	6	them
						6	when they

4 Detecting the First Language of Second Language Writers Using Automated Indices of Cohesion, Lexical Sophistication, Syntactic Complexity and Conceptual Knowledge

Scott A. Crossley and
Danielle S. McNamara

Introduction

Can we reliably predict the first language (L1) of a text written by a second language (L2) writer? Do aspects of the L2 writer's L1 leak through sufficiently such that it can be detected? As discussed in the first chapter of this volume, intuition lends to the assumption that experienced L2 teachers would be able to predict, with some accuracy, the L1 of an L2 writer. Indeed, if particular linguistic features and rhetorical strategies transfer from an L1 to an L2 in predictable ways, the language may be even more apparent to a teacher who shares the same L1 with the student writer. Similarly, if the linguistic features and rhetorical strategies transfer reliably and with sufficient frequency, crosslinguistic influences should be detectable by computational linguistic indices.

With this notion in mind, the objective of this study is to examine the degree to which the L1 of an L2 writer can be detected using computational linguistic indices. We use the computational tool, Coh-Metrix (McNamara &

Graesser, in press), to identify linguistic differences in a corpus of L2 essays written in English by a variety of L1 speakers (Czech, Finnish, German and Spanish). We then develop a statistical model to classify the language background of the writer. Such an approach not only allows us to detect the linguistic patterns associated with specific language backgrounds, but also allows us to test the strength of these differences in classifying texts into specific language groups. Because a statistical model would allow us to predict L1 background with a degree of accuracy that potentially exceeds chance, the success of these models in turn would provide support for theoretical arguments related to crosslinguistic influences (Jarvis, 2010).

Our approach in this study is deeply steeped in theories of cross-linguistic influence (CLI), which is defined as the influence of a person's knowledge of one language on the use or knowledge of another language. Likely the most common approach for analyzing L1 and L2 writing is to search for interlingual differences between L1 and L2 writers and for intralingual similarities within each group (Jarvis & Pavlenko, 2008). Past research has demonstrated that CLI affects almost all areas of linguistic and communicative competence including the lexicon, syntactic constructions, text cohesion and conceptual knowledge (Jarvis & Pavlenko, 2008). Our goal is to investigate these areas of linguistic and communicative competence to explore both interlingual differences and intralingual similarities.

Because the effects of the writer's L1 on the L2 can be quite subtle and are often obscured by other factors (Jarvis & Pavlenko, 2008), simple analyses of data (such as hand counts and intuitive judgments) may not detect faint, patterned differences between L2 texts (Reid, 1992). Thus, for this study, we employ more advanced computational indices that are capable of examining both deep- and surface-level language variables related to lexical sophistication, syntactic complexity, conceptual knowledge and cohesion. Such indices can prove beneficial when investigating the effects of crosslinguistic influences (Crossley & McNamara, 2009).

Computational Tools

While not always the motivation for the development of computational tools, the need exists for quantitative methods with which to analyze the deeper processes, contexts and purposes of discourse, such as analyzing student writing from a CLI perspective (Connor, 2004). Computational tools, unlike hand counts and subjective judgments, allow for the analysis of a large number of texts and the examination of the linguistic practices and processes of different language communities and the language products they create (Connor, 2004; Hyland, 2000). We argue that the best approach to quantifiably investigate the written processes and products manifested by a community of L2 writers in reference to their L1 is through the use of computational tools that have the capability to not only analyze a large number of texts quickly and uniformly, but also tap into deeper linguistic variables related to crosslinguistic influence.

Although uncommon in crosslinguistic influence studies, computational tools have proven to be beneficial in analyzing L2 texts. Computational tools are generally used in conjunction with document classification and machine learning. Researchers employing such approaches use statistical methods to develop algorithms that allow for the mathematical classification of texts. The linguistic data that have traditionally informed text classification models have been lexical in nature (e.g. word frequencies, type/token ratios or part of speech tags). However, more modern computational tools can also measure syntactic complexity, cohesion and conceptual knowledge. The computational tool that currently best represents such approaches is Coh-Metrix (McNamara & Graesser, in press). The Coh-Metrix framework contains a variety of computational components such as lexicons, pattern classifiers, part of speech taggers, syntactic parsers and semantic interpreters that allow for the automatic measurement of linguistic variables. The tool has been validated in a variety of studies that investigated text readability, lexical growth, discourse types and coherence (Crossley *et al.*, 2007, 2008, 2009, 2010).

More relevantly, Coh-Metrix variables have been used successfully to distinguish English essays written by native speakers from essays written by Spanish-speaking learners of English (Crossley & McNamara, 2009). Crossley and McNamara's method of analysis was not only to compare differences between L1 and L2 writing samples, but to also use supervised classification models to predict group membership. Crossley and McNamara focused only on lexical differences related to lexical sophistication (e.g. word frequency, meaningfulness, hypernymy and polysemy) and cohesion (e.g. argument overlap, motion verbs, givenness, causal verbs and locational nouns) to distinguish between L1 and L2 writers. To classify texts as belonging to either the L1 or L2 group, they used a discriminant (function) analysis (DA), which is a supervised classification algorithm that predicts group membership based on expected differences in variable strengths between the two groups. Crossley and McNamara first divided the essays in their corpus into training and test sets based in a 50/50 split. They used the essays in the training set to train the DA model. The reported model from the training set was then applied to the test set to determine how well the model could predict whether the essay was written by a native speaker of English or Spanish speaker writing in English on an independent corpus. Their results demonstrated that a model based on seven lexical variables (word hypernymy, argument overlap, incidence of motion verbs, word frequency, word polysemy, word givenness and age-of-acquisition scores) provided the highest degree of accuracy, classifying 79% of the text into their correct groupings.

Unlike previous studies, the Crossley and McNamara (2009) study signaled the potential to investigate language classification using linguistic features other than word frequencies, errors and parts of speech. In this chapter, we pursue an approach similar to that used in Crossley and McNamara study, but one that considers a greater number of linguistic features across a greater range of texts written in English by a larger number of L1 speakers. Also, unlike the Crossley and McNamara study, our interest is not in examining differences between L2 and L1 writers, but rather in detecting the L1 of an L2 writer. Thus, we seek to discover linguistic features of L2 writers that are relatively invariant within their specific L2 group, but vary among the L2 groups. If clear patterns of linguistic differences emerge between different language groups who are writing in an L2, we will then have additional evidence to support theories of crosslinguistic influences (Jarvis & Pavlenko, 2008).

Methods

In order to examine potential crosslinguistic influences between L2 writers of English, we extracted a sample of L2 essays from the International Corpus of Learner English (ICLE) and used the results from Coh-Metrix as a foundation for a statistical analysis of the data. Because our interest is in determining potential L1 influences, we selected L2 writers who came from diverse L1 backgrounds. Our selected corpus comprised four L1 backgrounds from four different language families: Czech (Slavic), Finnish (Finno-Ugric), German (Germanic) and Spanish (Italic). Thus, we use between-group comparisons (comparisons between people with different language backgrounds) to investigate if the use of the target language differs based on L1 background, or in other words, if the linguistic behavior in the target language is group specific (Jarvis & Pavlenko, 2008). We use the findings from this analysis to examine the linguistic structure of the L2 essays and consider the implications the findings have for the role of crosslinguistic influences in written language production and the strengths of computational tools to detect the language backgrounds of L2 writers.

Sample Selection

The ICLE was designed to meet certain criteria including learner level and rhetorical style. These criteria were implemented in order to make data interpretation easier and allow for clear conclusions as to the kind of errors or differences produced and under what conditions (Granger *et al.*, 2009). The ICLE was designed to consider learner variables such as age (university students in their 20s), learning context (EFL) and mother tongue. It was also designed to consider task variables such as medium (writing), genre (academic essays), field (general) and essay length (between 500 and 1000 words). The most common prompts used in the ICLE corpus are found in

Table 4.1 Most common essay topics in ICLE

- Some people say that in our modern world, dominated by science, technology and industrialization, there is no longer a place for dreaming and imagination. What is your opinion?
- Marx once said that religion was the opium of the masses. If he was alive at the end of the 20th century, he would replace religion with television.
- In his novel *Animal Farm*, George Orwell wrote All men are equal: but some are more equal than others. How true is this today?
- Feminists have done more harm to the cause of women than good.

Table 4.2 Descriptive statistics for the L2 corpora

Language	Mean number of words	Standard deviation	Texts in corpus
Czech	865.022	249.975	183
Finnish	739.947	250.384	229
German	514.159	259.070	296
Spanish	640.528	189.211	195

Table 4.1. The majority of the essays contained in the ICLE are argumentative essays that allow for discourse-orientated as well as grammatical and lexical investigation. To ensure equivalence, we selected only those essays that were argumentative essays. For our sample, we selected all available argumentative essays for each language group (Czech, Finnish, German and Spanish). Descriptive statistics for the selected samples are located in Table 4.2. It is worth mentioning that while the differences between text length in the L2 corpora appear relatively large, the Coh-Metrix indices we report on in this study are normalized for text length.

Statistical Analysis

To examine the hypothesis that there are linguistic differences that differentiate L2 texts based on the L1 of the writer, we conducted a series of stepwise linear discriminant analyses (DA). To obtain benchmark classification results, we conducted a DA on the total essay set without using cross-validation techniques (hereafter referred to as the *total set*). We then conducted a DA using 10-fold cross-validation techniques with embedded feature selection (hereafter referred to as the *10 CV set*). Ten-fold cross-validation provides optimal reliability and efficiency in testing classification models (Lecocke & Hess, 2006; Molinaro *et al.*, 2005) by dividing the data into 10 similarly sized partitions. In each fold of the analysis, one partition is held back as a test set, while the other nine partitions are used to train a model. The model from the training set is then used to classify the data in the held-back set. This procedure is repeated 10 times allowing all data to be classified independently of the training sets. The DA in this study analyzed the different languages in the data (the essays written by Czech, Finnish, German and Spanish writers of English) to examine if linguistic features could distinguish among L2 writers with different L1s.

For the statistical analysis, we selected variables from each measure reported by Coh-Metrix *a priori*. We selected variables *a priori* to avoid issues of multicollinearity that are common with the indices reported by Coh-Metrix (Crossley & McNamara, 2009; Crossley & McNamara, in press). For instance, the Coh-Metrix word frequency measure reports on over 100 indices computed from the CELEX database (Baayen *et al.*, 1995). The word frequency indices can be computed at the sentence level, the paragraph level and the text level. The indices can also be computed for all the words in the sample or only the content words. Additionally, the indices can be computed for the CELEX written corpus, the CELEX spoken corpus or a combination of the two. Lastly, the indices can be computed using raw scores, logarithmic scores, mean scores or standard deviations. When combined, these variations produce the 100 plus word frequency indices available in Coh-Metrix. Similar variations can be found in Coh-Metrix indices related to lexical overlap measures, semantic co-referentiality measures, word information measures, minimal edit distance measures and measures of connectives, spatiality and temporality. In past studies, the potential for multicollinearity has been controlled for using simple correlations, tolerance checks, and variance inflation factors (Crossley & McNamara, 2009; Crossley & McNamara, in press). However, such studies relied solely on a single training and test set for cross-validation avoiding the need for multiple feature selection. Embedded feature selection requires that features be selected at each fold of the DA analysis. If all the indices available in Coh-Metrix were used in an embedded 10-fold cross-validation analysis, a different index from each measure could potentially be selected for each fold, making interpretation of the model difficult.

For our *a priori* feature selection, we chose one index from each Coh-Metrix measure of interest. These measures included cohesion measures (connectives, word overlap, semantic co-referentiality, minimal edit distance), measures of lexical sophistication (word frequency, word familiarity, hypernymy, polysemy), measures of syntactic complexity (number of words before the main verb, syntactic similarity) and measures of conceptual knowledge (spatiality and temporality). We selected individual indices based on their strength in text analyses as found in previous studies (e.g. Crossley *et al.*, 2008; Crossley & McNamara, 2009, in press; McCarthy & Jarvis, 2010; McNamara *et al.*, 2010; Myers *et al.*, 2010) and, in cases where previous studies provided no clear choice, we selected indices that sampled the greatest number of linguistic items (i.e. word concreteness scores for all words versus word concreteness scores for content words only). All the selected indices have relevant correlates in language transfer studies (Jarvis & Pavlenko, 2008). The selected indices along with the constructs they measure are briefly discussed below. For a full overview of how these indices are measured in Coh-Metrix, see Crossley and McNamara (2009).

Cohesion

Cohesion is a crucial aspect of understanding language structure and how connections between propositions in a text can lead to coherent texts. Cohesion also plays an important role in distinguishing differences between L1 and L2 writers (Ferris, 1994; Silva, 1993). The features of cohesion that we investigate in this study are lexical co-referentiality (*stem overlap binary adjacent sentences*), semantic co-referentiality using Latent Semantic Analysis (*LSA sentence to sentence all combination mean score*), given/new information using Latent Semantic Analysis (*LSA average proportion of given information in each sentence*), minimal edit distances (*MED content stems mean score*), causality (*ratio of causal particles to causal verbs*), connectives (*incidence of positive temporal connectives*), and logical operators (*logical operators incident score*). Lexical and semantic co-referentiality are important indicators of cohesion that have been shown to aid in text comprehension and reading speed (Douglas, 1981; Kintsch & van Dijk, 1978; Rashotte & Torgesen, 1985). MED measures the location of specific words in sentences relative to their location in other sentences (with higher scores indicating lower cohesion and greater distance; McCarthy *et al.*, 2009). Given/new information relates to the amount of information available for recovery from the preceding discourse (Halliday, 1967). Causality is relevant to texts that depend on causal relations between events and actions (i.e. stories with an action plot or science texts with causal mechanisms) and is also relevant at the sentential level in order to show causal relationship between simple clauses (Pearson, 1974–1975). Connectives play an important role in the creation of cohesive links between ideas and clauses (Crismore *et al.*, 1993; Longo, 1994) and provide clues about text organization (van de Kopple, 1985) while logical operators relate directly to the density and abstractness of a text and correlate to higher demands on working memory (Costerman & Fayol, 1997).

Lexical Sophistication

The lexical items that we examine in this study involve lexical representation, lexical accessibility and lexical activation. These lexical features are important in forming links between words within and across languages. Their use is informed through frequency effects, language proficiency and order of acquisition. From a transfer position, lexical background activation can be primed by formal and typological similarities between the L1 and the target language (Jarvis & Pavlenko, 2008). Specifically, the lexical indices that we investigate are word information features (*word concreteness, familiarity, imagability and meaningfulness for every word*), hypernymy (*average of word hypernymy*), polysemy (*average of word polysemy*), word frequency (*average CELEX content word frequency by logarithm in sentence*) and lexical diversity (*Measure of Text Length and Diversity; MTLD*). Word information measures assess lexical constructs such as word salience (familiarity), word abstractness (concreteness), the evocation of mental and sensory images (imagability), the number of word associations attributable to a word (meaningfulness) and intuited order of lexical acquisition (age of acquisition; Salsbury *et al.*, 2011). Polysemy refers to the number of senses a word contains and is an important indicator of the text's ambiguity. Hypernymy refers to the number of levels a word has in a conceptual, taxonomic hierarchy and is related to text abstractness (Crossley *et al.*, 2007). Word frequency indices are signals of lexical sophistication (Linnarud, 1986; Silva, 1993). Lexical diversity is indicative of the range of vocabulary deployed by a speaker or writer with past studies demonstrating that more proficient L2 writers produce texts with greater lexical diversity (Engber, 1995; Grant & Ginther, 2000; Jarvis, 2002).

Syntactic Complexity

Recent studies into the potential for transfer at the level of syntax have demonstrated robust support for the notion of syntactic transfer. Transfer effects have been noted in adverbial placement, relative clauses and cleft constructions (Jarvis & Pavlenko, 2008). The syntactic features that we examine in our study include syntactic complexity (*mean number of words before the main verb*) and syntactic similarity (*sentence syntax similarity all sentence combinations mean*). Texts with difficult syntactic constructions include the use of embedded constituents and are often structurally dense, syntactically ambiguous, or ungrammatical (Graesser *et al.*, 2004). As a consequence, they are more difficult to process and comprehend (Perfetti *et al.*, 2005). Conversely, more uniform syntactic constructions result in less complex syntax that is easier for the reader to process (Crossley *et al.*, 2008).

Conceptual Knowledge

Various studies have demonstrated that crosslinguistic influences are affected by differences in language-mediated concepts and language specific patterns in framing. The development of L2-mediated concepts is influenced, among other things, by linguistic transparency and concept salience (Jarvis & Pavlenko, 2008). The four conceptual patterns that we will examine are spatiality (*number of motion verbs per 1000 verb phrases*) and temporality (*aspect repetition score*). Spatiality and motion help to construct a text and ensures that the situational model of the text is well structured and clearly conveys text meaning (Kintsch & van Dijk, 1978; Zwaan *et al.*, 1995). Aspect conveys the dynamics of the point itself such as the point being ongoing or completed

(Klein, 1994) and helps maintain information in working memory (Magliano & Schleich, 2000).

Analysis

ANOVA

An ANOVA was conducted using the selected Coh-Metrix measures as the dependent variables and the essays from the total set as the independent variables. The ANOVA was used to collect descriptive statistics for the selected variables (presented in Table 4.3 and ordered by effect size) and to analyze differences in the selected variables between the language groups. All the selected indices reported significant differences between the selected language groups.

Variable Selection

The stepwise DA selected variables based on a statistical criterion that retains the variables that best classify the grouping variable and helps control for potential multicollinearity. For our analysis, the significance level for a variable to enter or to be removed from the model was set at 0.05. For the total set, the stepwise DA retained 15 variables as significant predictors and removed four variables. For each fold in our 10 CV analysis, the DA retained 14 of the same variables retained in the total set as significant predictors. In addition, one variable was retained in two of the folds but not in the other eight while another variable was retained in one fold only and not in the other nine. Three variables were not retained in any of the folds. The selected variables and their retention information for both the total set and 10 CV set are provided in Table 4.4.

Accuracy of Model

We report the findings from our DA using an estimation of the accuracy of the analysis. We made this estimation by plotting the correspondence between the groupings (the L2 writers' L1) using the total set and the 10 CV set. Discriminant analyses on both sets used stepwise feature selection. For the 10 CV set, the stepwise feature selection was embedded within each fold of the cross-validation. The classification results from the total set and the 10 CV set are reported in Table 4.5.

The classification results demonstrate that the discriminant analysis correctly allocated 610 of the 902 essays in the total set (df = 9, n = 902,) χ^2 = 909.911, p < 0.001) for a classification accuracy of 67.6% (chance for this analysis is 25%). The reported Kappa = 0.565, indicates a moderate agreement between the actual essay classification and the predicted essay classification

Table 4.3 Means, F values, and effect sizes for the L2 essays in the total set*

Variables	Czech	Finnish	German	Spanish	$F(3, 899)$	η^2
Word concreteness every word	299.413	293.844	308.583	291.985	132.440	0.307
Word imagability every word	326.031	319.861	333.644	318.452	109.451	0.268
Number of motion verbs	82.384	101.652	146.696	80.227	100.268	0.251
Causal particles/verbs	0.452	0.587	0.527	0.993	63.900	0.176
Lexical diversity MTLD	82.075	90.258	104.791	85.313	56.889	0.160
LSA givenness	0.320	0.318	0.279	0.310	48.629	0.140
Stem overlap	0.253	0.307	0.207	0.346	44.703	0.130
Word meaningfulness every word	355.176	347.907	354.825	345.459	42.716	0.125
CELEX content word frequency	1.469	1.272	1.201	1.236	40.061	0.118
No. words before the main verb	3.352	4.204	4.722	4.687	32.663	0.098
LSA sentence to sentence mean	0.141	0.179	0.134	0.179	26.249	0.081
Aspect repetition score	0.917	0.862	0.912	0.865	20.681	0.065
Sentence syntax similarity	0.107	0.082	0.078	0.070	19.747	0.062
Positive temporal connectives	7.843	8.001	10.708	7.702	18.850	0.059
Logical operator incidence score	62.433	52.989	52.582	49.260	16.969	0.054
Word familiarity every word	593.996	592.970	594.640	593.396	12.411	0.040
Word polysemy	4.054	4.014	3.857	3.880	8.866	0.029
MED content stems mean	0.878	0.899	0.913	0.901	8.161	0.027
Word hypernymy	1.593	1.601	1.546	1.581	4.408	0.015

*For all indices $p < 0.001$.

Table 4.4 Variable retention in total set and 10 CV set

Variable	Retained in total set DA	Number of folds retained in 10 CV set
Word concreteness every word	+	10
Word imagability every word	+	10
Number of motion verbs	+	10
Causal particles/verbs	+	10
Lexical diversity MTLD	+	10
LSA givenness	+	10
Stem overlap	−	2
Word meaningfulness every word	+	10
CELEX content word frequency	+	10
Number of words before the main verb	+	10
LSA sentence to sentence mean	+	10
Aspect repetition score	+	10
Sentence syntax similarity	+	1
Incidence of positive temporal connectives	−	0
Logical operator incidence score	+	10
Word familiarity every word	+	10
Word polysemy	−	0
MED content stems mean	−	0
Word hypernymy	+	10

Table 4.5 Predicted text type versus actual text type results from total set and 10 CV set

Actual text type	Predicted text type			
Total set	Czech	Finnish	German	Spanish
Czech	**134**	33	6	10
Finnish	34	**141**	13	39
German	17	31	**224**	25
Spanish	22	51	11	**111**
10 CV set	Czech	Finnish	German	Spanish
Czech	**136**	32	7	8
Finnish	40	**133**	13	41
German	18	31	**223**	25
Spanish	24	58	11	**102**

Table 4.6 Precision and recall finding (total set and 10 CV set)

Total set

Text set	Recall	Precision	F1
Czech	0.732	0.647	0.687
Finnish	0.621	0.551	0.584
German	0.754	0.882	0.813
Spanish	0.569	0.600	0.584

10 CV Set

Text set	Recall	Precision	F1
Czech	0.743	0.624	0.678
Finnish	0.586	0.524	0.553
German	0.751	0.878	0.809
Spanish	0.523	0.580	0.550

for the total set. For the 10 CV set, the discriminant analysis correctly allocated 594 of the 902 essays (df = 9, n = 902, χ^2 = 855.810, p < 0.001) for an accuracy of 65.8% (chance for this analysis is also 25%). The reported Kappa = 0.542, indicates a moderate agreement between the actual essay classification and the predicted essay classification for the 10 CV set.

As is also common, this study reports its results in terms of recall and precision. Recall scores are computed by tallying the number of hits over the number of hits+misses. Precision is the number of correct predictions divided by the sum of the number of correct predictions and false positives. This distinction is important because if an algorithm predicted everything to be a member of a single group it would score 100% in terms of recall, but only by claiming members of the other group. If this happened, then the algorithm would score low in terms of precision. By reporting both values, we can better understand the overall accuracy of the model. The precision, recall, and F1 scores[1] of the model for predicting the L1 for the L2 texts written in English can be found in Table 4.6. The average F1 score of the model for the total set was 0.667. The average F1 score for the 10 CV set was 0.647. The results provide strong evidence that the linguistic features of essays can be used to classify L2 essays based on the L1 of the writer.

Pairwise Comparisons

As part of the ANOVA, a series of pairwise comparisons were conducted to examine specific differences between essays written in English by native speakers of Czech, Finnish, German and Spanish, for each selected Coh-Metrix index. Those results are reported below for the variables retained in each fold of the 10-fold CV and summarized in Table 4.7.

Word concreteness. The results from the word concreteness scores indicate that all language pairs except for Spanish to Finnish showed significant differences. The concreteness scores reveal that German writers tend to use the most concrete words, while Spanish writers use the least concrete words.

Word imagability. Like the word concreteness scores, the word imagability scores show that all language pairs except for Spanish to Finnish showed significant differences. The imagability scores reveal that German writers tended to use words that were more imagable, whereas Spanish writers used the least imagable words.

Motion verbs. The findings from the motion verb index demonstrate that all language groupings except for the Spanish to Czech groupings showed significant differences. Spanish essays exhibited the fewest motion verbs while German essay exhibited the most.

Table 4.7 Pairwise comparisons between language groupings*

Coh-Metrix Index	Significant difference
Word concreteness	GE>CZ>(FN=SP)
Word imagability	GE>CZ>(FN=SP)
Motion verbs	GE>FN>(CZ=SP)
Causal verbs and particles	SP>FN>GE>CZ
Lexical diversity	GE>FN>(SP=CZ)
LSA given/new	(CZ=FN)>SP>GE
Stem overlap	SP>FN>CZ>GE
Word meaningfulness	(CZ=GE)>FN>SP
Celex word frequency	CZ>(FN=SP=GE), FN>GE
Syntactic complexity	(GE=SP)>FN>CZ
LSA sentence to sentence	(SP=FN)>(CZ=GE)
Temporal cohesion	(CZ=GE)>(FN=SP)
Logical operators	CZ>(FN=GE)>SP
Word familiarity	(GE=CZ)>(SP=FN)
Word hypernymy	(FN=CZ)>GE, (CZ=SP)>GE

*CZ=Czech, FN=Finnish, GE=German, SP=Spanish

Note: The significant difference column presents the statistically significant differences between the means according to the pairwise comparisons. For example, GE>CZ>(FN=SP) indicates that the mean for the FN group does not differ significantly from that of the SP group, while both of these means are significantly lower than the mean for the GE and CZ group. Additionally, the mean for the GE group is significantly higher than the CZ group.

Causal verbs and particles. The causal verbs and particles incidence scores indicate that all language groupings showed significant differences in their causal cohesion, Spanish essays contained the most causal cohesion while Czech essays contained the least.

Lexical diversity. The results reveal that all language pairs except for Spanish and Czech yielded significant differences in lexical diversity. German essays contained the greatest lexical diversity while Czech essays contained the least lexical diversity.

LSA given/new. The given/new findings reveal that the German writers showed significant differences with all the other L2 language writers and that Spanish and Czech writers also differed significantly. Czech writers used the most given information while German writers used the least.

Stem overlap. The results of the noun overlap scores show that all language groups demonstrated significant differences from one another. German essays contained the least noun overlap while Spanish essays contained the most noun overlap.

Word meaningfulness. The results reveal all language groupings except for German and Czech showed significant differences in their use of meaningful words. The Czech writers used words with the highest meaningfulness scores, while the Spanish writers used words with the lowest meaningfulness scores.

CELEX word frequency. The results indicate that all language groupings except for Spanish to Finnish and Spanish to German yielded significant differences in their use of frequent words. German essays contained the least frequent words while Czech essays contained the most frequent words.

Syntactic complexity. The findings reveal that all language groupings expect for German to Spanish demonstrated significant differences. German essays contained the most number of words before the main verb phrase, while Czech essays contained the fewest words before the main verb phrase.

LSA sentence to sentence. No differences were noted between Czech and German writers or between Spanish and Finnish writers for semantic co-referentiality. Significant differences were reported for all other language pairs. Spanish writers wrote essays containing the most semantic co-referentiality while German writers wrote essays containing the least.

Temporal cohesion. The findings reveal that all language groupings except for German to Czech and Finnish to Spanish exhibited significant differences in temporal cohesion. Finnish writers displayed the lowest amount of temporal cohesion while Czech writers exhibited the greatest.

Logical operators. The results demonstrate that Czech essays, when compared with all other language groupings, showed significant differences in their incidence of logical operators (*and, if* and *or*). No differences were reported between Finnish and German. The Czech writers used the most logical operators, while the Spanish used the fewest logical operators.

Word familiarity. The findings indicate that German and Czech essays, when compared with all other language groupings, showed significant differences in word familiarity. No differences were noted between Spanish and Finnish essays. German essays contained the highest word familiarity scores, while Finnish essays had the lowest word familiarity scores.

Word hypernymy. The findings from the hypernymy index show that all language groupings except for the Finnish to Czech and Czech to Spanish comparisons demonstrated significant differences. German essays contained the least specific words while Finnish essays contained the most specific words.

Discussion and Conclusion

This study has demonstrated that linguistic indices related to cohesion, lexical sophistication, syntactic complexity and conceptual knowledge can significantly predict group membership based on a writer's L1. The study thus provides supporting evidence for theories of crosslinguistic influence and the use of linguistic features to inform language detection algorithms. Specifically, this study shows that four different languages from four different language families can be predicted with varying degrees of success based on interlingual differences that exist between the groups and on intralingual similarities within each group. Our classifier performed best in categorizing German essays and worst in categorizing Finnish and Spanish essays.

Our analysis demonstrated that the strongest predictors for distinguishing the writing samples in our corpus were generally lexical in nature (word concreteness, word imagability, lexical diversity, word frequency, word meaningfulness, word familiarity and word hypernymy) followed by indices of text cohesion (causality, givenness, stem overlap, semantic co-referentiality and logical operators). Our analysis also indicated that indices related to conceptual knowledge (motion verbs and aspect repetition) and one index of syntactic complexity (number of words before the main verb) were also important predictors for predicting the L1 of an L2 writer. Below, we discuss these linguistic features in relation to the manner in which they help characterize writers from different language backgrounds.

Czech. When compared with the other language groups investigated, the portrait of Czech writers that emerges from this analysis is that of writers who do not heavily depend on cohesive elements to connect aspects of the text together, with the exception of logical operators. Hence, they tend not to use a great deal of word overlap or causality but they do tend to use connectives. Czechs write in a manner that does not indicate a high degree of lexical sophistication, producing a low variety of words that are frequent, concrete, imagable, meaningful and familiar. An exception to this trend is the production of highly polysemous words. However, this latter attribute may be the result of their tendency to use frequent words, which are more polysemous (Davies & Widdowson, 1974). Czech writing is also low in syntactic complexity. Conceptually, Czech writers appear prone to use less spatiality and higher degrees of temporality than the other language groups in this study. We, thus, see a group of writers that produce texts that are linguistically less complex and less cohesive when compared with Finnish, German and Spanish writers. Language distance may provide a potential explanation for these differences in that languages that are further apart (as in the case of English and Czech when compared with German and Spanish) generally share fewer features and thus afford less transfer of linguistic items (Biskup, 1992).

Finnish. The results of our study show that Finnish texts are represented as demonstrating an average use of cohesive devices when compared with the other language groups. From a lexical perspective, Finnish essays do appear to contain a higher degree of lexical sophistication, especially in reference to word concreteness, word meaningfulness, word familiarity and word hypernymy. Finnish writers do not demonstrate either simple or complex syntactic structures, but instead produce syntactic structures that are of average complexity in comparison with the other languages sampled. From a conceptual standpoint, Finnish writers produce texts that seem to include an average amount of text spatiality and lower temporality and intentionality. The findings that Finnish writers produce texts with limited syntactic complexity as well as low temporality and intentionality supports, to a degree, the notion that Finns over-simplify their writing (Ventola & Mauranen, 1991). However, their use of words with greater lexical sophistication complicates this prior supposition.

German. In general, German writers, as compared to the other language groups sampled, seem to produce texts of lower lexical cohesion with little emphasis on stem overlap, semantic co-referentiality and given information. Essays by German writers do, however, contain a higher number of positive temporal connectives (i.e. *after, later, next*). In contrast to the lower lexical cohesion, German writers appear to produce texts with a high degree of lexical sophistication evidenced in their use of infrequent words and high lexical diversity. However, this finding is tempered by the properties of the words, which demonstrate that they are more concrete, more meaningful, more familiar, less specific and less ambiguous. Syntactically, German writers produce complex sentences and German essays contain a greater amount of spatial and temporal information. The findings suggest that German writers of English may emphasize content over form (Clyne, 1987) unlike other writers who may try to make the text more readable. Such an argument is supported by low lexical diversity scores, the use of infrequent words, lower argument overlap and greater syntactic complexity. In contrast, high values for word concreteness, imagability, meaningfulness and familiarity, along with low values for word senses, provides evidence that German writers may focus on content.

Spanish. The findings of this study illustrate that Spanish writers, in comparison with the other language groups investigated, show relatively high degrees of lexical cohesion in their essays, especially in reference to stem overlap, semantic co-referentiality and causal cohesion. Spanish essays only exhibit low cohesion in reference to logical operators and connectives. In terms of lexicon, Spanish writers produce frequent words that are lexically sophisticated (i.e. low concreteness, meaningfulness, familiarity scores). The words produced are also relatively unambiguous. Unlike Czech and Finnish essays, Spanish essays exhibit greater syntactic complexity. Conceptually, Spanish essays demonstrate low spatiality and temporality. Overall, Spanish writers appear to produce lexically cohesive texts that demonstrate a high degree of linguistic sophistication (both lexical and syntactic). Spanish texts, when compared with German texts, thus seem to focus more on form as compared to content. The low incidence of connectives and logical operators likely supports the notion that Spanish writing is loosely coordinated (Montaño-Harmon, 1988).

While our overall accuracy in categorizing essays into their appropriate language group was well above chance, our study is not without limitations. There are indications that the corpus from which we selected our samples (the ICLE) might be biased by the proficiency levels of the writers who comprise specific language groups (see Chapter 5, this volume). If differences in proficiency level exist between language groups, our analysis may not be classifying texts based on linguistic features intrinsic to a language population, but rather intrinsic to a proficiency level. However, as reported by Bestgen *et al.*, linguistic features can be used successfully in automated L1 group identification tasks for populations that are controlled for proficiency. Additionally, we did not control for the potential impacts of errors on the indices used in this study. A greater number of spelling errors on the part of one L1 group could, for example, lead to higher lexical diversity scores (Granger & Wynne, 1999). As well, syntactic errors on the part of writers could also affect the parser used in Coh-Metrix and, as a result, indices of syntactic similarity (Lonsdale & Strong-Krause, 2003). Another limitation of our approach is that we did not analyze crosslinguistic performance congruity. Such an approach requires an examination of the learners' L1 in reference to reported differences in their L2 production and analysis of the L1 and the L2 for performance similarities. If similarities were found between the linguistic features in the L1 and the linguistic features in the L2, then we would have stronger evidence of crosslinguistic influences. Such an approach would further the findings that we report in this study and provide for a greater understanding of why these differences occur in reference to the patterns of the writer's L1.

An additional study that would also prove beneficial, especially in reference to the validity of computational tools to discriminate between L1 essay groupings, would involve a comparison of human judgments to machine judgments of authorship attribution. A comparison of human capability to distinguish L1 authorship to that of a computational tool would provide important convergent validity for the use of the computational and statistical analyses employed in this study to discriminate among authorship groupings. Lastly, while Coh-Metrix reports on a variety of automated linguistic features, it is not representative of all linguistic features. Additional features related to semantic categories, lexical arguments, collocation accuracy and basic category use (among others) may prove beneficial in detecting the L1 of L2 writers.

In conclusion, it is important to note that our approach toward language detection examined both intergroup heterogeneity and intragroup homogeneity as evidence of crosslinguistic influences in our sampled language groups. That is to say, we examined groups of language speakers that spoke different first languages (L1) under the assumption that their L1 would influence their second language (L2) production such that differences between the groups were evident as were similarities within the groups. Our support for this hypothesis is founded on differences in the linguistic features found in the groups' L2 production (i.e. the English essays). Our results strongly support the notion that linguistic features reliably differ in predictable ways among the essays we sampled from the four different language backgrounds. These findings provide support for theories of crosslinguistic influences as well as support for using computational indices to detect the L1 of L2 writers.

Acknowledgments

This research was supported by the Institute for Education Sciences (IES R305G020018-02; IES R305A080589). Any opinions, findings and conclusions or recommendations expressed in this material are those of the authors and do not necessarily reflect the views of the IES.

Note

(1) The F1 scores function as a weighted average of the precision and recall scores. F1 scores are calculated by multiplying the precision and recall scores, dividing that number by the sum of the precision and recall scores, and multiplying that value by 2.

References

Baayen, R.H., Piepenbrock, R. and Gulikers, L. (1995) *The CELEX Lexical Database (Release 2) [CDROM]*. Philadelphia, PA: Linguistic Data Consortium, University of Pennsylvania.

Biskup, D. (1992) L1 influence on learners' renderings of English collocations: A Polish/German empirical study. In P.J.L. Arnaud and H. Béjoint (eds) *Vocabulary and Applied Linguistics* (pp. 85–93). Basingstoke: Macmillan.

Clyne, M. (1987) Cultural differences in the organization of academic texts. *Journal of Pragmatics* 11, 211–247.
Connor, U. (2004) Intercultural rhetoric research: Beyond texts. *Journal of English for Academic Purposes* 3, 291–304.
Costerman, J. and Fayol, M. (1997) *Processing Interclausal Relationships: Studies in Production and Comprehension of Text*. Hillsdale, NJ: Lawrence Erlbaum Associates.
Crismore, A., Markkanen, R. and Steffensen, M.S. (1993) Metadiscourse in persuasive writing: A study of texts written by American and Finnish university students. *Written Communication* 10, 39–71.
Crossley, S.A. and McNamara, D.S. (2009) Computational assessment of lexical differences in L1 and L2 writing. *Journal of Second Language Writing* 18, 119–135.
Crossley, S.A. and McNamara, D.S. (in press) Predicting second language writing proficiency: The role of cohesion, readability, and lexical difficulty. *Journal of Research in Reading*.
Crossley, S.A., Louwerse, M.M., McCarthy, P.M. and McNamara, D.S. (2007) A linguistic analysis of simplified and authentic texts. *The Modern Language Journal* 91, 15–30.
Crossley, S.A., Greenfield, J. and McNamara, D.S. (2008) Assessing text readability using cognitively based indices. *TESOL Quarterly* 42, 475–493.
Crossley, S.A, Salsbury, T. and McNamara, D.S. (2009) Measuring L2 lexical growth using hypernymic relationships. *Language Learning* 59, 307–334.
Crossley, S.A., Salsbury, T. and McNamara, D.S. (2010) The role of lexical cohesive devices in triggering negotiations for meaning. *Issues in Applied Linguistics* 18, 55–80.
Davies, A. and Widdowson, H.G. (1974) Reading and writing. In J.B.P. Allen and S.P. Corder (eds) *The Edinburgh Course in Applied Linguistics: Techniques in Applied Linguistics* (pp. 155–201). London: Oxford University Press.
Douglas, D. (1981) An exploratory study of bilingual reading proficiency. In S. Hudelson (ed.) *Learning to Read in Different Languages* (pp. 33–102). Washington, DC: Washington Center for Applied Linguistics.
Engber, C.A. (1995) The relationship of lexical proficiency to the quality of ESL compositions. *Journal of Second Language Writing* 4, 139–155.
Ferris, D.R. (1994) Lexical and syntactic features of ESL writing by students at different levels of L2 proficiency. *TESOL Quarterly* 28, 414–420.
Granger, S. and Wynne, M. (1999) Optimising measures of lexical variation in EFL learner corpora. In J. Kirk (ed.) *Corpora Galore* (pp. 249–257). Amsterdam: Rodopi.
Granger, S., Dagneaux, E., Meunier, F. and Paquot, M. (2009) *The International Corpus of Learner English. Handbook and CD-ROM* (2nd edn). Louvain-la-Neuve: Presses Universitaires de Louvain.
Grant, L. and Ginther, A. (2000) Using computer-tagged linguistic features to describe L2 writing differences. *Journal of Second Language Writing* 9, 123–145.
Graesser, A.C., McNamara, D.S., Louwerse, M.M. and Cai, Z. (2004) Coh-Metrix: Analysis of text on cohesion and language. *Behavior Research Methods, Instruments, and Computers* 36, 193–202.
Halliday, M.A.K. (1967) Notes on transitivity and theme in English. *Journal of Linguistics* 3, 199–244.
Hyland, K. (2000) *Disciplinary Discourses: Social Interactions in Academic Writing*. Harlow: Pearson.
Jarvis, S. (2002) Short texts, best-fitting curves and new measures of lexical diversity. *Language Testing* 19, 57–84.
Jarvis, S. (2010) Comparison-based and detection-based approaches to transfer research. In L. Roberts, M. Howard, M. Ó Laoire and D. Singleton (eds) *EUROSLA Yearbook 10* (pp. 169–192). Amsterdam: Benjamins.

Jarvis, S. and Pavlenko, A. (2008) *Crosslinguistic Influence in Language and Cognition*. New York: Routledge.

Lecocke, M. and Hess, K. (2006) An empirical study of univariate and genetic algorithm-based feature selection in binary classification with microarray data. *Cancer Informatics* 2, 313–327.

Linnarud, M. (1986) *Lexis in Composition: A Performance Analysis of Swedish*. Lund, Sweden: Liber Forlag Malmo.

Longo, B. (1994) Current research in technical communication: The role of metadiscourse in persuasion. *Technical Communication* 41, 348–352.

Lonsdale, D. and Strong-Krause, D. (2003) Automated rating of ESL essays. In *Proceedings of the NAACL 2003 Workshop* (pp. 61–67). Morristown, NJ: Association for Computational Linguistics.

Kintsch, W. and Van Dijk, T.A. (1978) Toward a model of text comprehension and production. *Psychological Review* 85, 363 – 394.

Klein, W. (1994) *Time in Language*. London: Routledge.

Magliano, J.P. and Schleich, M.C. (2000) Verb aspect and situation models. *Discourse Processes* 29, 83–112.

McNamara, D.S., Crossley, S.A. and McCarthy, P.M. (2010) Linguistic features of writing quality. *Written Communication* 27, 57–86.

McNamara, D.S. and Graesser, A.C. (in press) Coh-Metrix: An automated tool for theoretical and applied natural language processing. In P.M. McCarthy and C. Boonthum (eds) *Applied Natural Language Processing and Content Analysis: Identification, Investigation, and Resolution*. Hershey, PA: IGI Global.

McCarthy, P.M., Guess, R.H. and McNamara, D.S. (2009) The components of paraphrase evaluations. *Behavior Research Methods* 41, 682–690.

McCarthy, P.M. and Jarvis, S. (2010) MTLD, vocd-D, and HD-D: A validation study of sophisticated approaches to lexical diversity assessment. *Behavior Research Methods* 42, 381–392.

Molinaro, A.M., Simon, R. and Pfeiffer, R.M. (2005) Prediction error estimation: A comparison of resampling methods. *Bioinformatics* 21, 3301–3307.

Montaño-Harmon, M. (1988) Discourse features in the compositions of Mexican English as a second language. Mexican-American Chicano, and Anglo high school students: Considerations for the formulation of educational policy. PhD thesis, University of Southern California, Los Angeles.

Myers, J.C., McCarthy, P.M., Duran, N.D. and McNamara, D.S. (2010) The bit in the middle and why it's important: A computational analysis of the linguistic features of body paragraphs. *Behavior Research Methods* 41, 201–209.

Pearson, P.D. (1974–75) The effects of grammatical complexity on children's comprehension, recall, and conception of certain semantic relationships. *Reading Research Quarterly* 10, 155–192.

Perfetti, C.A., Landi, N. and Oakhill, J. (2005) The acquisition of reading comprehension skill. In M.J. Snowling and C. Hulme (eds) *The Science of Reading: A Handbook* (pp. 227–247). Oxford: Blackwell.

Rashotte, C.A. and Torgesen, J.K. (1985) Repeated reading and reading fluency in learning disabled children. *Reading Research Quarterly* 20, 180–188.

Reid, J. (1992) A computer text analysis of four cohesion devices in English discourse by native and nonnative writers. *Journal of Second Language Writing* 1, 79–107.

Salsbury, T., Crossley, S.A. and McNamara, D.S. (2011) Psycholinguistic word information in second language oral discourse. *Second Language Research* 27, 343–360.

Silva, T. (1993) Toward an understanding of the distinct nature of L2 writing: The ESL research and its implications. *TESOL Quarterly* 27, 657–675.

van de Kopple, W.J. (1985) Some exploratory discourse on metadiscourse. *College, Composition and Communication* 36, 82–93.

Ventola, E. and Mauranen, A. (1991) Non-native writing and native revising of scientific articles. In E. Ventola (ed.) *Functional and Systemic Linguistics: Approaches and Uses* (pp. 457–492). Berlin: Mouton de Gruyter.

Zwaan, R.A., Magliano, J.P. and Graesser, A.C. (1995) Dimensions of situation-model construction in narrative comprehension. *Journal of Experimental Psychology: Learning, Memory, and Cognition* 21, 386–397.

5 Error Patterns and Automatic L1 Identification

Yves Bestgen, Sylviane Granger and Jennifer Thewissen

Introduction

The strong version of the Contrastive Analysis Hypothesis rested on the 'difference equals difficulty principle'. That is to say, learner errors can be predicted on the basis of differences between their mother tongue (L1) and the target language (L2). Although this strong version has been abandoned, research in error analysis and more recently, computer-aided error analysis has demonstrated that a sizable proportion of errors are L1-induced (see results of studies by Chuang & Nesi, 2006; Díez-Bedmar & Papp, 2008; Hawkins & Buttery, 2010; Neff & Bunce, 2005). It would thus seem reasonable to use error patterns as a clue to L1 identification. However, a survey of the literature shows that errors have rarely been used as a profiling criterion for this purpose, although they are one of the standard variables used in other types of stylometric studies, notably those that aim to determine learners' proficiency level (see Dikli, 2006 for a survey of automated scoring systems). The aim of this chapter is to investigate the extent to which error patterns can be relied on for automatic L1 identification.

Two recent studies have used errors as a sole or additional feature for the purposes of L1 identification. Koppel *et al.* (2005) based their investigation on five sub-corpora of the first version of the *International Corpus of Learner English* (L1 Russian, Czech, Bulgarian, French and Spanish). Using a mixture of features (several error types as well as function words, letter *n*-grams, and rare POS bigrams), they achieved an automatic identification rate of 80%. In their conclusion, the authors add an important caveat, which is that they may have taken 'unfair advantage of differences in overall proficiency among the different sub-corpora' (Koppel *et al.*, 2005: 627). They give as an example Bulgarian learners who were considerably less error prone than the Spanish learners. However, their investigation brings out a number of distinctive patterns that can be exploited for identifying the L1 of particular learner populations, such as the unnecessary doubling of consonants by Spanish learners or the overuse and misuse of *indeed*, which is characteristic of French learners. In a subsequent investigation, Wong and Dras (2009) used the same five sub-corpora as Koppel *et al.*, to which they added two native languages (i.e. Chinese and Japanese) from the second version of the *International Corpus of Learner English*. They used three types of syntactic errors (subject–verb disagreement, noun–number disagreement and misuse of determiners) and obtained accuracy rates that were slightly though significantly higher than the 14% majority class baseline.[1] However, when combined with other features (function words, character *n*-grams and POS *n*-grams), syntactic errors did not demonstrate any improvement in classification accuracy. ANOVA tests were run for each error type. The results show significant differences in both raw and relative frequencies for only one error category: determiner misuse. Overall, Czech and Chinese learners display significantly more such errors than French and Spanish learners, a fact that the authors attribute to the absence or less extended use of articles in their mother tongue.

Although the results of those two studies are mixed, they illustrate the potential of errors as L1 identification features, thus providing an impetus for further research. The two studies suffer from a number of weaknesses that need to be addressed, in particular as regards the actual selection of error types and the methods used to identify them. Research so far has been based on a highly restricted number of error types (often formal and syntactic) selected on rather weak grounds. Koppel *et al.* give a very practical justification for this, namely that 'they can be identified with relative ease' (Koppel *et al.*, 2005: 626). However, automatic identification of errors with spell- and grammar-checkers is far from fool-proof. This is acknowledged by Wong and Dras, who report 'a relatively high false positive rate of 48.2% in determiner misuse errors' (Wong & Dras, 2009: 58). They give a more theoretical explanation for the selection of their three syntactic error types, claiming to have chosen them because they are 'amongst the frequently observed syntactic error types in nonnative English which it has been argued are attributable to language transfer' (Wong & Dras, 2009: 53). This claim is not very convincing in the case of disagreement errors which are at least partly developmental (Osborne, 2008), a factor which may explain the lack of significant differences between the three L1 groups for these error types. In their conclusion, the authors mention two desiderata for future research in the field: 'using more error types' and designing 'a method for more accurately identifying them' (Wong & Dras, 2009: 60).

In the current study we try to address some of the shortcomings of earlier studies by making use of manually error-tagged samples from the *International Corpus of Learner English* (Granger *et al.*, 2009), annotated on the basis of the *Louvain Error Tagging System* (Dagneaux *et al.*, 1998) which covers a wide range of error types. In the section 'Data and Methodology', we describe the corpus data and error annotating system used. The following section 'Automatic Identification of the L1 Groups' gives an outline of the statistical methods employed for the automatic L1 identification and presents the classification results. Next, in the section 'Bringing Proficiency into the Equation' we tackle the possible impact of proficiency level differences on the results. The section 'Fine-Grained Qualitative Analysis' then provides a fine-grained analysis of the most discriminatory error patterns, while the 'Conclusion' section concludes our chapter and suggests avenues for future research.

Data and Methodology

The learner corpus data used in this study were taken from the *International Corpus of Learner English (ICLEv2)*, which contains essays written by learners of English from 16 mother tongue backgrounds (Granger et al., 2009). The texts selected for the present study were all written by French-, German- and Spanish-speaking EFL learners (henceforth FR, GE, SP), are argumentative in nature, and vary between 500 and 900 words in length. A total of 223 learner essays were selected, amounting to c. 50,000 tokens per L1 group. The detailed breakdown of the learner corpus sample used here is presented in Table 5.1.

The rather limited size of the corpus sample can be explained by the fact that each of the texts was exhaustively error tagged (i.e. annotated for errors, in accordance with the latest version of the *Louvain Error Tagging Manual*; Dagneaux et al., 1998).[2] The Louvain error tagging system is hierarchical: it includes a total of seven main error domains,[3] the majority of which are broken down into further error subcategories. The main error domains are briefly described in Table 5.2.

Examples (1) and (2) below target error subcategories, more specifically spelling errors (FS) which are part of the formal error domain, and verbs used with an erroneous dependent preposition, which belong to the lexico-grammatical domain (XVPR). As can be seen from the examples, the error tag is written between brackets and placed in front of the erroneous element while the correction is presented between dollar signs after the error:[4]

(1) *The fast spread of television can transform it into a double-edged* **(FS) wheapon $weapon$**. *(SP)*
(2) *The classroom must often have* **(XVPR) resembled to $resembled$** *a 'Chamber of Horrors'. (GE)*

Table 5.1 *ICLE* corpus sample

L1 background	Number of learner essays	Total tokens
FR	74	50,195
GE	71	49,856
SP	78	51,397
Total	223	151,448

Table 5.2 The Louvain error tagging system

Error tags	Definition	Description
F	Formal errors	Spelling or morphological errors that result in a nonexistent English word (+ homophones)
G	Grammatical errors	Errors that break the general rules of English grammar
L	Lexical errors	Errors involving the semantic properties of words or phrases (conceptual, collocational or connotative)
X	Lexico-grammatical errors	Errors that violate the lexico-grammatical properties of words, that is, erroneous dependent prepositions, complementation patterns or countable/uncountable noun confusion.
Q	Punctuation errors	Errors that target punctuation problems, for example, confusion between punctuation markers, missing or redundant markers
W	Word redundant/missing/order errors	Unnecessary use of words, missing necessary words, or misordered words
S	Style errors	Sentence fragments and incomprehensible sentences

Along with its seven main error domains, the Louvain system comprises a total of 54 error subtags. A number of these tags (six in total) were excluded from the present analysis, however, because they occurred with too low a frequency (i.e. in fewer than 10 different texts). A full list of the error tags used in our study is included in the appendix (the six excluded error tags are not represented).

Automatic Identification of the L1 Groups

In what follows, we first present the statistical measures that were chosen to best tackle our research question, namely the possibility of automatically identifying the learners' L1 on the basis of the errors found in the *ICLE* learner corpus sample. The success rate with which the L1s were identified along with the error types which best discriminate the L1 groups will be described in a second stage.

Statistical Methods

In keeping with the work carried out in this book, we have used the statistical method known as Discriminant Analysis (DA) to find out whether errors can be relied upon to automatically classify a text according to its L1.[5] This classification technique, which aims at selecting the variables (in our case errors) that best discriminate between given groups, is detailed in Chapter 1 and in the chapter preceding ours. Two elements that are specific to our study are in need of additional attention, however.

First, having a large number of potential (L1) predictors (i.e. 46 error types in total) in relation to the number of observations (i.e. 223 learner texts) may lead to the problem known as overfitting (e.g. Hawkins, 2004; Schiavo & Hand, 2000). Overfitting occurs when a statistical model (which is formed by the variables included in the prediction of group membership) is excessively specialized to account for the particular sample at hand, therefore lowering the predictive power of the discriminant analysis. In order to circumvent the problem of overfitting, researchers are advised to first carry out a procedure to select the best group of predictors (Schiavo & Hand, 2000: 302). It is noteworthy that such a procedure does not prevent overfitting, but only reduces it by limiting the number of variables used in the model. However, it brings other benefits which, in themselves, serve to justify its use: it facilitates the identification of the variables that will help discriminate between the groups and should ensure that the discriminant analysis is more successful than if carried out on the basis of all the variables (Louw & Steel, 2006). In order to do so, we have chosen an automatic selection procedure known as Stepwise analysis. To start off, the model does not contain any predictor. At each step, the algorithm adds the variable with the highest discriminatory power. However, because adding variables to the model modifies the discriminatory power of the other variables present, the algorithm each time checks that the variable with the lowest discrimination still significantly contributes to the analysis. If not, the variable is taken out of the model. The procedure ends when none of the variables that are not yet in the model are significant enough to be included. The significance level to enter the model or to be removed from the model is 0.05 so as to avoid the selection of too many variables in comparison with the number of texts.

Second, in order to evaluate the effectiveness of DA in the selection of new variables, we used the Leave-one-out cross-validation technique (LOOCV) which classifies each text on the basis of the model derived from the DA for the other 222 texts (Lachenbruch & Mickey, 1968). This step results in an unbiased estimate, ensuring that if the model were to be applied to new texts taken from the same learner population, the rate of accurately classified texts would be similar to the one reported by the LOOCV procedure.

Combining the stepwise and LOOCV methods is not without problems, however. The statistical packages available apply the stepwise procedure and thus select the best set of variables on the basis of the dataset as a whole. It is only afterwards that the LOOCV is performed. Thus, when the LOOCV is performed, the model that is used to classify each text has partially been constructed on the basis of this text. A consequence of this is that the LOOCV is favorably biased; that is, it provides an estimation of the classification accuracy that is overly optimistic. To find a way around this problem, we used the procedure advocated by Schulerud and Albregtsen (2004), which involves excluding each text one by one *before* actually selecting the variables with the stepwise analysis. In other words, 223 stepwise analyses were carried out, each time leaving one text out. The variables selected on this basis were used to build the best model for the 222 texts. We then determined how this model classified the 223rd text. This ensures an unbiased LOOCV measure despite the use of the stepwise procedure.

Results

L1 Group Identification

Table 5.3 presents the results for the L1 group identification obtained by combining the stepwise and LOOCV techniques. In this analysis the stepwise procedure was set to iterate through no more than 22 steps. In this way, a maximum of 22 error types could be incorporated into the prediction model and, consequently, the ratio between the number of variables in the model and the number of cases (or texts) in the training set was limited to 1 variable per 10 cases. The bolded figures presented diagonally in the table give the number of texts that were accurately classified in each L1 group: 48 FR texts, 51 GE texts and 47 SP texts.

It appears from Table 5.3 that error types can indeed lead to successful L1 group identification. The overall score for accurate classification is 65% (i.e. 146 out of the 223 texts) which is a very satisfactory result in view of the fact that chance would have set the score at approximately 33%. Looking at the individual L1 backgrounds, we see that the number of texts which have been accurately classified is quite similar in the three groups. However, what also stands out is that the discriminant analysis classified very few FR and

Table 5.3 L1 group identification scores for FR, GE and SP texts

Actual L1	Predicted L1			Total
	FR	GE	SP	
FR	**48**	21	5	74
GE	13	**51**	7	71
SP	15	16	**47**	78
Total	76	88	59	223

GE texts in the SP group (i.e. 5 FR and 7 GE texts were classified as SP), while quite a high number of GE and SP texts were classified as FR (i.e. 13 and 15 respectively); similarly a number of FR and SP texts were identified as belonging to the GE group (i.e. 21 and 16 respectively). What this indicates is that when DA classifies a text as SP, its decision is in general more accurate than when it classifies a text as being either FR or GE. This may also be interpreted as meaning that while error profiles generally enable us to clearly distinguish the Spanish group from its counterparts, it may be more difficult to tease apart a French text from a German text.

Identifying L1 discriminatory error types

To determine which specific error types are the most useful to differentiate texts written by speakers of the three L1s, we followed Schulerud and Albregtsen (2004) and relied on the number of times that a given variable is selected across the folds of a cross-validation with the internal stepwise feature selection procedure. We assumed that any error type that is selected in more than half of these stepwise DAs is potentially useful. Each of these error types was then submitted to a Student–Newman–Keuls post-hoc test to determine whether their mean relative frequency (out of 100 tokens) differed significantly across the three L1 groups. Table 5.4 provides all the error

Table 5.4 Discriminatory error types for the three L1 backgrounds

Sign. diff.	Error category	Mean relative frequency		
		FR	GE	SP
SP>FR>GE	LS	1.79614	1.48447	2.69455
SP>GE>FR	LP	0.63539	0.79587	1.10214
SP>(FR=GE)	GA	0.50257	0.33697	1.14883
SP>(FR=GE)	FS	0.62141	0.79184	1.61050
SP>(FR=GE)	GPU	0.09966	0.06123	0.24312
SP>(FR=GE)	XVPR	0.10129	0.09632	0.27498
SP>(FR=GE)	GDD	0.02048	0.01416	0.06117
GE>(FR=SP)	GADJO	0.00775	0.03733	0.00943
GE<(FR=SP)	GNN	0.22731	0.11789	0.23780
GE<FR	LCLS	0.17842	0.08718	0.12460
FR>(GE=SP)	QL	0.16064	0.03337	0.04836
FR<(GE=SP)	LCS	0.06320	0.10906	0.11787

Note: The sign. diff. column presents the statistically significant differences between the means according to the Student–Newman–Keuls procedure. For example, GE>(FR=SP) indicates that the mean for the FR group does not differ significantly from that of the SP group, while both of these means are significantly lower than the GE mean. The numbers in the FR, GE and SP columns represent the respective group means.

types that have passed these two selection tests as well as the statistical results of the mean comparison tests.

Table 5.4 shows seven error types to be strongly associated with the SP group: spelling errors (FS), lexical errors on single words (LS) and phrases (LP), as well as erroneous article use (GA), erroneous-dependent prepositions used with verbs (XVPR), unclear pronominal reference (GPU)[6] and erroneous demonstrative determiners (GDD). Errors involving the order of adjectives (GADJO) are more typical of the GE group. Strongly associated with the FR population are punctuation errors of the QL type (i.e. use of a conjunction of coordination instead of a punctuation marker, or of a punctuation marker instead of a conjunction of coordination, as in *he took the books* (QL) *and $,$ the records and the computers*). Some of the other error categories found in Table 5.4 are less frequent in one of the L1 groups than in the other two (cf. noun number disagreement errors (GNN) and subordinating conjunction errors (LCS)). A last error category (LCLS) distinguishes between just two of the three groups: single logical connectors are significantly fewer in the GE than in the FR group, neither of which show significant differences from the SP group. These results show that the error types that play a part in L1 identification are extremely diverse, which justifies widening the error base beyond the traditional spelling and agreement errors.

The above analysis suggests that it is possible to successfully discriminate the learners' L1 backgrounds on the basis of error types. However, like Koppel *et al.* (2005), we acknowledge that proficiency level differences between the three L1 groups may have played a part in the discriminant analysis. In the following section we investigate the possible impact of proficiency differences on the good L1 identification rates obtained above.

Bringing Proficiency into the Equation

Because the learners whose writing is included in the *ICLE* corpus were in their third or fourth year of undergraduate university studies, the data were initially believed to be representative of advanced learner writing. However, following a pilot study carried out by the Centre for English Corpus Linguistics in which a professional rater was asked to assign a Common European Framework score (henceforth CEF) to 20 texts randomly selected from each of the 16 mother tongue backgrounds, it was revealed that the corpus as a whole actually 'falls in the intermediate-advanced range' (Granger, 2004: 130).[7] In view of this finding, it is important to establish whether the reasonably successful automatic identification of the three L1 groups presented in Table 5.3 might be due to possible differences in proficiency level between the mother tongue populations. Two questions will be investigated in relation to this issue, the first being whether there are indeed significant differences in the level of English proficiency between the FR, GE and SP groups. If so, we will determine whether error profiles can nevertheless be used to successfully discriminate between subgroups of learners with the same level of proficiency but with a different L1.

CEF Rating Procedure

Because the *ICLE* does not include any built-in information on *individual* learners' level of proficiency in English, we had each of the 223 learner essays assessed by two professional raters who were both involved in the assessment of writing at the University of Cambridge Local Examinations Syndicate (UCLES).[8] A consequence of this methodology is that what we have termed 'proficiency level' is in fact a description of the quality of one single essay produced by each individual learner, rather than a more independent assessment of the learners' overall proficiency in English as would have been obtained if they had taken a standardized proficiency test such as TOEFL, for instance.[9] Importantly also, errors were a feature that the raters took into account when assessing the quality of the essays, as accuracy was part of the criteria they had to rate, along with elements pertaining to complexity and coherence and cohesion. Table 5.5 details the specific linguistic competences that were assessed for each text.

Both raters were asked to assign a CEF grade to each of the linguistic components in Table 5.5. The scores they could choose from ranged from the lower intermediate to the most advanced CEF levels, that is, B1, B2, C1 or C2.[10] In addition, the raters also attributed a holistic score to each text so as to convey their overall impression of the quality of the 223 essays. It was made possible for raters to use + or – signs to further specify quality within each proficiency level (e.g. vocabulary control = B2–, grammatical accuracy = C1+ etc).[11] The scores thus obtained were recorded using an 11-point numerical scale (i.e. B1– = 0.67, B1 = 1, B1+ =1.33 etc until C2 = 4,[12] cf. Table 5.6) so as to calculate the degree of correlation between the grades given by the two raters. The correlation between both raters on this 11-point scale reached $r = 0.69$. Overall,

Table 5.5 Linguistic competences considered in the rating procedure

Linguistic competence	Linguistic domain represented
Vocabulary control	Accuracy in lexical choice
Grammatical accuracy	Accuracy in grammatical use
Orthographic control	Accuracy in spelling and punctuation
Vocabulary range	Complexity, that is, range and richness of lexical knowledge
Coherence and cohesion	Accuracy of the chosen coherence and cohesion devices and complexity, that is, range of coherence and cohesion devices used

Table 5.6 11-point numerical scale

Holistic CEF score	B1−	B1	B1+	B2−	B2	B2+	C1−	C1	C1+	C2−	C2
Numerical value	0.67	1	1.33	1.67	2	2.33	2.67	3	3.33	3.67	4

Table 5.7 Interpreting mean scores to assign final CEF score

Mean score	Final CEF score assigned
Lower than 1.5	B1
Exactly 1.5	B1
Between 1.51 and 2.5	B2
Exactly 2.5	B2
Between 2.51 and 3.5	C1
Exactly 3.5	C1
Between 3.51 and 4	C2

Table 5.8 Converting mean numerical scores into the final CEF score

	Txt	Holistic score Rater 1	Holistic score Rater 2	Mean score	Final CEF score
Initial CEF scores	SP49	C1+	B2		
Numerical values	SP49	3,33	2	**2,67**	**C1**

both raters completely agreed on a total of 102 texts (46%); they reached near agreement (i.e. a maximal difference of one band score as in B2–C1 or C1–C2) on 87 texts (39%) and disagreed by more than one band score (e.g. B1–C1) on 34 texts (15%). In accordance with the language testing guidelines described in Alderson et al. (2001), the 34 texts on which the two raters substantially disagreed were submitted to a third rater, who was given the same descriptors and guidelines as her first two colleagues.

In order to attribute one final CEF score to each text and so as to be able to stratify the corpus sample accordingly, we computed the mean of the holistic scores given by the two (or three) raters (each holistic score had been given a numerical value, as shown in Table 5.6). The mean was then reinterpreted in terms of CEF score, as shown in Table 5.7.

A concrete example of how this procedure was conducted is given in Table 5.8 for one of the SP texts whose final CEF score was calculated to be C1.

Impact of Proficiency Level on the Discriminant Analysis Results

A one-way between-groups analysis of variance (ANOVA) was carried out to determine whether the mean CEF scores in the three L1 groups (see Table 5.9) differed significantly or not. The ANOVA indicated that there

Table 5.9 Mean CEF scores in the three L1 groups

	N	Mean	Std Dev	Minimum	Maximum
SP	78	**1.44**	0.64	0.67	3.00
FR	74	**2.64**	0.67	1.44	4.00
GE	71	**3.03**	0.87	0.83	4.00

are highly significant differences in mean CEF scores between the groups ($F(2, 220) = 96.14$; $p < 0.0001$). The Student–Newman–Keuls post-hoc test revealed that all three group means actually differ significantly from each other, namely all three learner populations display a different level of proficiency in English. As can be noted, however, the difference between the SP group and the FR/GE groups is much more marked than that between the FR and GE groups themselves.

Table 5.10 gives the breakdown of the number of texts per proficiency in each of the L1 sub-corpora. The SP group is overwhelmingly representative of the lower intermediate level B1 (i.e. 68% of all SP essays are B1); the FR learners are mainly situated between B2 (45%) and C1 (41%), while the GE population is well within the advanced C1 (42%) and C2 (31%) range. It is difficult to determine whether the differences in the mean proficiency scores between the L1 groups are specific to the *ICLE* sample used here or whether they can be generalized to these three populations as a whole. The latter option is plausible given that these results were confirmed by the rating of ICLE as a whole (Granger *et al.*, 2009), which also highlighted the closeness of the FR and GE data in comparison with the SP group, which was found to be at a lower level of proficiency. The differences in proficiency level can partly explain the effectiveness of the discriminant analysis in distinguishing between the groups on the basis of errors as there is a very strong correlation ($r = -0.81$; $p < 0.0001$) between the total number of errors (out of 100 tokens) and the CEF score (as an 11-point scale). The horizontal *x*-axis in Figure 5.1 represents the total number of errors (out of 100 tokens) while the vertical *y*-axis stands for the CEF score (in numerical values). As can be seen, the SP population (represented by the triangles) is clustered on the right-hand side of the *x*-axis with a high number of errors and toward the lower

Table 5.10 Text breakdown per L1 and proficiency level

	B1	B2	C1	C2	Total
SP	**53**	18	7	0	78
FR	5	**33**	**30**	6	74
GE	8	11	**30**	**22**	71
Total	66	62	67	28	223
	29.60	27.80	30.04	12.56	100.00

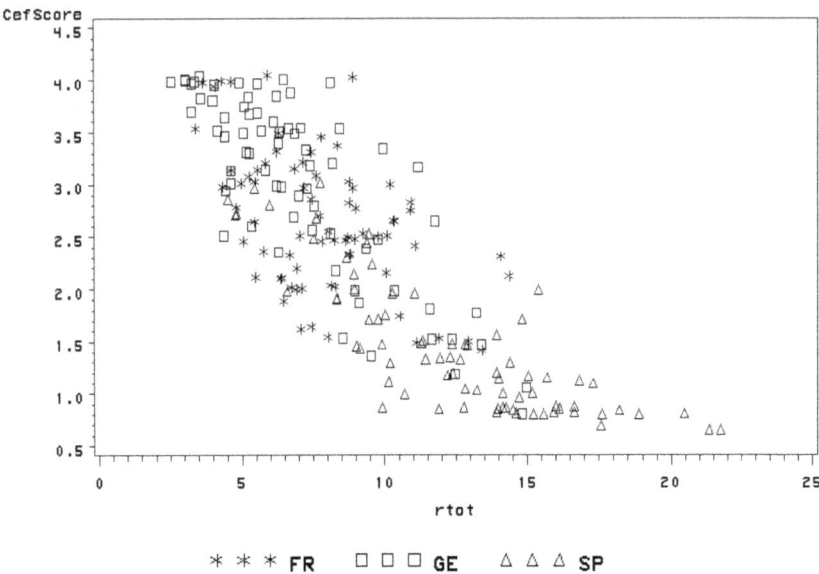

Figure 5.1 Scatterplot for the correlation between the total errors and the CEF score

end of the *y*-axis for low CEF proficiency scores. On the other hand, the FR and GE groups (represented by the stars and squares, respectively) are more difficult to tease apart. It follows from this observation that, in order to distinguish the SP learners from their FR and GE counterparts, the discriminant analysis can rely on this clear difference in proficiency levels. What can also be concluded, therefore, is that one cannot exclude the possibility that automatic L1 group identification may at some level be based on proficiency-level differences.

Controlling for Proficiency Level

In order to control for the possible impact of proficiency-level differences on the 65% accurate classification score obtained for the data as a whole (cf. Table 5.3), we selected a group of learners with the same proficiency level but with a different L1. The same analyses as were carried out earlier on the FR, GE and SP data as a whole (i.e. Stepwise and LOOCV) were conducted on the 30 FR and 30 GE texts that were assessed as C1. As indicated in Table 5.10 above, this is the CEF category for which we have the highest number of texts in two different L1 groups. However, because the analysis is carried out on a small data sample, the results should be cautiously interpreted and seen as preliminary.

The LOOCV results are given in Table 5.11. In total, 75% of texts (i.e. 22 FR and 23 GE) were accurately classified, with chance setting the score at 50%.

Table 5.11 L1 group identification for C1 FR and GE texts

	To L1		
From L1	FR	GE	Total
FR	**22**	8	30
GE	7	**23**	30
Total	29	31	60

Table 5.12 Discriminatory error types for the C1 FR and GE texts

Sign. diff.	Error types	FR	GE
FR>GE	QL	0.158	0.035
FR>GE	GNN	0.231	0.083
GE>FR	FS	0.530	0.808

Note: The sign. diff. column presents the statistically significant differences between the relative error means as reported by the Student–Newman–Keuls procedure.

To determine which specific error types are the most useful to differentiate texts written by speakers of the two L1s, we relied on the method that was outlined in the section 'Identifying L1 discriminatory error types'. Table 5.12 provides the three error types that have passed the two selection tests as well as the statistical results of the mean comparison tests. Strongly associated with the FR C1 group are punctuation errors of the QL type (i.e. use of 'and' instead of a punctuation marker or of a punctuation marker instead of 'and') and noun number disagreement errors (GNN) (these two error types were also more typical of the FR texts than of the GE texts in Table 5.4, which presented the discriminatory errors for the corpus sample as a whole). As for spelling errors (FS), these are more tightly associated with the GE than the FR C1 population.

This small-scale analysis, which would need to be replicated on a larger corpus, suggests that errors can be used for successful automatic L1 group identification even for populations that have been controlled for proficiency.

Fine-Grained Qualitative Analysis

An important point we wish to put forward here is that successfully identifying L1 groups on the basis of errors is not tantamount to saying that the discriminatory error types all necessarily result from transfer from the L1. Many other factors can be at play here to explain why certain L1 populations commit more errors than other L1 groups, such as differences in the level of English proficiency reached by the L1 populations or different English teaching methods (some of which may be more accuracy oriented while others may be more communication-oriented). Each error category may thus include errors that are the result of many different processes, including though not restricted to transfer. In order to identify potential transfer errors among the errors committed, we carried out a more fine-grained analysis which involved analyzing a number of 'error couples', that is, errors together with their suggested corrections. Examples include the *'his-its'* couple, which pertains to the GDO category (grammatical errors on possessive determiners) or *'increase of-increase in'* which belongs to the XNPR error category (noun used with an erroneous dependent preposition). An ANOVA test was used to compare the mean frequencies of the error couples in the three L1 sub-corpora. This enabled us to identify the couples that were significantly more frequent in one corpus than in the other two. In spite of the many comparisons being carried out and because this is an exploratory qualitative study, a rather liberal 0.05 significance value was adopted. Importantly, this procedure can only be applied if a couple occurs frequently enough in the data. We set the frequency threshold at seven occurrences in the whole corpus sample.

Figure 5.2 shows the number of error couples that are significantly more frequent in one population than in the other two. As can be seen, the SP sub-corpus clearly stands out as containing the most L1-salient couples.

Table 5.13 lists the couples that occur significantly more frequently in the SP, FR and GE sub-corpora, respectively. The error couples presented below

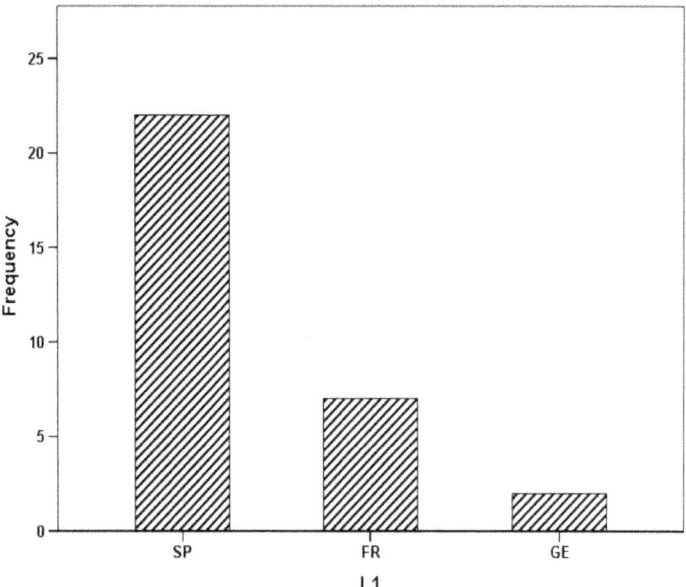

Figure 5.2 Frequency of L1-discriminatory error/correction couples in the three sub-corpora

Table 5.13 Error couples

Dependent	F Value	Prob F	Mean	N	Level
SP > [FR = GE]					
r_theX0	23.61	<0.0001	.	.	.
r_theX0	23.61	.	0.660	78	SP
r_theX0	23.61	.	0.249	74	FR
r_theX0	23.61	.	0.120	71	GE
r_0Xit	13.29	<0.0001	.	.	.
r_0Xit	13.29	.	0.038	78	SP
r_0Xit	13.29	.	0.003	71	GE
r_0Xit	13.29	.	0.000	74	FR
r_inXon	8.42	0.0003	.	.	.
r_inXon	8.42	.	0.035	78	SP
r_inXon	8.42	.	0.004	71	GE
r_inXon	8.42	.	0.002	74	FR
r_thisXthese	8.42	0.0003	.	.	.
r_thisXthese	8.42	.	0.027	78	SP
r_thisXthese	8.42	.	0.004	71	GE
r_thisXthese	8.42	.	0.000	74	FR
r_0Xthe	8.39	0.0003	.	.	.
r_0Xthe	8.39	.	0.271	78	SP
r_0Xthe	8.39	.	0.135	74	FR
r_0Xthe	8.39	.	0.092	71	GE
r_haveXhas	7.65	0.0006	.	.	.
r_haveXhas	7.65	.	0.025	78	SP
r_haveXhas	7.65	.	0.004	74	FR
r_haveXhas	7.65	.	0.000	71	GE
r_0Xby	7.65	0.0006	.	.	.
r_0Xby	7.65	.	0.026	78	SP
r_0Xby	7.65	.	0.004	74	FR
r_0Xby	7.65	.	0.000	71	GE
r_commaXfull stop	7.47	0.0007	.	.	.
r_commaXfull stop	7.47	.	0.097	78	SP
r_commaXfull stop	7.47	.	0.035	74	FR
r_commaXfull stop	7.47	.	0.030	71	GE
r_it_sXit_is	7.24	0.0009	.	.	.
r_it_sXit_is	7.24	.	0.059	78	SP
r_it_sXit_is	7.24	.	0.010	71	GE

(*continued*)

Table 5.13 (continued)

Dependent	F Value	Prob F	Mean	N	Level
SP > [FR = GE]					
r_it_sXit_is	7.24	.	0.005	74	FR
r_enterpriseXcompany	6.92	0.0012	.	.	.
r_enterpriseXcompany	6.92	.	0.013	78	SP
r_enterpriseXcompany	6.92	.	0.000	71	GE
r_enterpriseXcompany	6.92	.	0.000	74	FR
r_otherXanother	6.84	0.0013	.	.	.
r_otherXanother	6.84	.	0.014	78	SP
r_otherXanother	6.84	.	0.000	71	GE
r_otherXanother	6.84	.	0.000	74	FR
r_commaXcolon	5.54	0.0045	.	.	.
r_commaXcolon	5.54	.	0.050	78	SP
r_commaXcolon	5.54	.	0.019	74	FR
r_commaXcolon	5.54	.	0.012	71	GE
r_itXquestion mark	5.46	0.0048	.	.	.
r_itXquestion mark	5.46	.	0.015	78	SP
r_itXquestion mark	5.46	.	0.000	71	GE
r_itXquestion mark	5.46	.	0.000	74	FR
r_full stopX0	5.38	0.0052	.	.	.
r_full stopX0	5.38	.	0.094	78	SP
r_full stopX0	5.38	.	0.004	71	GE
r_full stopX0	5.38	.	0.002	74	FR
r_0Xa	5.19	0.0063	.	.	.
r_0Xa	5.19	.	0.082	78	SP
r_0Xa	5.19	.	0.037	71	GE
r_0Xa	5.19	.	0.027	74	FR
r_speciallyXespecially	5.19	0.0063	.	.	.
r_speciallyXespecially	5.19	.	0.016	78	SP
r_speciallyXespecially	5.19	.	0.000	71	GE
r_speciallyXespecially	5.19	.	0.000	74	FR
r_0Xthey	4.82	0.0089	.	.	.
r_0Xthey	4.82	.	0.015	78	SP
r_0Xthey	4.82	.	0.000	71	GE
r_0Xthey	4.82	.	0.000	74	FR
r_lifesXlives	4.79	0.0092	.	.	.
r_lifesXlives	4.79	.	0.025	78	SP
r_lifesXlives	4.79	.	0.005	71	GE

Dependent	F Value	Prob F	Mean	N	Level
SP > [FR = GE]					
r_lifesXlives	4.79	.	0.000	74	FR
r_areXis	4.59	0.0112	.	.	.
r_areXis	4.59	.	0.022	78	SP
r_areXis	4.59	.	0.005	74	FR
r_areXis	4.59	.	0.002	71	GE
r_notXno	4.47	0.0125	.	.	.
r_notXno	4.47	.	0.011	78	SP
r_notXno	4.47	.	0.002	74	FR
r_notXno	4.47	.	0.000	71	GE
r_increase_ofXincrease_in	4.31	0.0145	.	.	.
r_increase_ofXincrease_in	4.31	.	0.017	78	SP
r_increase_ofXincrease_in	4.31	.	0.004	74	FR
r_increase_ofXincrease_in	4.31	.	0.000	71	GE
r_don_tXdo_not	4.30	0.0147	.	.	.
r_don_tXdo_not	4.30	.	0.060	78	SP
r_don_tXdo_not	4.30	.	0.019	74	FR
r_don_tXdo_not	4.30	.	0.018	71	GE
FR > [SP = GE]					
r_indeedX0	21.62	<.0001	.	.	.
r_indeedX0	21.62	.	0.075	74	FR
r_indeedX0	21.62	.	0.008	71	GE
r_indeedX0	21.62	.	0.003	78	SP
r_ellipsis(…)Xfull stop	9.12	0.0002	.	.	.
r_ellipsis(…)Xfull stop	9.12	.	0.077	74	FR
r_ellipsis(…)Xfull stop	9.12	.	0.033	78	SP
r_ellipsis(…)Xfull stop	9.12	.	0.002	71	GE
r_ellipsis(…)Xfull stop	7.78	0.0005	.	.	.
r_ellipsis(…)Xfull stop	7.78	.	0.021	74	FR
r_ellipsis(…)Xfull stop	7.78	.	0.000	71	GE
r_ellipsis(…)Xfull stop	7.78	.	0.000	78	SP
r_commaXand	7.66	0.0006	.	.	.
r_commaXand	7.66	.	0.083	74	FR
r_commaXand	7.66	.	0.029	78	SP
r_commaXand	7.66	.	0.019	71	GE
r_butXhowever	6.80	0.0014	.	.	.
r_butXhowever	6.80	.	0.141	74	FR
r_butXhowever	6.80	.	0.078	71	GE

(continued)

Table 5.13 (continued)

Dependent	F Value	Prob F	Mean	N	Level
FR > [SP = GE]					
r_butXhowever	6.80	.	0.073	78	SP
r_communityXeu	6.24	0.0023	.	.	.
r_communityXeu	6.24	.	0.036	74	FR
r_communityXeu	6.24	.	0.002	78	SP
r_communityXeu	6.24	.	0.000	71	GE
r_hisXits	4.11	0.0176	.	.	.
r_hisXits	4.11	.	0.016	74	FR
r_hisXits	4.11	.	0.003	78	SP
r_hisXits	4.11	.	0.002	71	GE
GE > [SP = FR]					
r_full stopXquestion mark	5.09	0.0069	.	.	.
r_full stopXquestion mark	5.09	.	0.025	71	GE
r_full stopXquestion mark	5.09	.	0.009	74	FR
r_full stopXquestion mark	5.09	.	0.000	78	SP
r_kidsXchildren	4.56	0.0115	.	.	.
r_kidsXchildren	4.56	.	0.037	71	GE
r_kidsXchildren	4.56	.	0.005	78	SP
r_kidsXchildren	4.56	.	0.002	74	FR

should be interpreted as follows: 'r_theX0', for instance, stands for the relative frequency of the couple involving the use of the definite article *the* where the zero article should have been used instead, for example, *they haven't access to* **(GA) the 0** *education and probably most of them will dye before they were 15 or 16, while the children of the manager who bought them, go to* **(GA) the 0** *university in Europe* (SP).

A close look at the SP error couples shows that a number of them can safely be assumed to be transfer related. The '0Xit' and '0Xthey' couples, illustrated by examples 3 through 5 below, can be explained by the fact that Spanish nearly always omits personal pronouns in subject position, a possibility that does not exist in French or German. It is symptomatic that all '0Xthey' errors and all but one '0Xit' errors are found in the SP sub-corpus.

(3) *Finally* **0** *must be added that in our days it is necessary for a country to be (…)*
(4) *by the other hand* **0** *is very difficult for a person who have hurt any harm damage to prove it*
(5) *particular and daily objects become so artificial that* **0** *<they> lose their primitive charm.*

Similarly, the 'otherXanother' couple (cf. example 6) is most probably due to the fact that Spanish uses the same word *otro* for both *other* and *another* (cf. also Cowan & Leeser, 2007, who report similar results for this feature). Similarly, 'inXon' errors (cf. example 7) can be assumed to be due to the fact that both *in* and *on* are translated into Spanish by the same preposition *en*.

(6) *it is clear that a person who is born in Africa or in any other Third World country will have more problems to develop than* **other** <**another**> *who is born in Europe.*

(7) *All words, tones, images which appear* **in** <**on**> *television are controlled by someone.*

Determiner errors are complex and would require a more detailed investigation than is possible within the framework of this study. It is clear, however, that transfer may play a part in several of the error couples involving articles, for example in 0Xa errors, as Spanish often uses the zero article where English as well as French and German use the indefinite article.[13] Several of the FR couples also appear to be transfer-related, such as the overuse and misuse of *indeed*, already noted by Granger and Tyson (1996) and Koppel et al. (2005).

A sizable proportion of the SP error couples, however, are more likely to be developmental than transfer related. This is the case with certain number errors such as 'lifesXlives' or 'areXis' and punctuation errors where learners have used a comma instead of a full stop ('commaXfull stop'), thus producing a run-on sentence as illustrated in example 8:

(8) *Dreams are the instruments of imagination,* <.> *through them we begin to give shape to all the formless ideas than wander in (...)*

The inappropriate use of contractions in academic texts, apparent from the 'it'sXit is' and 'don'tXdo not' pairs are unlikely to be linked to the learners' L1 but might rather be a sign of novice writing. It is symptomatic that most of the errors are also found in the other two sub-corpora, though in much smaller numbers, most likely because the Spanish texts are scored lowest.

The fine-grained analysis has shown that certain L1 discriminatory error couples do indeed appear to result from transfer from the L1 but other errors that also contribute to L1 group discrimination do not necessarily find their source in transfer processes. Importantly, this indicates that discriminant analysis (as well as any other supervised classification technique such as Support Vector Machines) has the ability to rely on any type of information that will help toward group identification, whatever the theoretical relevance of the information in question may be (in our case, the fact that L1 discrimination is due to transfer).

Conclusion

This chapter has shown that the error patterns found in error-tagged learner corpora can indeed be used as a reliable source of information in L1 authorship profiling studies. The good L1 identification scores obtained here may be due to the fact that, as advised by Wong and Dras (2009), we drew on a wide array of errors ranging from the more traditional spelling and agreement errors to the more covert lexical, lexico-grammatical and punctuation error types, all of which were manually identified. Besides considering the valuable evidence yielded by error frequencies, we also felt it necessary to dig deeper into the qualitative aspect of the errors committed and to concretely identify a number of L1-salient error couples. Such a fine-grained approach is also advocated by Baroni and Bernardini in translation studies to automatically distinguish translated texts from original texts: 'the analysis should be carried out at a more detailed level, studying the impact not only of broad categories but also of specific elements (e.g. a certain pronoun or a certain punctuation mark)' (Baroni & Bernardini, 2006: 271).

Because of its exploratory nature, our study also displays a number of caveats, however. First, the learner corpus sample is admittedly limited in size. Additionally, the fact that only three L1 backgrounds were considered is very likely to have had an influence on the high percentage of accurately classified texts (see Chapters 2 and 3 in this volume for more on this issue). However, the complexity of the analyses carried out would not have easily allowed for the inclusion of more language backgrounds. Another question that has not been broached in this chapter has to do with whether errors actually contribute in a significant way to authorship studies when compared with other features such as function words, *n*-grams or POS patterns. This question is tackled in Chapter 6.

An important point highlighted by our study is the importance of controlling for other phenomena such as differences in proficiency levels that influence error frequency and, consequently, the subsequent discriminant analysis results. As shown in our analysis, the discriminant analysis was most successful in distinguishing the SP group—the group with the lowest level of proficiency—from the FR and GE groups, whose proficiency profiles are more homogeneous. What the fine-grained analysis further revealed is that the SP sub-corpus was also the one to include the most traces of potential transfer-related errors. These observations can be linked to a claim often made in SLA studies according to which reliance on transfer is inversely proportional to proficiency level; that is, the lower the proficiency level, the more learners rely on transfer from their L1 (cf. e.g. Taylor, 1975; Zhang, 2003).[14] A more extensive study would need to be carried out on a wider number of L1 backgrounds and range of proficiency levels for this claim to be further substantiated.

Besides SLA, the evidence gathered from error patterns may be of relevance for a number of other fields. Pedagogically, the identification of L1-salient error types can help teachers zoom in on learner-corpus-attested areas of difficulty. This is a valuable practice across the proficiency range as it can benefit beginner and intermediate learners, who frequently commit errors, as well as advanced learners, to try and erase the more visible signs of their nonnativeness. Other applications that derive from the study of L1 patterns include improved scoring algorithms for e-rating tools (Granfeldt et al., 2005) as well as heightened security by helping toward the identification of phishing texts, for example. To this end, however, it remains to be seen whether high classification accuracy can be obtained from errors that have been automatically rather than manually 'identified'.

Notes

(1) The majority class baseline is the proportion of correctly classified texts when all the texts are classified in the most frequent class in the data.
(2) The error-tagging procedure was carried out within the framework of a PhD dissertation that is under completion at the Centre for English Corpus Linguistics (Thewissen, 2011).
(3) The Louvain taxonomy includes an additional main category, namely infelicities (tagged Z), which target odd-sounding yet nonerroneous language, and which were excluded from the discriminant analysis results reported below.
(4) The error tags and corrections were inserted into the learner texts with the help of the *Université catholique de Louvain Error Editor (UCLEE)*, that is, a computer software program which includes (a) an error tag menu from which the analyst can select the appropriate tag and (b) an error correction box which speeds up the inclusion of the corrections in the texts (for more details on this, see Dagneaux et al., 1998).
(5) The statistical analyses were all carried out using SAS v9.1 (SAS Institute, Cary, NC).
(6) Although we have included unclear pronominal reference in the grammatical error category, this is an error that actually targets the discourse dimension of learner writing, for example, *But there are also imprisoned people waiting for their execution who are innocent. They never had a fair trial and a real chance to get out of* (GPU) *it $jail¢$. These people often do not have enough money to get their own attorney.*
(7) See Granger et al. (2009) for a detailed account of the proficiency-level breakdown for each of the 16 ICLE mother tongue backgrounds.
(8) The rating procedure carried out for the 223 texts investigated here (described in Thewissen, 2011) is distinct from the pilot study reported in Granger et al. (2009) for each of the 16 ICLE L1 backgrounds (20 texts per L1 background were given a CEF score).
(9) Recent studies (i.e. Wulff & Römer, 2009; Carlsen, forthcoming; Thewissen, 2011) have shown that *individual* learners' proficiency level is a variable that learner corpus research has paid little attention to so far and that it would need to be more tightly controlled for in future corpus compilation work.
(10) The CEF includes a total of six proficiency levels which can be broken down into three groups of two, namely A1 and A2 (=basic users; elementary proficiency learners), B1 and B2 (=independent users; intermediate proficiency learners), C1 and C2

(=proficient users; advanced proficiency learners). We started the rating procedure at level B1 because the CEF specifies that learners need a B1 proficiency level to attempt essay writing.
(11) The essays were presented to the raters in a random order (the same random order for both raters). The judges were given clear rating guidelines and carried out the rating procedure completely independently, that is, they never met to discuss results, and were not told how many L1 backgrounds were represented in the data.
(12) The scale is an 11-point rather than 12-point scale as the data did not include any C2+ score.
(13) Díez-Bedmar and Papp (2008: 155) give the following example: *Maria tiene Ø coche* vs **Mary has Ø car.*
(14) Note that some scholars have made the opposite claim (cf. e.g. Håkansson *et al.*, 2002).

References

Alderson, J.C., Clapham, C. and Wall, D. (2001) *Language Test Construction and Evaluation*. Cambridge: Cambridge University Press.
Baroni, M. and Bernardini, S. (2006) A new approach to the study of translationese: Machine-learning the difference between original and translated text. *Literary and Linguistic Computing* 21, 259–274.
Carlsen, C. (forthcoming) Proficiency level: A fuzzy variable in computer learner corpora.
Chuang, F-Y. and Nesi, H. (2006) An analysis of formal errors in a corpus of Chinese student writing. *Corpora* 1, 251–271.
Council of Europe (2001) *Common European Framework of Reference for Languages: Learning, Teaching, Assessment*. Cambridge: Cambridge University Press.
Cowan, R. and Leeser, M. (2007) The structure of corpora in SLA research. In R. Facchinetti (ed.) *Corpus Linguistics 25 Years on* (pp. 289–304). Amsterdam, NY: Rodopi.
Dagneaux, E., Denness, S. and Granger, S. (1998) Computer-aided error analysis. *System: An International Journal of Educational Technology and Applied Linguistics* 26, 163–174.
Díez-Bedmar, M.B. and Papp, S. (2008) The use of the English article system by Chinese and Spanish learners. In G.S. Gilquin, S. Papp and M.B. Díez-Bedmar (eds) *Linking Up: Contrastive and Learner Corpus Research* (pp. 147–175). Amsterdam: Rodopi.
Dikli, S. (2006) An overview of automated scoring of essays. *The Journal of Technology, Learning, and Assessment* 5, accessed 22 July 2010. http://www.jtla.org.
Granfeldt, J., Nugues, P., Persson, E., Persson, L., Kostadinov, F., Ågren, M. and Schlyter, S. (2005) Direkt profil: A system for evaluating texts of second language learners of French based on developmental sequences. In *Proceedings of the Second Workshop on Building Educational Applications Using Natural Language Processing* (pp. 53–60). Ann Arbor, MI.
Granger, S. (2004) Computer learner corpus research: Current status and future prospects. In U. Connor and T.A. Upton (eds) *Applied Corpus Linguistics: A Multidimensional Perspective* (pp. 291–231). Amsterdam: Rodopi.
Granger, S. and Tyson, S. (1996) Connector usage in the English essay writing of native and non-native EFL speakers of English. *World Englishes* 15, 19–29.
Granger, S., Dagneaux, E., Meunier, F. and Paquot, M. (2009) *The International Corpus of Learner English. Handbook and CD-ROM* (2nd edn). Louvain-la-Neuve: Presses Universitaires de Louvain.
Håkansson, G., Pienemann, M. and Sayehli, S. (2002) Transfer and typological proximity in the context of L2 processing. *Second Language Research* 18, 250–273.

Hawkins, D.M. (2004) The problem of overfitting. *Journal of Chemical Information and Computer Sciences* 44, 1–12.
Hawkins, J. and Buttery, P. (2010) Criterial features in learner corpora: Theory and illustrations. *English Profile Journal* 1, 1–23.
Koppel, M., Schler, J. and Zigdon, K. (2005) Determining an author's native language by mining a text for errors. In *Proceedings of the Eleventh ACM SIGKDD International Conference on Knowledge Discovery in Data Mining* (pp. 624–628). Chicago: Association for Computing Machinery.
Lachenbruch, P.A. and Mickey, R.M. (1968) Estimation of error rates in discriminant analysis. *Technometrics* 10, 1–11.
Louw, N. and Steel, S.J. (2006) Variable selection in kernel Fisher discriminant analysis by means of recursive feature elimination. *Computational Statistics and Data Analysis* 51, 2043–2055.
Neff van Aertselaer, J. and Bunce, C. (2005) An account of lexico-grammatical errors in Spanish EFL writers' argumentative texts: Data from the International Corpus of Learner English Error Tagging Project. In M. Genis and E. Orduna (eds) *Actas del III Congreso de ACLES* (pp. 697–705). Madrid: Universidad Antonio de Nebrija.
Osborne, J. (2008) Phraseology effects as a trigger for errors in L2 English: The case of more advanced learners. In F. Meunier and S. Granger (eds) *Phraseology in Foreign Language Learning and Teaching* (pp. 67–83). Amsterdam: Benjamins.
Schiavo, R.A. and Hand, D.J. (2000) Ten more years of error rate research. *International Statistical Review* 68, 295–310.
Schulerud, H. and Albregtsen, F. (2004) Many are called, but few are chosen: Feature selection and error estimation in high dimensional spaces. *Computer Methods and Programs in Biomedicine* 73, 91–99.
Taylor, B.P. (1975) The use of overgeneralisation and transfer learning strategies by elementary and intermediate students of ESL. *Language Learning* 25, 73–107.
Thewissen, J. (2011) Accuracy across proficiency levels: Insights from an error-tagged EFL learner corpus. PhD thesis, Centre for English Corpus Linguistics, Université catholique de Louvain.
Wong, S-M.J. and Dras, M. (2009) Contrastive analysis and native language identification. In *Proceedings of the Australasian Language Technology Association* (pp. 53–61). Cambridge, MA: The Association for Computational Linguistics.
Wulff, S. and Römer, U. (2009) Becoming a proficient academic writer: Shifting lexical preferences in the use of the progressive. *Corpora* 4, 115–133.
Zhang, W. (2003) Error analysis of college students' writing. *US-China Foreign Language* December, 52–60.

Appendix

Error tags used in the present study

Error tags	Definition	Learner-corpus-attested examples
F	**Form errors**	
FS	Form spelling	*The fast spread of television can transform it into a double-edged* (FS) *wheapon $weapon$.**
FM	Form morphology	*It is* (FM) *unpossible $impossible$.*
G	**Grammatical errors**	
GDD	Grammar determiner demonstrative	(GDD) *This $These$ elements cannot be separated.*
GDO	Grammar determiner possessive	*People accept jobs according to how much they get paid but not according to* (GDO) *his $their$ preferences.*
GDI	Grammar determiner indefinite	*He does not have* (GDI) *some any expectations.*
GPP	Grammar pronoun personal	*The big majority of children have a computer or a video-game, with which* (GPP) 0 *$they$ spend (waste, in my opinion) a great number of hours.*
GPI	Grammar pronoun indefinite	*A lower-class man is not on an equal footing with his middle- or upper-class* (GPI) *one $counterpart$.*
GPF	Grammar pronoun reflexive and reciprocal	*They didn't need to communicate* (GPF) *themselves 0 outside their homes.*
GPR	Grammar relative and interrogative pronouns	*The government took several measures to stop the strikes, (GPR) that $which$ was not effective.*
GPU	Grammar pronoun unclear reference	*But there are also imprisoned people waiting for their execution who are innocent. They never had a fair trial and a real chance to get out of* (GPU) *it $jail$. These people often do not have enough money to get their own attorney.*

Error tags	Definition	Learner-corpus-attested examples
GA	Grammar article	(GA) The 0 life is beautiful.
GNN	Grammar noun number	Bearing in mind that sex equality is one of the great (GNN) reason $reasons$ for fights in most places around the world (...)
GNC	Grammar noun case	Behind the (GNC) Berlin's wall $Berlin wall$.
GADJCS	Grammar adjective comparative/ superlative	The role that women should play in a (GADJCS) more fair $fairer$ present-day society.
GADJN	Grammar adjective number	The last sentences have been (GADJN) favourables $favourable$ to women.
GADJO	Grammar adjective order	A (GADJO) leather black small $small black leather$ handbag.
GADVO	Grammar adverb order	They (GADVO) see only $only see$ other criminals.
GVAUX	Grammar verb auxiliary	So if there is an army it (GVAUX) might $should$ be professional, and formed by people who believe in that and want to dedicate their lives to it.
GVM	Grammar verb morphology	It is generally (GVM) agree $agreed$ today that we live in a world where television plays an important part.
GVN	Grammar verb number	How do you think that a man (GVN) react $reacts$ when he hears that a woman is shocked when she receives a letter beginning with 'Dear Sirs'?
GVNF	Grammar verb nonfinite/finite	(GVNF) To travel $Travelling$ by public transport is recommended.
GVT	Grammar verb tense	He learned a profession in the prisson, and now he (GVT) wrote $writes$ poetry and (GVT) took $takes$ part in the publication of a prisson's journal.
GVV	Grammar verb voice	This seems impossible to (GVV) be achieved $achieves$.
GWC	Grammar word class	We are going to review the following subjects: Labour discrimination, the right to vote, the fight against male (GWC) chauvinist $chauvinistic$ behaviours.

(continued)

Error tags	Definition	Learner-corpus-attested examples
L	**Lexical errors**	
LCC	Lexical conjunction coordination	Life is not only work (LCC) or and study.
		(continued)
LCS	Lexical conjunction subordination	There is also the ethical question (LCS) if $whether$ people generally have the right to manipulate living beings.
LCLS	Lexis logical connector single	The second important point is the notion of 'risks' taken by the worker. (LCLS) Indeed 0 we often hear that 'in the public service you earn less money than in the private'.
LCLC	Lexis logical connector complex	(LCLC) In consequence to this $Consequently$, people are very busy and tired.
LS	Lexical error on single words	Resorting to violence might be somehow a (LS) comprehensible $understandable$ reaction.
LP	Lexical phrase errors	I was riding my bike through the village when I met a Turk, who was (LP) of middle age $middle-aged$.
X	**Lexico-grammatical errors**	
XADJPR	Adjectives used with wrong/ missing dependent preposition	How many public places are easily (XADJPR) accessible for $accessible to$ wheelchairs?
XNCO	Nouns used with wrong complementation	Students have the (XNCO) possibility to leave $possibility of leaving$.
XNPR	Nouns used with wrong/missing dependent preposition	He has a (XNPR) thirst of $thirst for$ knowledge.
XNUC	Errors on countable/ uncountable nouns	The tremendous (XNUC) progresses $progress$ realized by science have disrupted our habits and our way of living.
XVCO	Verbs used with wrong complementation	What about the people who cannot (XVCO) afford going $afford to go$ to these kind of centres?

Error tags	Definition	Learner-corpus-attested examples
XVPR	Verbs used with wrong/missing dependent preposition	The classroom must often have (XVPR) resembled to $resembled$ a 'Chamber of Horrors'.
W	**Word missing/redundant/order errors**	
WRS	Word redundant single	Actual life is very complicate and (WRS) extremely 0 full of worries.
WRM	Word redundant multiple	Others comment that (WRM) the fact is that 0 once you are inside, if you like it, you can even re-enlist.
WM	Word missing	The future soldiers make an strict physical training and (WM) 0 sit some exams.
WO	Word order	Think about (WO) how would be your house $how your house would be$ without the last century's inventions.
S	**Style errors**	
SU	Sentence unclear	(SU) Beggars of reflection have power and very often they use it in such a wrong way that make of imagination become slaves or just disappear$?$.
SI	Sentence incomplete	(SI) Another example. $Another example is:$ Yesterday we spoke about the Gulf War (...)
Q	**Punctuation errors**	
QC	Punctuation confusion	Some creative people make the most of their spare time by imagining or even building things (QC), $.$ others create works of art which are fruits of their inmost beings.
QM	Punctuation missing	Physically (QM) 0 $,$ you do not run any risks but it is very dangerous for your mind.
QR	Punctuation redundant	Women were seen conducting affairs, and bringing negotiations to satisfactory conclusions in what men always claimed to be (QR) : 0 'a man's world'.
QL	Punctuation lexical	He took the books (QL) and $,$ the records and the computers.

*The examples are replicated as in the original. In cases where the examples contain multiple errors, only the error that represents the tag being illustrated is highlighted.

6 The Comparative and Combined Contributions of *n*-Grams, Coh-Metrix Indices and Error Types in the L1 Classification of Learner Texts

Scott Jarvis, Yves Bestgen, Scott A. Crossley, Sylviane Granger, Magali Paquot, Jennifer Thewissen and Danielle McNamara

Introduction

Chapters 3 through 5 of this book have given an indication of the levels of L1 detection accuracy that can be attained through classification analyses whose predictor variables are individual words and multiword sequences (or *n*-grams, see Chapter 3), measures of coherence, lexical semantics and lexical diversity (or Coh-Metrix (CM) indices, see Chapter 4 and McNamara & Graesser, in press), and the types and numbers of errors that learners make in their L2 English writing (see Chapter 5). The results of these analyses show L1 classification accuracies from roughly 54% for *n*-grams to roughly 65% for both errors and CM indices. All three analyses were performed with data extracted from the International Corpus of Learner English (ICLE; see Granger *et al.*, 2009) using similar selection criteria (e.g. argumentative essays between 500 and 1000 words in length), but they differ in relation to the number of texts analyzed (2033 in the *n*-gram analysis, 903 in the CM analysis, and 223 in the error analysis) as well as in relation to the number of L1s under investigation (12, 4 and 3, respectively). The purpose of the present chapter is to perform a series of L1 detection analyses on essays from three language groups (French, German and Spanish), applying the features (or variables) from all three studies to a single dataset in order to examine both the comparative and combined usefulness of *n*-grams, CM indices and error measures for this type of research.

Previous research has reported findings that are only indirectly relevant to the focus of the present investigation. The most relevant studies are those by Koppel *et al.* (2005) and Wong and Dras (2009). Like the present study, both of these studies performed classification tasks on texts extracted from the ICLE. The classification tasks in these studies were presumably more challenging than the ones we will be performing in the present study as they involved the classification of five and seven L1 backgrounds, respectively, as compared with the three we deal with in the present chapter. The study by Koppel *et al.* (2005) relied on a combination of four types of variables including 400 function words, 200 frequent letter *n*-grams, 185 error categories and 250 rare part-of-speech bigrams. In a combined analysis using all four types of variables, their 10-fold cross-validation showed an L1 classification accuracy of 80% (for five L1 backgrounds). The study by Wong and Dras (2009) used a slightly different set of predictor variables, including 400 function words, 500 character *n*-grams, three error categories and 650 part-of-speech *n*-grams. In a combined analysis using all four types of variables, they achieved an L1 classification accuracy of 74% (for seven L1 backgrounds), but they were also able to achieve this same level of classification accuracy through a combined analysis using only the function words and parts-of-speech *n*-grams, leaving out of the analysis character *n*-grams and error categories.

The variables examined in these two studies partially overlap with those to be examined in the present chapter. For example, the pool of word *n*-grams used in this chapter includes several of the function words investigated by Koppel *et al.* (2005) and Wong and Dras (2009), but our pool of *n*-grams also extends to content words and to multiword sequences of content and function words (see the section '*n*-Grams') – variables that the two previous studies did not examine. The error categories examined in this chapter also overlap to some degree with the error categories included in the two previous studies. However, the errors examined in the present study were hand-tagged, whereas those in the previous studies were identified through computer-automated error tagging – a process that Wong and Dras report as having a false-positive rate of as high as 48%. Comparisons between these two studies and the present investigation are also limited by the fact that these studies did not include CM indices (whereas the present study does), and the present study does not consider letter *n*-grams or part-of-speech *n*-grams (whereas the previous studies did).

Extrapolating from these two previous studies to the extent possible, we expect that a classification analysis involving a combination of multiple types of variables will result in a higher level of L1 classification accuracy than an analysis involving only a single type of variable. However, the results of Wong and Dras (2009) also suggest that the inclusion of some types of variables, such as error categories, will not necessarily lead to higher levels of classification accuracy beyond that achieved with a combination of other types of variables.

The accuracy rate of 80% achieved by Koppel *et al.* (2005) is a benchmark level that we hope to achieve in the combined analysis in the present study, but the differences between our study and that of Koppel *et al.* create a number of challenges. Although the smaller number of L1s in the present study makes our classification task simpler, differences in the classifiers, variables and text selection criteria used in the two studies might give their study certain advantages. The classifier they used was Support Vector Machines (SVM), which does not have such strict constraints on the ratio of variables to cases as does the Discriminant Analysis classifier we will use. The fact that Koppel *et al.* were able to include over 1000 variables in their L1 classification model – whereas we will be limiting our models to just 22 variables – might mean that their model is more sensitive to L1-related influences than ours will be. A further possibility is that the inclusion of so many variables in the Koppel *et al.* study may have also resulted in excessive overfitting, meaning that their model might be overly tailored to account for the specific data they analyze, but might not apply well to future cases. If this is the case, then their results could be overly optimistic, which is another factor that would make it difficult for our analysis to reach as high a level of L1 classification accuracy as they achieved. Related to this is our observation that Koppel *et al.* appear not to have limited their data to a single genre (e.g. argumentative texts), as we have done in previous chapters and will do in the present chapter. Insofar as the occurrence of linguistic features varies by genre, if the different genres in the data used by Koppel *et al.* were not equally distributed across L1 groups, then this would have increased the between-groups variance in their data and thus artificially inflated their L1 classification accuracy.

In summary, the limited, relevant literature suggests that a classification analysis involving more than one type of variable will likely lead to a higher level of L1 classification accuracy than an analysis involving only one type of variable; however, the literature gives conflicting findings concerning whether a combined analysis involving the three types of variables that we will be examining will lead to an improvement over a combination of just two types of variables. Finally, the previous research by Koppel *et al.* (2005) and Wong and Dras (2009) suggests that our combined analysis could lead to levels of L1 classification accuracy in the range of 70–80%, or perhaps even higher (given the smaller number of L1s we are dealing with), but major differences between our method and those of past studies do not allow for a straightforward prediction.

The purpose of the present chapter is to determine how effective *n*-grams, CM indices and error variables are – both separately and combined – for L1 detection purposes. To address this question, we conducted five separate analyses: an *n*-gram analysis, a CM analysis, an analysis based on error variables, a combined analysis involving all three types of variables and a combined analysis involving just *n*-grams and CM indices. These analyses are described in the following sections.

Corpus

Whereas we were able to rely on completely automated measures for determining *n*-gram frequencies and the values of CM indices, our error variables required human error tagging, which is a time-consuming and expensive process. Because the 223 texts used in Chapter 5 are the only texts for which we have error variables, we chose precisely these texts for our combined and comparative analyses in the present study. Here, we reproduce Table 6.1 from Chapter 5 in order to show the breakdown of the texts in question. As the table shows, the native languages of the learners who produced these texts include French (FR), German (GE) and Spanish (SP), with similar numbers of texts per L1 background, as well as similar overall numbers of words produced by the learners from each L1 background.

n-Grams

One noteworthy characteristic of the *n*-gram approach to L1 detection is that it allows for the use of a very large number of predictor variables. However, the use of a large number of variables in multivariate tests such as Discriminant Analysis (DA) requires an even larger number of cases

Table 6.1 *ICLE* corpus sample

L1 background	Number of learner essays	Total tokens
FR	74	50,195
GE	71	49,856
SP	78	51,397
Total	223	151,448

(e.g. texts). The *n*-gram analyses in Chapter 3 of this book used a pool of 722 variables, from which as many as 200 were included in the resulting L1 prediction models. Such a large number of predictors was made possible by the fact that the analysis rested on over 2000 texts. In the current study, which is designed to compare the L1 predictive power of three groups of features (i.e. *n*-grams, CM indices and error categories), the number of available texts is limited to the 223 that are error-tagged. We will henceforth refer to these 223 texts as the Error Corpus. Because of the smaller number of available texts in the Error Corpus, we found it optimal to reduce the pool of *n*-grams (from the 722 used in Chapter 3) to 50, a number just slightly higher than the number of error categories (i.e. 46; see Chapter 5).

This reduction was achieved in two ways. First, *n*-grams occurring in fewer than 10 different texts were excluded. This reduced the total number of *n*-grams from 722 to 575. Second, a first (*a priori*) DA was run on an independent sample of ICLE texts that did not overlap with but was as similar as possible to the Error Corpus. These texts consisted of the 126 French, 112 German and 67 Spanish texts analyzed in Chapter 3 that are not part of the Error Corpus. It is noteworthy that this independent sample of 305 texts was selected by means of similar criteria as those used for selecting the Error Corpus: argumentative texts of lengths roughly 500–1000 words. Our *a priori* analysis allowed us to select (from the 575 *n*-grams in the previous step) the 50 *n*-grams that were the most useful predictors of whether the texts in the independent sample were written by French, German or Spanish speakers. To select the 50 best *n*-grams, we followed a procedure used in Chapters 2, 4 and 5 (see also Schulerud & Albregtsen, 2004). This involved determining how frequently each *n*-gram was selected in a 305-fold leave-one-out cross-validation (LOOCV) of the 305 texts in the independent sample and choosing the 50 *n*-grams most often selected as those that will be used in the present study. The 50 retained *n*-grams as well as the number of times that they were selected in the LOOCV stepwise procedure are shown in Table 6.2. As can be extrapolated from this table, 22 of the retained *n*-grams were unigrams (i.e. single words), 19 were bigrams, nine were trigrams and none were 4-grams.

To obtain benchmark classification results, we submitted these 50 *n*-grams to a stepwise DA of the independent sample of 305 texts described in the preceding paragraph. As has been pointed out in each of the preceding chapters, the proper type of cross-validation for a stepwise DA involves conducting a stepwise analysis within each fold of a multifold cross-validation. This avoids overly optimistic levels of classification accuracy (i.e. bias) and provides classification results that are reliably indicative of how well the model will apply to future data (e.g. Lecocke & Hess, 2006: 316; Molinaro *et al.*, 2005: 3303). As was done in Chapter 5, in the present study we used LOOCV with stepwise feature selection embedded within each fold of the cross-validation.

Table 6.2 Variable retention in the 223 LOOCV stepwise procedure

n-Gram	n	n-Gram	n	n-Gram	n	n-Gram	N	n-Gram	n
I	305	other hand	287	able to	175	in my opinion	117	it would	66
this	305	also	284	is not the	162	do not know	115	going to	60
will	305	whole	277	however	159	both	109	way of	57
often	305	become	274	of all	158	I would like	94	that this	52
to	304	things	269	it is very	157	all over the	93	something	48
some	302	think that	268	we	147	it is true	91	in fact	43
to do	301	of a	207	in which	127	of	86	not only	41
could	298	the most	199	is	125	has to be	73	between	39
and they	296	that	189	they have to	120	will be	72	able	39
for	295	not have	183	we can	119	seems to	71	see	37

The parameters of the stepwise procedure were set as follows. First, the significance (or alpha) level for a variable to enter the model or to be removed from the model was set at 0.05. Second, the stepwise procedure was set to iterate through no more than 22 steps. In this way, a maximum of 22 *n*-grams could be incorporated into the prediction model and, consequently, the ratio between the number of variables in the model and the number of cases (or texts) in the training set was limited to 1 variable per 10 cases.

The results of the LOOCV with embedded stepwise feature selection showed that 205 (or 67.2%) of the 305 texts in the independent sample were classified correctly as having been written by native speakers of French, German or Spanish. A confusion matrix showing the relationship between the learners' actual L1s and their predicted L1s is given in Table 6.3.

Next, we used the same pool of 50 *n*-grams and the same LOOCV and stepwise parameters and procedures described above to test how well they

Table 6.3 L1 group identification scores for FR, GE and SP texts in the independent sample

	Predicted L1			
Actual L1	FR	GE	SP	Total
FR	**84 (67%)**	28	14	126
GE	17	**79 (71%)**	16	112
SP	18	7	**42 (63%)**	67
Total	119	114	72	305

Table 6.4 L1 group identification scores for FR, GE and SP texts

Actual L1	Predicted L1			Total
	FR	GE	SP	
FR	**45 (61%)**	11	18	74
GE	15	**46 (65%)**	10	71
SP	19	9	**50 (64%)**	78
Total	79	66	78	223

can predict the L1 backgrounds of the texts in the Error Corpus. The results of this analysis are shown in Table 6.4 in the form of a confusion matrix, which indicates that large majorities of the texts predicted to have been written by French, German and Spanish speakers, respectively, were indeed written by the same. More generally, the results indicate that 141 (or 63.2%) of the 223 texts in the Error Corpus were classified correctly (df = 4, n = 223, χ^2 = 94.164, p < 0.001; Cohen's Kappa = 0.448), which is statistically above the level of chance (33% for a classification task involving three L1s) and also substantially higher than the baseline of 35% (i.e. the number of correct hits that would be obtained if each text were classified as a member of the largest L1 group). It is perhaps worth mentioning that the n-gram classification accuracy achieved in this study is higher than that obtained in Chapter 3, which was 53.6%. However, this is to be expected given that the present classification task required the classifier to distinguish among only three L1s, whereas the classification task in Chapter 3 involved the differentiation of 12 L1s.

To determine which specific n-grams are the most useful for differentiating texts written by speakers of the three L1s, we followed Schulerud and Albregtsen (2004) in relying on the number of times that a given variable is selected across the folds of a cross-validation with internal stepwise feature selection. In the present case, we examined how many times out of the 223 folds of the LOOCV each of the 50 n-grams was selected by the embedded stepwise DA procedure. We deemed any n-gram that was selected in more than half of the folds to be particularly useful for L1 detection purposes. Each n-gram that met this criterion was then submitted to a one-way ANOVA and a Student–Newman–Keuls (SNK) post-hoc test to determine whether the mean relative frequency of this n-gram differed significantly across the three L1 groups. Table 6.5 lists all of the n-grams that passed both usefulness tests.

As seen in Table 6.5, the two n-grams that stand out as being particularly useful for L1 detection purposes are *of* and *this*. The mean usage frequencies for both of these words show a significant separation of all three groups. The remaining n-grams listed in Table 6.5 set one group apart from

Table 6.5 Results of the ANOVAs and the SNK tests for the selected variables

Diff sign	n-Grams	FR	GE	SP
FR>SP>GE	of	37.391	28.158	33.549
SP>FR>GE	this	7.951	5.507	9.783
GE<(FR=SP)	is	19.079	14.112	21.533
GE<(FR=SP)	we	8.158	3.714	9.098
GE<(FR=SP)	think that	1.067	0.305	1.130
GE<(FR=SP)	in which	0.590	0.175	0.700
GE>(FR=SP)	I	5.236	13.203	6.059
FR>(GE=SP)	become	1.380	0.533	0.634
FR>(GE=SP)	will	6.292	2.674	3.175
SP>(FR=GE)	to do	0.418	0.527	1.676
SP<(FR=GE)	often	1.103	1.068	0.261

Note: The diff sign column presents the statistically significant differences between the means according to the Student–Newman–Keuls procedure. For example, GE>(FR=SP) indicates that the mean for the FR group does not differ significantly from that of the SP group, while both of these means are significantly lower than the mean for GE. The numbers in the FR, GE and SP columns represent group means.

the other two, but do not distinguish between those other two. Five of the *n*-grams are shown to isolate German speakers from the other two groups, whereas only two *n*-grams isolate French speakers from the other two, and only two *n*-grams isolate Spanish speakers from the other two groups. Another important observation is that most of the *n*-grams we have identified in this analysis as being useful for L1 detection purposes are unigrams (or single words); the list in Table 6.5 includes only three bigrams and no trigrams.

An important caveat to the results presented in Table 6.5 is that significant mean differences across L1 groups do not guarantee that individuals within those groups will behave uniformly with respect to the variables in question. In other words, intragroup homogeneity can be low even when intergroup heterogeneity is high (cf. Jarvis, 2000, 2010), and this can of course have a negative impact on L1 classification accuracy even where significant differences exist between groups. The flipside of this caveat is also important to consider: Variables can contribute significantly (though perhaps not substantially) to classification accuracy even in the absence of significant between-group differences. In any event, the results we have presented here suggest that the *n*-grams we have listed in Table 6.5 are apparently quite useful for this particular classification task.

CM Indices

For the present study, we used the same pool of CM indices discussed in Chapter 4. Because this pool consists of only 19 variables, no further reduction of this pool is necessary to maintain an acceptable ratio of variables to cases in relation to the 223 texts in the Error Corpus. As described in Chapter 4, the CM indices were selected from measures of word concreteness, word imagability, word familiarity, word polysemy, word hypernymy, word meaningfulness, lexical diversity and various other measures of meaning, meaningfulness, cohesion and syntactic complexity. To conduct our CM analysis of the Error Corpus, we submitted these 19 variables to precisely the same LOOCV and stepwise parameters and procedures described in the preceding section. The purpose of this analysis was to test how well an L1 prediction model built on CM indices can predict the L1 backgrounds of the texts in the Error Corpus. The results of this analysis in the form of a confusion matrix are shown in Table 6.6.

This table shows that a clear majority of the French, German and Spanish texts were classified correctly by L1 background. The overall classification accuracy is 143 out of 223, or 64.1% (df = 4, n = 223, χ^2 = 114.050, $p < 0.001$; Cohen's Kappa = 0.461), which is a relatively high level of accuracy in view of the fact that a chance level of accuracy would have been approximately 33%, and a baseline level of accuracy would have been 35% (see previous section). This is also slightly higher than the classification accuracy of 63.2% obtained in the corresponding n-gram analysis discussed in the preceding section, despite the fact that the n-gram analysis included a larger pool of potentially useful variables for L1-group discrimination. However, the differences in classification accuracy between the n-gram analysis and the CM analysis were not significant (as determined by a paired-samples t-test: $t[222] = 0.226, p > 0.050$).

In order to examine the usefulness of the CM indices more closely, we followed the same procedures used in the n-gram analysis. This involved a consideration of the number of times each variable was selected across the folds of the LOOCV with internal stepwise variable selection. That is, we examined how many times out of the 223 folds of the cross-validation each

Table 6.6 L1 group identification scores for FR, GE and SP texts

Actual L1	Predicted L1			
	FR	GE	SP	Total
FR	**52 (70%)**	6	16	74
GE	13	**47 (66%)**	11	71
SP	30	4	**44 (56%)**	78
Total	95	57	71	223

Table 6.7 Results of the ANOVAs and the SNK tests for the selected variables

Diff sign	CM index	FR	GE	SP
GE>SP>FR	Word imagability every word	315.419	330.013	318.591
GE>SP>FR	Word meaningfulness every word	342.136	352.823	345.891
GE>FR>SP	Lexical diversity MTLD	91.336	106.583	83.308
SP>FR>GE	Stem overlap	0.403	0.296	0.516
GE>(FR=SP)	Number of motion verbs	93.072	135.903	80.992
GE>(FR=SP)	Aspect repetition score	0.848	0.914	0.879
SP>(FR=GE)	Causal particles/verbs	0.550	0.525	0.984
SP>(FR=GE)	LSA givenness	0.298	0.295	0.316
FR<(GE=SP)	Word familiarity every word	591.550	593.872	593.220

of the 19 CM indices was selected by the embedded stepwise DA procedure. As before, we deemed any variable that was selected in more than half of the folds to be potentially useful for L1 detection purposes. Each CM index that met this criterion was then submitted to a one-way ANOVA and SNK post-hoc test to determine whether the mean relative frequency of this variable differed significantly across the three L1 groups. Table 6.7 shows the nine CM indices that passed both usefulness tests.

The seemingly most noteworthy indices in Table 6.7 are the first four, which are measures of word imagability, word meaningfulness, lexical diversity and stem overlap (see Chapter 4 for a fuller description of what these mean and how they were measured). These four variables significantly differentiate all three L1 groups from one another. The remaining five variables distinguish one group from the other two, but do not differentiate between the other two. As mentioned earlier, the criteria we have used for identifying useful variables for L1 detection are not completely unproblematic, but these nine CM indices do appear to be particularly useful for the classification of the texts in the Error Corpus according to the L1s of their writers.

Error Categories

The error-based analysis of the Error Corpus is described in detail in Chapter 5. We recap the main results of that analysis here in order to facilitate our examination of the comparative contributions of *n*-grams, CM indices and error categories to this type of research. The error categories were applied to a DA analysis of the Error Corpus in the same way described in relation to *n*-grams and CM indices. The pool of error categories includes

46 variables dealing with errors in word form, word meaning, word usage (e.g. collocational constraints), word order, punctuation, coherence and various other areas of grammar and style. These 46 variables were submitted, as before, to a stepwise DA that was embedded within an LOOCV process. All parameters were set in the same way as in the preceding analyses, with the maximum number of stepwise iterations within each fold of the LOOCV set to 22 so as to prevent an L1 classification model that would exceed 22 variables (i.e. 10% of the number of texts). The results of the error-based analysis are shown in Table 6.8 in the form of a confusion matrix.

As in the two previous analyses, the error-based analysis resulted in a strong majority of correct L1 group identifications for each of the three L1 groups. The overall L1 classification accuracy for the error-based analysis is 65.5%, or 146 out of the 223 texts (df = 4, n = 223, χ^2 = 110.985, $p < 0.001$; Cohen's Kappa = 0.484). This is somewhat higher than the classification accuracies obtained in the n-gram (63.2%) and CM analyses (64.1%), but the differences are not significant ($t[222]$ = 0.512, $p > 0.050$ for errors vs. n-grams; $t[222]$ = 0.317, $p > 0.050$ for errors vs. CM indices).

For present purposes, the most useful of the error categories were defined as those that were selected in over half of the 223 folds of the LOOCV and for which significant differences across the means of the three L1 groups could be found. The 12 error categories that met both criteria are listed in Table 6.9. Of these, the first two variables, lexical single errors and lexical phrase errors, are particularly noteworthy in that they significantly differentiate the means of all three groups from one another. In five of the error categories, the Spanish speakers stand out for their significantly higher rate of errors than the other two L1 groups produce. In other cases, the German speakers, on the one hand, and French speakers, on the other, show a significantly higher or lower number of errors than the other two groups. For one variable, single logical connector errors, the German group produces significantly fewer errors than the French group, but neither the German group nor the French group shows significant differences from the Spanish group.

Table 6.8 L1 group identification scores for FR, GE and SP texts

Actual L1	Predicted L1			Total
	FR	GE	SP	
FR	**48 (65%)**	21	5	74
GE	13	**51 (72%)**	7	71
SP	15	16	**47 (60%)**	78
Total	76	88	59	223

Table 6.9 Results of the ANOVAs and the SNK tests for the selected variables

Diff sign	Error category	FR	GE	SP
SP>FR>GE	Lexical single errors	1.796	1.484	2.695
SP>GE>FR	Lexical phrase errors	0.635	0.796	1.102
SP>(FR=GE)	Article errors	0.503	0.337	1.149
SP>(FR=GE)	Spelling errors	0.621	0.792	1.611
SP>(FR=GE)	Unclear pronominal reference	0.100	0.061	0.243
SP>(FR=GE)	Verbs used with the wrong dependent preposition	0.101	0.096	0.275
SP>(FR=GE)	Demonstrative determiner errors	0.020	0.014	0.061
GE>(FR=SP)	Adjective order errors	0.008	0.037	0.009
GE<(FR=SP)	Noun number errors	0.227	0.118	0.238
GE<FR	Single logical connector errors	0.178	0.087	0.125
FR>(GE=SP)	Punctuation mark instead of lexical item and vice versa	0.161	0.033	0.048
FR<(GE=SP)	Subordinating conjunction errors	0.063	0.109	0.118

Combined Analysis

Whereas a comparison of the three preceding analyses suggests that *n*-grams, CM indices and error categories are roughly equally effective as predictors of learners' L1 backgrounds in a DA analysis, the next critical question is whether a DA analysis that draws simultaneously from all three types of variables would be more effective than an analysis based on one type alone. This is the question we address in the present section. In order to perform the combined analysis, we brought together the 50 *n*-grams, 19 CM indices and 46 error categories into a single variable pool and submitted it to a DA using the same parameters and procedures as before. The fact that the combined pool now included 115 variables is not ideal given that there are only 223 texts in the Error Corpus. Nevertheless, we did not consider this fact to be overly problematic given that our stepwise parameters were set so as to avoid statistical models involving relationships among more than 22 variables. Thus, we maintained a ratio of 10 texts for every variable in each model that was constructed. As with our prior analyses, we submitted the pool of variables to a DA using LOOCV with stepwise feature selection embedded within each fold of the cross-validation. The alpha level for

Table 6.10 L1 group identification scores for FR, GE and SP texts

	Predicted L1			
Actual L1	FR	GE	SP	Total
FR	**63 (85%)**	3	8	74
GE	11	**56 (79%)**	4	71
SP	15	5	**58 (74%)**	78
Total	89	64	70	223

the stepwise procedure was set at 0.05 for variables to enter or to be removed from the model, and the stepwise procedure was set to iterate through no more than 22 steps.

The results of the combined analysis are shown in Table 6.10. The confusion matrix shows the relationship between the actual L1 backgrounds of the texts in the Error Corpus and the classification of the texts during the LOOCV. As can be seen in the table, strong majorities of the texts in each L1 group were classified correctly, and this is especially true of the texts written by French speakers (i.e. 85%). Overall, 177 out of the 223 texts were classified correctly by L1 background (df = 4, n = 223, χ^2 = 219.196, $p < 0.001$; Cohen's Kappa = 0.690). The overall classification accuracy was thus 79.4%, which is not only significantly higher than the level of chance (33.3%) and the baseline (35%), but is also significantly higher than any of the previous analyses that were based on a single type of variable: 63.2% for n-grams alone ($t[222] = 4.483$, $p < 0.001$), 64.1% for CM indices alone ($t[222] = 4.350$, $p < 0.001$) and 65.5% for error variables alone ($t[222] = 4.261$, $p < 0.001$). The L1 classification accuracy of 79.4% in our combined analysis also comes very close to the rate of 80.2% achieved in the combined analysis performed by Koppel et al. (2005), which seems remarkable in light of the fact that our model was limited to 22 variables, whereas that of Koppel et al. included 1035. On the other hand, our classification task concerned only three L1 backgrounds, whereas theirs involved five L1s, which does make the classification task in our analysis somewhat less challenging.

Although there are different ways of constructing what might be regarded as an optimal model in a classification task of this type, the model we present as the optimal set of L1 predictors for the Error Corpus was constructed as follows. First, we calculated the number of times across the 223 folds of the LOOCV each variable was included by the stepwise procedure in its DA model of L1 classes. (Recall that the stepwise procedure allowed only 22 variables in any given model – within any given fold of the LOOCV.) From the pool of 115 variables, it turned out that 74 were not selected in any of the 223 folds. Of the remaining 41, some were selected in as few as one fold, whereas others were selected in all the folds. Table 6.11 shows the number of times (or the number of LOOCV folds in which) each of these

Table 6.11 Variable retention in the 223 LOOCV stepwise procedure

Variable	n	Variable	n
Error: unclear pronominal reference	223	Error: lexical phrase errors	80
Error: spelling errors	223	Error: demonstrative determiner errors	70
Error: punctuation instead of word & vice versa	223	Error: noun number errors	64
Error: verbs used with wrong dependent prep	223	Error: verb number errors	61
CM: causal particles/verbs	223	Error: sentence unclear	48
CM: motion verbs	223	CM: positive temporal connectives	34
CM: word concreteness	223	n-Gram: *between*	34
n-Gram: *become*	223	Error: missing punctuation	26
n-Gram: *to do*	223	Error: morphological errors	10
n-Gram: *think that*	223	Error: confusion of punctuation marks	10
CM: aspect repetition	222	n-Gram: *way of*	10
n-Gram: *we*	222	n-Gram: *it is very*	4
Error: single logical connector errors	221	Error: adjectives used w/ wrong dependent prep	3
CM: word hypernymy	220	CM: logical operator incidence	3
n-Gram: *for*	217	Error: adjective comparative/superlative errors	1
n-Gram: *some*	185	CM: content stems	1
CM: word familiarity	158	n-Gram: *we can*	1
n-Gram: *and they*	157	n-Gram: *not have*	1
n-Gram: *often*	152	n-Gram: *going to*	1
Error: article errors	150		
Error: word redundant errors	133		
n-Gram: *however*	117		

41 variables was selected. Variables selected in more than half of the folds of the LOOCV are listed on the left side of the table, and variables selected in fewer than half are listed on the right side of the table.

There are 22 variables on the left side of the table, which is coincidentally precisely the number of variables we wish to include in our optimal L1 prediction model, as this is 10% of the number of texts (i.e. 222) in the training set used in each fold of the LOOCV. These are therefore the 22 variables we present as our final solution, but we show them in a different order in Table 6.12 in order to offer an additional perspective of their usefulness. In Table 6.12, these variables are listed according to F values obtained through a series of one-way ANOVAs, where each variable was tested for significant differences across the group means of the three L1 groups. The rightmost column of the table shows the results of an SNK post-hoc text, which indicates more precisely where the differences exist.

It appears from the results shown in Tables 6.11 and 6.12 that the three types of variables are roughly equally important to this final model. Although the final model includes more n-grams ($n = 9$) than error categories ($n = 7$) or CM indices ($n = 6$), some of the strongest L1 predictor variables in the model are CM indices and error categories.[1] It is interesting to note that the last three variables listed in Table 6.12 do not show any significant differences at all across the means of the three L1 groups, yet these three variables do nevertheless contribute to the model's ability to identify the L1s of the texts in the Error Corpus, as attested by the fact that they were selected as many as 220 times (in the case of word hypernymy) in the 223 folds of the LOOCV, where the stepwise procedure selected only those variables whose unique contribution to the model significantly improved the model's L1 prediction ability. It is also interesting to note that the final model presented here does not include any of the n-grams, CM indices or error categories described earlier that show significant differences across all three groups. As seen in Table 6.12, the differences are primarily between one group and the two others, without any significant differences between those two other groups. Despite the lack of such variables in the present combined analysis, it is noteworthy that the variables we have retained work together in such a way as to provide a substantially more powerful model of L1 prediction than was found in any of the prior analyses based on a single type of variable.

A Truncated Combined Analysis

In view of the analyses presented so far, it seems uncontroversial that an L1 prediction model that includes multiple types of predictors is superior to a model consisting of predictor variables of only one type. However, one question that remains is whether all three types of variables are needed to achieve optimal results. Recall that Wong and Dras (2009) found that a combination of just two types of variables (i.e. function words and parts-of-speech n-grams) led to equally high levels of L1 classification accuracy as a combination of three or even four types of variables. In the Wong and Dras study, the inclusion of error variables, for example, did not improve the model beyond what was achieved through function words and n-grams

Table 6.12 Results of the ANOVAs and the SNK tests for the selected variables

Variable	F	p	FR (means)	GE (means)	SP (means)	Diff sign
CM: word concreteness	51.04	<0.001	289.411	304.810	291.914	GE>(FR=SP)
CM: motion verbs	36.64	<0.001	93.072	135.903	80.992	GE>(FR=SP)
Error: article errors	36.51	<0.001	0.503	0.337	1.149	SP>(FR=GE)
Error: spelling errors	32.70	<0.001	0.621	0.792	1.610	SP>(FR=GE)
Error: unclear pron ref	23.86	<0.001	0.100	0.061	0.243	SP>(FR=GE)
CM: causal particles/verbs	23.05	<0.001	0.550	0.525	0.984	SP>(FR=GE)
Error: verbs w/ wrong prep	20.29	<0.001	0.101	0.096	0.275	SP>(FR=GE)
Error: punctuation <> word	17.52	<0.001	0.161	0.033	0.048	FR>(GE=SP)
n-Gram: *to do*	14.31	<0.001	0.418	0.527	1.676	SP>(FR=GE)
n-Gram: *become*	10.47	<0.001	1.380	0.533	0.634	FR>(GE=SP)
CM: word familiarity	10.00	<0.001	591.550	593.872	593.220	FR<(GE=SP)
n-Gram: *we*	9.54	<0.001	8.158	3.714	9.098	GE<(FR=SP)
n-Gram: *often*	9.17	<0.001	1.103	1.068	0.261	SP<(FR=GE)
CM: aspect repetition	7.72	0.001	0.848	0.914	0.879	GE>(FR=SP)
n-Gram: *think that*	6.71	0.002	1.067	0.305	1.130	GE<(FR=SP)
n-Gram: *however*	6.54	0.002	0.561	1.154	0.594	GE>(FR=SP)
Error: single log connector	5.18	0.006	0.178	0.087	0.125	FR>GE
n-Gram: *for*	5.01	0.007	8.207	9.823	7.641	GE>(FR=SP)
n-Gram: *some*	4.04	0.019	2.735	1.892	3.121	SP>GE
n-Gram: *and they*	3.01	0.052	0.349	0.285	0.684	Nonsignificant
Error: word redundant	2.61	0.076	0.030	0.056	0.059	Nonsignificant
CM: word hypernymy	1.69	0.186	1.583	1.540	1.585	Nonsignificant

alone. An important caveat is that they used only three error variables (subject–verb disagreement, noun–number disagreement and misuse of determiners) whereas our analysis includes 46 error variables – so it is perhaps to be expected that their error variables would be of limited usefulness. A second caveat is that the error variables used by Wong and Dras were tagged through a computer-automated procedure, whereas the errors analyzed in this chapter were hand-tagged. As mentioned earlier, problems associated with computer-automated error tagging may have further limited the usefulness of the error variables used by Wong and Dras. Nevertheless, we use their findings as a point of departure for the present section, in which we examine whether a combination of *n*-grams and CM indices – without error categories – enables a level of L1 classification accuracy that is comparable to that of a combined analysis involving all three types of variables.

Our interest in the effectiveness of a combined analysis that excludes error categories is also motivated by practical considerations. That is, whereas *n*-grams and CM indices can be extracted from the data through automated means, accurate error tagging requires human intervention in the form of careful reading and annotation, and usually also requires at least two raters for each text for purposes of reliability. Accurate and reliable error tagging is thus very time-consuming and expensive. One wonders, therefore, how much error categories really contribute to L1 detection beyond what other types of variables contribute. If the benefit is small, then error tagging might not be worth the effort. This is the question we address in the present section.

To conduct this analysis, we combined the 50 *n*-grams and 19 CM indices described earlier into a single pool of variables. This pool of variables was then submitted to a DA analysis of the Error Corpus using stepwise variable selection embedded within each fold of an LOOCV. As before, the stepwise parameters were set to a significance criterion of 0.05 for variable entrance and removal, and the number of iterations was limited to 22.

The results of this analysis are shown in Table 6.13. As in prior analyses, the proportion of correctly classified texts for each L1 group is quite high,

Table 6.13 L1 group identification scores for FR, GE and SP texts

Actual L1	Predicted L1			
	FR	GE	SP	Total
FR	**53 (72%)**	6	15	74
GE	16	**50 (70%)**	5	71
SP	23	7	**48 (62%)**	78
Total	92	63	68	223

and this is especially true of the texts written by French and German speakers. Nevertheless, the overall number of correct classifications is lower than what was achieved in the analysis in the previous section involving not just *n*-grams and CM indices, but also error categories. Whereas the results of the previous analysis showed an overall L1 classification accuracy of 79.4%, the present analysis achieved only 67.7% accuracy, correctly classifying 151 of the 223 texts (df = 4, *n* = 223, χ^2 = 130.766, $p < 0.001$; Cohen's Kappa = 0.516). The differences in classification accuracy between the full combined analysis and the truncated combined analysis are both considerable and statistically significant ($t[222] = 3.707$, $p < 0.001$), suggesting that the potential contribution of error categories to L1 detection is anything but trivial. Concerning its usefulness in relation to the analyses based on a single variable type, the truncated combined analysis achieved a higher level of accuracy than any of the single-variable-type analyses, but the differences are not significant (truncated combined analysis vs. *n*-gram analysis: $t[222] = 1.293$, $p > 0.05$; truncated combined analysis vs. CM analysis: $t[222] = 1.181$, $p > 0.05$; truncated combined analysis vs. the error-based analysis: $t[222] = 0.535$, $p > 0.05$).

Table 6.14 Results of the ANOVAs and the SNK tests for the selected variables

Variable	F	p	FR (means)	GE (means)	SP (means)	Diff sign
CM: word concreteness	51.04	<0.001	289.411	304.810	291.914	GE>(FR=SP)
CM: motion verbs	36.64	<0.001	93.072	135.903	80.992	GE>(FR=SP)
CM: stem overlap	27.93	<0.001	0.403	0.296	0.516	SP>FR>GE
CM: causal particles/verbs	23.05	<0.001	0.550	0.525	0.984	SP>(FR=GE)
n-Gram: *to do*	14.31	<0.001	0.418	0.527	1.676	SP>(FR=GE)
n-Gram: *become*	10.47	<0.001	1.380	0.533	0.634	FR<(GE=SP)
CM: word familiarity	10.00	<0.001	591.550	593.872	593.220	FR>(GE=SP)
n-Gram: *we*	9.54	<0.001	8.158	3.714	9.098	GE<(FR=SP)
n-Gram: *often*	9.17	<0.001	1.103	1.068	0.261	SP<(FR=GE)
CM: aspect repetition	7.72	0.001	0.848	0.914	0.879	GE>(FR=SP)
n-Gram: *think that*	6.71	0.002	1.067	0.305	1.130	GE<(FR=SP)
n-Gram: *however*	6.54	0.002	0.561	1.154	0.594	GE>(FR=SP)
n-Gram: *for*	5.01	0.007	8.207	9.823	7.641	GE>(FR=SP)

For purposes of consistency across the sections of this chapter, and in hopes of providing useful benchmarks for future research in this area, we examined the results of the combined analysis of n-grams and CM indices in order to identify the variables that are seemingly the most useful in combination with one another for L1 classification. As before, we used two criteria for this purpose. First, we identified which variables were selected by the stepwise DA procedure in more than half of the folds of the LOOCV. Then, we submitted these variables to a series of one-way ANOVA and SNK tests in order to determine which of these variables show significant differences across the means of the three L1 groups. We found that 16 variables met the first criterion, and 13 of these met the second criterion, as well. The 13 variables that met both criteria are listed in Table 6.14 in the order of the strength of their F values, with more precise information about the location of the differences given in the rightmost column. This table shows that there is only one variable (CM stem overlap) that shows significant differences across the means for all three L1 groups. It is interesting to note that this is not the variable with the highest F value.

Discussion and Conclusions

This chapter has investigated the comparative and combined contributions of n-grams, CM indices and error categories in the identification of the L1 backgrounds of learner texts. In terms of the comparative dimension, our analyses have shown that L1 prediction models based on predictor variables of a single type are fairly powerful, leading to L1 classification accuracies of between 63% and 66% for the 223 texts in the Error Corpus, which were written by learners from three L1 backgrounds (French, German and Spanish). The analysis based on error categories reached the highest classification accuracy (65.5%), followed by the analysis based on CM indices (64.1%) and finally the analysis based on n-grams (63.2%). However, this range of results is quite narrow and the differences are not significant. We thus conclude on the basis of the present results that n-grams, CM indices and error categories are roughly equally effective, by themselves, for L1 detection purposes. Nevertheless, they do not correctly classify all of the same texts, and it would be interesting in future studies to conduct a more in-depth examination of the ways in which the three types of analysis complement one another in relation to the L1 classification of individual learner texts and whether, for example, one type of analysis might be better for detecting certain L1s, whereas another type of analysis might be better for detecting others (cf. Tables 6.4, 6.6 and 6.8).

Concerning the effectiveness of a combination of all three types of variables in a single analysis, our results have confirmed the general finding of Koppel *et al.* (2005) and Wong and Dras (2009) that an L1 prediction model that includes multiple types of variables is substantially more powerful than one constructed from a single type. Our combined analysis of three types of variables showed an L1 classification accuracy of 79.4%. This comes very close to the 80.2% mark set by Koppel *et al.* We see the 80% mark as an important threshold for classification research as it gives a clear indication that (1) the data contain strong and consistent patterns (i.e. a signal) associated with the classes in question; (2) the variables included in the model capture a good portion of that signal; and (3) the specific classifier used (DA, in the present case) is effective in tuning into that signal.

Because of the relative difficulty of deriving error variables in comparison with *n*-grams and CM indices, and in order to determine how important error categories are for L1 identification, we also conducted an analysis based on a combination of just *n*-grams and CM indices, leaving out error categories. The results of this analysis produced an L1 classification accuracy of 67.7%, which is slightly (though not significantly) better than the classification accuracies for the analyses based on a single type of variable, but much worse (significantly) than the classification accuracies for the analysis based on all three types of variables. Because *n*-grams and CM indices can be extracted and calculated through automated means, using a combination of both types of variables for this type of research seems clearly warranted, even if the classification improvement is only slight in relation to analyses based on *n*-grams alone or CM indices alone. More importantly, however, the results of this study strongly point to the value of including error categories along with *n*-grams and CM indices. Rather than searching for alternatives to error variables, therefore, we believe that this area of research would benefit more from efforts directed toward the pursuit of higher levels of accuracy in automated error tagging (cf. Wong & Dras, 2009).

While conducting each of the several analyses in this chapter, we attempted to identify the most useful variables for predicting whether a text was written by a learner from one particular L1 background or another. The set of variables differed somewhat between the single-type analyses and combined analyses, but 15 of the 22 variables chosen as the optimal model for the combined analysis of *n*-grams, CM indices and error categories were also among the optimal variables identified in the single-type analyses and in the truncated combined analysis (i.e. the analysis based on just *n*-grams and CM indices). These 15 variables include six error categories (unclear pronominal reference, spelling errors, punctuation mark instead of lexical item and vice versa, verbs used with the wrong dependent preposition, article errors and single logical connector errors), five *n*-grams (*to do, become, we, often* and *think that*), and four CM indices (causal particles/verbs, motion verbs, word familiarity and aspect repetition). Because they loaded into the optimal models of multiple analyses, we believe that these 15 variables are of a general usefulness for differentiating argumentative texts written by French-, German- and Spanish-speaking learners of English.[2] Whether these variables reflect direct L1 influence, however, is another question.

Although the three groups of writers have different L1s, there may be other relatively consistent differences between these groups that affect their use of L2 English, and which therefore enhance L1 classification accuracy independently of L1 influence per se. Such factors would therefore confound L1 effects (see e.g. Jarvis, 2000; Jarvis & Pavlenko, 2008). As discussed in Chapter 5, the Spanish group appears to be, on the whole, less proficient than the French and German groups. This fact raises doubts about whether some of the 15 variables described earlier as being of general usefulness really do reflect L1 influence versus merely proficiency differences. Nowhere is this more problematic than in the case of the error categories, where the Spanish speakers produced significantly more errors than the other two groups in relation to five of the six error categories identified in the previous paragraph as being of general usefulness for L1 classification. Inasmuch as errors decrease with increases in proficiency, the effects of proficiency appear to combine with and thus confound the effects of the L1, at least for some of the variables we have examined. As mentioned in previous chapters, there may also be other confounding factors that coincide with L1 differences, such as differences in the specific topics that the writers wrote about,[3] differences in the nature of their English language training, and differences in the types and amounts of exposure they have had to English both inside and outside the classroom. From this perspective, the L1 classification accuracy of 79.4% that we achieved in our combined analysis of all three types of variables may be an overestimation of the strength of the signals emanating from the learners' L1s.

On the other hand, it is at least theoretically possible that the L1 signals in the data are actually stronger than what we have been able to tune into in this study. Because of the relatively small size of the Error Corpus, for example, the number of variables we could include in our DA model was quite limited. We do not know what the optimal number of variables is for capturing the L1 signals in the data, but it is likely to be at least somewhat larger than the limit of 22 imposed on the models in this study.

Besides the optimal number of variables, we are also not completely sure as to what the ideal set of variables is. In this study, we have used only three types of variables: *n*-grams, CM indices and error categories. There are a number of additional types of variables that might carry L1-specific patterns, such as parts-of-speech patterns (Estival *et al.*, 2007; Koppel *et al.*, 2005; Mayfield Tomokiyo & Jones, 2001; Wong & Dras, 2009), the types of grammatical constructions learners produce (cf. Bohnacker & Rosén, 2008; Odlin, 1990), the level of formality with which they write, how much they elaborate on the context (cf. Montaño-Harmon, 1991; Reppen & Grabe, 1993; Thatcher, 2000) and so forth. By expanding our pool of variables to include additional features that distinguish the learners' L1s from one another, we are likely to achieve even higher levels of L1 classification accuracy in a combined analysis.

It is also possible that higher levels of L1 classification accuracy could be achieved even with just the three types of variables already included in our study. Our use of stepwise procedures in the present study seems to have worked well for selecting variables from a larger pool, but the outcome of a stepwise procedure is always strongly affected by which variable the procedure happens to choose first from that pool. If our stepwise procedures had begun with different variables than the ones that were first selected, it is possible (though not necessarily likely) that the ensuing models would have been even more effective in L1 classification than the ones we have presented. In order to determine whether this is the case, it would be necessary to use a variable selection procedure that involves all possible subsets of variables. This was beyond the scope of the present investigation, but it is certainly worth pursuing in future studies.

A final reason why the L1 signals in the data might theoretically be stronger than what we have found is that the present study has used only one of many available classifiers (see e.g. Jockers & Witten, 2010; Kotsiantis, 2007). The classifier used in the present study and throughout this book is DA. This is an effective classifier; in fact, in a comparison of DA with a large number of other classifiers, Jarvis (2011) shows that DA produces the very highest L1 classification accuracy for the classification task that is the focus of Chapter 3 of this book (i.e. an *n*-gram analysis of texts written by speakers of 12 L1s). Nevertheless, the effectiveness of a classifier depends considerably on the task it is given (e.g. Estival *et al.*, 2007), and it is possible that a different classifier or an ensemble of classifiers would have been able to perform the combined analysis of the present chapter more successfully than DA (alone). This is another question that we hope will be explored in future research.

As we have emphasized throughout this book, detection-based methodology appears to offer a great deal of promise to transfer research. Although high levels of accuracy in the L1 classification of learners' language samples is not sufficient evidence of L1 influence unless the effects of all potential confounds (e.g. proficiency differences between groups, differences in language exposure and training) have been ruled out – which is impossible with most existing learner corpora – the detection-based methodology nevertheless allows researchers to estimate the potential strength of the L1 signals in and across individual learner samples, and to identify the variables (or features of learners' language use) that carry those signals. These variables can then be further scrutinized in relation to whether they reflect patterns in the L1 itself and whether they also reflect the unique web of similarities, differences and zero relationships that exists only between a particular L1 and L2 (Jarvis, 2010; Ringbom, 2007). The analyses presented in this chapter and other chapters of this book have, we hope, opened the door more widely to future work in this area.

Notes

(1) A potential advantage that CM indices have over both *n*-grams and error categories is that the CM measures used in the present study consistently produce nonzero values for all texts, whereas *n*-gram and error variables frequently receive a value of 0, that is, when a particular *n*-gram or error category is not found in a given text. A high number of zero values can result in a floor effect that limits the variation across texts and thus impedes accurate text classification. This was not a serious problem with the *n*-grams and error categories used in the present study, however.
(2) Distinguishing among other L1s would most likely entail a different set of variables.
(3) Although this may be particularly relevant for the *n*-gram analyses, we did deal with this issue in the present study by discarding all topic-related *n*-grams.

References

Bohnacker, U. and Rosén, C. (2008) The clause-initial position in L2 German declaratives: Transfer of information structure. *Studies in Second Language Acquisition* 30, 511–538.

Estival, D., Gaustad, T., Pham, S.B., Radford, W. and Hutchinson, B. (2007) Author profiling for English emails. In *Proceedings of the 10th Conference of the Pacific Association for Computational Linguistics (PACLING 2007)* (pp. 31–39). Melbourne, Australia.

Granger, S., Dagneaux, E., Meunier, F. and Paquot, M. (2009) *The International Corpus of Learner English. Handbook and CD-ROM*. Version 2. Louvain-la-Neuve: Presses universitaires de Louvain.

Jarvis, S. (2000) Methodological rigor in the study of transfer: Identifying L1 influence in the interlanguage lexicon. *Language Learning* 50, 245–309.

Jarvis, S. (2010) Comparison-based and detection-based approaches to transfer research. In L. Roberts, M. Howard, M. Ó Laoire and D. Singleton (eds) *EUROSLA Yearbook 10* (pp. 169–192). Amsterdam: Benjamins.

Jarvis, S. (2011) Data mining with learner corpora: Choosing classifiers for L1 detection. In F. Meunier, S. De Cock, G. Gilquin and M. Paquot (eds) *A Taste for Corpora. Honour of Sylviane Granger* (pp. 131–158). Amsterdam: John Benjamins.

Jarvis, S. and Pavlenko, A. (2008) *Crosslinguistic Influence in Language and Cognition*. New York: Routledge.

Jockers, M.L. and Witten, D.M. (2010) A comparative study of machine learning methods for authorship attribution. *Literary and Linguistic Computing* 25, 215–223.

Koppel, M., Schler, J. and Zigdon, K. (2005) Determining an author's native language by mining a text for errors. In *Proceedings of the Eleventh ACM SIGKDD International Conference on Knowledge Discovery in Data Mining* (pp. 624–628). Chicago: Association for Computing Machinery.

Kotsiantis, S. (2007) Supervised machine learning: A review of classification techniques. *Informatica Journal* 31, 249–268.

Lecocke, M. and Hess, K. (2006) An empirical study of univariate and genetic algorithm-based feature selection in binary classification with microarray data. *Cancer Informatics* 2, 313–327.

Mayfield Tomokiyo, L. and Jones, R. (2001) You're not from 'round here, are you? Naive Bayes detection of non-native utterance text. In *Proceedings of the Second Meeting of the North American Chapter of the Association for Computational Linguistics (NAACL '01)*, unpaginated electronic document. Cambridge, MA: The Association for Computational Linguistics.

McNamara, D.S. and Graesser, A.C. (in press) Coh-Metrix: An automated tool for theoretical and applied natural language processing. In P.M. McCarthy and C. Boonthum (eds) *Applied Natural Language Processing and Content Analysis: Identification, Investigation, and Resolution*. Hershey, PA: IGI Global.

Molinaro, A.M., Simon, R. and Pfeiffer, R.M. (2005) Prediction error estimation: A comparison of resampling methods. *Bioinformatics* 21, 3301–3307.

Montaño-Harmon, M. (1991) Discourse features of written Mexican Spanish: Current research in contrastive rhetoric and its implications. *Hispania* 74, 417–425.

Odlin, T. (1990) Word order transfer, metalinguistic awareness, and constraints on foreign language learning. In B. VanPatten and J.F. Lee (eds) *Second Language Acquisition/Foreign Language Learning* (pp. 95–117). Clevedon: Multilingual Matters.

Reppen, R. and Grabe, W. (1993) Spanish transfer effects in the English writing of elementary school students. *Lenguas Modernas* 20, 112–128.

Ringbom, H. (2007) *Cross-Linguistic Similarity in Foreign Language Learning*. Clevedon: Multilingual Matters.

Schulerud, H. and Albregtsen, F. (2004) Many are called, but few are chosen: Feature selection and error estimation in high dimensional spaces. *Computer Methods and Programs in Biomedicine* 73, 91–99.

Thatcher, B.L. (2000) L2 professional writing in a US and South American context. *Journal of Second Language Writing* 9, 41–69.

Wong, S.-M.J. and Dras, M. (2009) Contrastive analysis and native language identification. In *Proceedings of the Australasian Language Technology Association* (pp. 53–61). Cambridge, MA: The Association for Computational Linguistics.

7 Detection-Based Approaches: Methods, Theories and Applications

Scott A. Crossley

The five studies reported in this volume provide strong evidence of the usefulness of a detection-based approach for classifying texts written in English based on the first language (L1) of the writer. Such an approach not only provides support for theories concerning crosslinguistic influences, but also yields important methodological innovations that will prove beneficial for future research that investigates language transfer, second language (L2) acquisition, language pedagogy, language assessment and forensic linguistics.

Historically, language detection methods have been employed to examine authorship attribution (e.g. whether Madison or Hamilton were the authors of the Federalist papers; Mosteller & Wallace, 1964). An important point of departure for the present volume is the notion that identifying an author's L1 is a type of authorship attribution. It differs slightly from classic authorship studies because we are not interested in identifying a particular author, but rather a class of authors based on the sharing of a similar L1. In doing so, the chapters in this volume are designed to discover features of the L1 that are relatively invariant across the group, but vary within groups. The notion underlying such an approach is that the emergence of clear differences in the patterns of language use among different language groups writing in an L2 can provide evidence of interlingual transfer (Kubota, 1998). Additionally, the approaches found in this volume depend on machine-learning algorithms for group classification, setting up a signal or pattern detection framework. The studies in this volume demonstrate that such a framework provides advantages for identifying subtle linguistic differences that exist between L1 groups that may not be observable in qualitative analyses.

As mentioned in Chapter 1 of this volume, there have been various studies that have used automatic text classification to detect the L1 backgrounds of L2 writers. Three studies, in particular, are informative from a methodological and theoretical position: Koppel *et al.* (2005), Tsur and Rappoport

(2007) and Wong and Dras (2009). Koppel *et al.* (2005) reported on a classification task that involved five L1 backgrounds, 1290 texts sampled from the ICLE (Granger *et al.*, 2009), and over 1000 linguistic features, which together attained a maximum classification accuracy of 80%. Tsur and Rappoport (2007) conducted an L1 classification analysis that was very similar to that of Koppel *et al.* (2005) but sampled a different selection of texts and focused primarily on letter bigrams and trigrams. Their highest level of L1 classification accuracy was 67%. Lastly, Wong and Dras (2009) also conducted a study similar to that of Koppel *et al.* and Tsur and Rappoport, However, unlike these previous studies, the Wong and Dras study included texts written by Chinese- and Japanese-speaking learners of English and analyzed a smaller sample of texts. Their highest level of L1 classification accuracy was 74%.

We regarded these previous studies as a springboard from which to further explore the potential to predict the L1 of L2 writers using machine-learning algorithms informed through the selection of suitable linguistic features. However, unlike these past studies our focus has not only been solely on classification accuracy (i.e. intra- and intergroup homogeneity), but also on cross-language congruity through narrowly defined L1-related patterns. Thus, while the studies reported in this volume do seek to accurately and reliably classify L2 writing samples based on the L1 of the writer, we have also been fundamentally interested in how these differences correspond to the writer's L1 and how these differences can be used to assess the degree of predictable crosslinguistic influence from one language to another. Also, unlike earlier studies, we improve the statistical approaches used by relying on a classifier that demonstrates higher accuracy and reliability in the given classification tasks (i.e. a discriminant function analysis classifier), using feature selection procedures to identify optimal sets of relevant classification features, and ensuring that the reported models do not suffer from excessive overfitting.

For instance, in Chapter 2 of this volume, Jarvis *et al.* reported on a detection-based study that focused on the use of single words to classify narrative descriptions written in English by L2 learners from five different language backgrounds. Jarvis *et al.* were able to correctly classify 76.9% of the texts based on the L1 of the participant. Such accuracy was well above chance demonstrating that a relatively small set of highly frequent words is capable of discriminating learners from different L1 backgrounds, even when their L1s are closely related to one another. These findings supported by corresponding qualitative analyses reported by Jarvis *et al.* yield evidence that the lexical styles of L1 speakers can transfer to their L2.

In Chapter 3 of this volume, Jarvis and Paquot explored the classification potential of multiword units (unigrams, bigrams, trigrams and quadrigrams) to classify texts written in English by 12 different L1 populations. Jarvis and Paquot secured their highest independent classification rate using unigrams (53% accuracy). Their analysis also demonstrated a negative trend in classification accuracy as a result of *n*-gram size (with quadgrams reporting an accuracy of just 22%). Their highest overall accuracy was obtained using a combination of *n*-grams (53.6%), though this accuracy was not statistically higher than that reported for unigrams. In general, Jarvis and Paquot found that a large number of L1 backgrounds can be distinguished relatively successfully from one another on the basis of *n*-grams alone, and that the optimal model consists of a well-chosen set of *n*-grams of different lengths. Such findings support the strength of *n*-grams to detect the L1 of L2 writers, even if the L2 writers come from closely related cultures and language backgrounds.

In Chapter 4, Crossley and McNamara used the computational tool Coh-Metrix to investigate the potential for linguistic indices related to cohesion, lexical sophistication, syntactic complexity and conceptual knowledge to predict the L1 of four groups of L2 writers. Crossley and McNamara were able to accurately classify 65.8% of the essays based on the writer's L1 using 14 of the 19 selected variables. Their analysis demonstrated that the strongest predictors of an L2 writer's L1 were lexical in nature, followed by indices of text cohesion, conceptual knowledge and syntactic complexity. Crossley and McNamara concluded that these types of linguistic features were strong indicators of both intergroup heterogeneity and intragroup homogeneity, providing support for the notion that linguistic features differ in predictable ways among L2 essays written by different L1 groups and that these differences can be used to reliably detect the L1 of L2 writers.

In Chapter 5, Bestgen, Granger and Thewissen investigated the use of learner errors as a method from which to classify the L1 of three groups of L2 writers. Their approach, which was novel in its use of hand-tagged error categories, yielded a classification accuracy of 65%, which was significantly above chance. The best predictors of L1 classification were spelling errors, lexical errors on single words and phrases, erroneous article use, erroneous dependent prepositions used with verbs, unclear pronominal references and erroneous demonstrative determiners. Bestgen *et al.* were careful to note that not all the errors in their analysis necessarily resulted from transfer; however, a careful analysis of the data did demonstrate that a number of the errors could safely be attributed to transfer effects. While the classification accuracy reported by Bestgen *et al.* was significantly above chance, the predictive ability of error categories does not appear to be greater than that reported for many of the linguistic features used in Chapters 2 through 4 (i.e. unigrams, bigrams, trigrams, cohesive devices, lexical items, syntactic features). This finding is somewhat surprising given the amount of attention the error analysis and L2 transfer has received in the past (e.g. Corder, 1967; George, 1972).

In the final study in this volume, Jarvis *et al.* compared the classification accuracy of each type of classification analysis found in this volume as well as examined the effect of combining all the selected features from Chapters 3 through 5. The purpose of this chapter was to compare the predictive ability of the individual approaches to classify L2 texts based on the L1 of the writer as well as investigate the comparative strength of the features when combined in a stepwise classification technique. Jarvis *et al.* used the corpus sampled in Bestgen *et al.* and predictors taken from the *n*-gram analysis, the Coh-Metrix analysis and the error tag analysis. They reported a classification accuracy of 63.2% for the *n*-gram analysis, 64.1% for the Coh-Metrix analysis and 65.5% for the error tag analysis. While all of these analyses reported classification rates that were significantly higher than chance and the baseline, none of these approaches demonstrated a classification accuracy that was significantly better than the others. In the final analysis, which combined all of the indices, Jarvis *et al.* report a classification accuracy of 79.4%, which was significantly higher than chance and the baseline and, importantly, significantly higher than the results from the individual analyses. The strongest predictors in this analysis were Coh-Metrix variables related to word concreteness and the use of motion verbs followed by error tag variables and *n*-gram variables. Jarvis *et al.* concluded that an L1 prediction model that includes multiple predictor variables was far superior to models based on a shorter range of variables. Additionally, Jarvis *et al.* found that a prediction model using all three of the variable categories was far more powerful than one that excluded one of those categories.

Overall, the studies reported in this volume demonstrate strong empirical support for detection-based methodologies as a technique for predicting the L1 of an L2 writer. The studies also provide some indication that the variables used to predict the L1 of the L2 writers are transfer related. While transfer may not explain all of the classification accuracy reported in these studies, it is certainly responsible for at least a moderate degree of the accuracy reported. However, as discussed in Chapter 6 of this volume, some of the classification accuracy could be attributable to proficiency level, the writing topics, English language training, and English language exposure. The possibility of overestimating the importance of transfer effects for these data promotes a cautious extrapolation of the causal effects attributable to the transfer of linguistic features from the L1 to the L2. However, the analyses in this volume do support the notion that intragroup homogeneity as well as intergroup heterogeneity are at play in the data such that similarities within L1 speakers and dissimilarities between L1 groups afford categorical classification based on linguistic patterns.

Additionally, it is clear in many of the chapters in this volume that cross-language congruity (i.e. similarities between TL use and L1) is evident, providing support for transfer-based arguments. Such evidence is available at the lexical, grammatical and *n*-gram level. Most of this evidence is qualitative in nature and not the result of detection-based methodologies. Thus, many of the studies in the volume promote a mixed-method approach involving an initial detection-based analysis followed by a comparison-based analysis in which an examination of the learners' L1 is undertaken in reference to reported differences in their L2 production in order to investigate performance similarities between the L1 and L2.

From a lexical perspective, in Chapter 2 of this volume, Jarvis *et al.* found that many of the unigrams predictive of writers' L1 could be linked to preferred word choices in their L1 and, when the words did not exist in the L1, the word's omission. For example, Spanish speakers tended to produce the word *police* as compared to *policeman*, likely as a result of the Spanish word *policia*. Likewise, Danes, Swedes and Finns were more likely to produce the word *away* because of phrasal verbs in each language respectively that overlap with the term *run away*. Portuguese and Spanish speakers were also more likely to use the word *escape* because of the cognate *escapar* found in each language. Perhaps more tellingly, Portuguese and Spanish speakers were more likely to use the word *arrive* (which corresponds to the word for *come* in their L1), while Finns and Swedes were more likely to use the word *come*, which has a parallel verb in both those languages. Additionally, Bestgen *et al.* (this volume) reported that Spanish writers would use the same word for *other* or *another* as the result of Spanish containing only one word for both these concepts (*otro*). Spanish writers are also more likely to translate *in* and *on* as one word because Spanish contains only one word for these concepts (*en*).

Grammatical differences attributable to transfer were also evidenced in post-hoc qualitative analyses in many of the studies contained in this volume. For instance, Jarvis *et al.* (Chapter 2 of this volume) reported that the writers in the Finnish group were more likely to use proper nouns (e.g. *Chaplin*) than other L1 groups and that Finnish writers used pronouns (e.g. *he*) less often than other writers from other L1 groups. Because Finnish has only a single pronoun for both he and she (=hän), Finnish writers of English may resort to using nouns more frequently than pronouns in order to avoid referential ambiguity. Likewise, Finnish writers were less likely to produce articles such as *a* and *the* because Finnish does not have an article system. Bestgen *et al.* (this volume) reported in their error analysis that Spanish speakers were more likely to have errors in which personal pronouns were omitted in the subject position (which is allowable in Spanish) or in which a zero article was used (which is also allowable in Spanish), while writers from different L1s (French and German) would use indefinite articles as found in their L1.

Post-hoc analyses of detection-based machine classification findings in this volume have also promoted the notion that *n*-grams are transferred from the L1 to the L2 such that common *n*-grams in the L1 come to serve specific, stylistic functions in the L2 (Paquot, 2010). For instance, Jarvis and Paquot (this volume) found that *n*-grams such as *as far as* were more commonly used by French writers, who have a parallel construction in their native language. The *n*-gram *on the contrary* was also produced at a higher rate by French writers likely because of the *n*-gram *au contraire* in French. Spanish and Italian writers were more likely to use the *n*-gram *we can* probably because of similar constructions in their L1s (*poder* and *potere*, respectively). Additionally, Spanish writers were more likely to use the *n*-gram *going to* probably as a result of overlap with the construction *a ir + verb* common in Spanish. Lastly, Finnish writers appear more likely to use the phrase *all the time* because it has conceptual overlap with the phrase *koko ajan*, which is common in Finnish.

Other features of language detection algorithms reported in this volume are more difficult to directly connect with theories of L2 transfer because many of the linguistic features reported are indirect representations of language at the lexical, syntactic and rhetorical level. These features, when combined with detection-based approaches for predicting the L1 of L2 writers, provide indirect evidence for transfer under the assumption that many transfer effects are too subtle, too complex, and too difficult to anticipate (Jarvis, this volume). Nowhere is this clearer than in the chapter written by Crossley and McNamara in which they used Coh-Metrix indices related to lexical sophistication, syntactic complexity, cohesion and conceptual knowledge to predict the L1 of L2 writers. Although these indices demonstrated great success at separating writers based on their L1, the interpretation of these differences is difficult to parse out. For instance, how do lexical measures such as word concreteness, word imagability, lexical diversity and word frequency capture subtle differences among the L1 lexicons of L2 writers? When Crossley and McNamara report that German writers have a higher degree of lexical sophistication, it is difficult to pinpoint which words, word combinations or frequency of words drive this finding and how the production of these features associates with crosslinguistic influences. Ostensibly, such a finding is likely related to the close family relation between English and German that would permit the greater use of cognates and, likely, the more accurate development of lexical networks. However, strong evidence supporting such a hypothesis is not easily available. Anecdotal evidence supporting some aspects of the Coh-Metrix findings are available, such as the notion that Spanish writing is loosely coordinated (Montaño-Harmon, 1988) or that Finns may oversimplify their writing (Ventola & Mauranen, 1991). However, such evidence is sparse and most is not based on strong empirical findings.

Being aware of such limitations, the authors in this volume have been careful to highlight that the detection-based techniques used in their analyses may not be detecting and classifying the L2 texts based on patterns attributable to transfer from the L1 to the L2 alone. Among the problems with the learner data contained in the ICLE is that it may not accurately represent a single proficiency level and that demographic information for the learners (e.g. levels of English language training and English language exposure) is unavailable. Thus, to some degree, the signal captured in the classification analyses may not be the result of differences between the L1s of the writers, but rather differences in learner-level variables. Such learner-level variables may create an overestimation of the strength of the signals that result from the L1. To what degree this overestimation may occur will require future studies that control for learner-level variables. However, there is evidence that differences in learner-level variables may not contribute too strongly to L1 classification rates. For instance, Jarvis *et al.* (Chapter 2, this volume) included learners from a variety of different proficiency levels and still reported strong classification rates (76.9% accuracy). Bestgen *et al.* (this volume) conducted a small-scale analysis of L2 texts controlled for proficiency level and found that rates of error occurrences within those texts could still be used for successful, automatic L1 group identification (with an accuracy of 75% reported for the classification model).

Examining the studies reported in this volume in combination with one another can also disquiet suspicion that proficiency level may play a role in text classification. For instance, Bestgen *et al.* reported that Spanish essays in a small sub-corpus of the ICLE were judged to be of lower proficiency than either French or German essays with German essays being evaluated as the highest proficiency. Such a finding would promote the notion that lower proficiency essays (i.e. Spanish essays) may emit detectable patterns that are not only transfer related, but are also related to proficiency level. Presumably, such patterns would aid a machine-learning algorithm in classification accuracy and, potentially, give Spanish essays an edge in classification accuracy because they would emit additional signals with which they could be classified. Not only that, there is a general consensus that transfer patterns are more prevalent at lower proficiency levels (Odlin, 1989; Poulisse & Bongaerts, 1994), which would also aid in signal detection. However, Spanish essays were generally classified at lower accuracy rates than the majority of languages sampled. For instance, Spanish essays had the lowest rates of classification when Coh-Metrix variables were used, when error tags were used, and when *n*-grams, Coh-Metrix variables, and error tags were combined. Spanish essays were also classified at a lower level than four other language groups when unigrams and multiword units (including unigrams) were used (see Table 7.1 for classification rates). Such findings call into question the notion that lower proficiency levels may lead to greater classification accuracy.

The research reported in this volume also supports the use of machine-learning algorithms for analyzing intergroup heterogeneity and intragroup homogeneity. The methods relied on in these studies (i.e. *n*-fold cross-validation, within fold feature selection and discriminant analysis) are powerful methods for researchers interested in language detection studies and crosslinguistic influences. The methods are also statistically rigorous and are reported in enough depth to promote future replication. What these studies demonstrate is that high classification rates can be acquired with few linguistic features (i.e. independent variables) with at least one study (Crossley & McNamara, this volume) relying on as few as 14 features. Additionally, the methods used in this volume have demonstrated that high classification rates

Table 7.1 Classification accuracies for each analysis using the ICLE corpus

Language	Unigrams	Multiword units (all n-grams)	Coh-Metrix Variables	Error analysis	Combined analysis
Bulgarian	55.0	47.9	x	x	x
Czech	53.4	52.6	74.3	x	x
Dutch	52.0	45.6	x	x	x
Finnish	49.6	47.9	58.6	x	x
French	48.0	51.0	x	64.8	**85.1**
German	47.8	51.6	**75.1**	71.8	78.9
Italian	41.9	41.9	x	x	x
Norwegian	59.6	59.3	x	x	x
Polish	**66.0**	**68.1**	x	x	x
Russian	45.8	53.5	x	x	x
Spanish	52.1	51.4	52.3	60.3	74.4
Swedish	47.0	49.3	x	x	x

are possible when many dependent variables are used. For instance, Jarvis et al. (this volume) reported classification rates of nearly 54% when classifying 12 different L2 writing groups. Lastly, many of the chapters found in this volume promote the notion that a feature's F value is not a sufficiently reliable indicator of usefulness in a classification model. Likely, this is the result of the potential for an F value's strength to be influenced by a single dependent variable such that a linguistic feature may report a high F value solely in response to that feature's ability to discriminate one group from five other groups, but not each individual group from all other groups. Additionally, the F value of an index as an indicator of its separation potential may overlap with features that have already been included in the model, making it less reliable in categorical models. Statistically, tests such as the Student–Newman–Keuls post-hoc tests reported in the chapters of this volume become indispensable at demonstrating where differences exist and aiding in additional qualitative analyses that assess cross-language congruity among L1s.

An important question discussed by Jarvis (Chapter 1, this volume) is the success of machine-learning algorithms to automatically classify documents as compared to the ability of human raters to accomplish the same task. A comparison between machine-learning judgments and human judgments would provide researchers with a greater understanding of the degree of subtlety captured by detection-based approaches and the strengths of expert raters at discerning faint, linguistic patterns that may transfer from a L1 to a L2. Although theoretical, it seems that human raters would be at a disadvantage when compared with machine-learning algorithms because of the subjectivity of human judgments and factors such as fatigue. However, such questions and their answers are best left to future, empirical studies.

Along with investigations into human capabilities to detect the language patterns of L2 writers of a specific L1, the research reported in the previous chapters provides a variety of research directions and application. From a research perspective, these studies provide evidence and new methodologies to support many of the enabling goals at the heart of crosslinguistic influence research discussed by Jarvis in the first chapter of this volume. For instance, this volume has provided a wealth of empirical discoveries involving linguistic differences between a variety of L1 writers writing in an L2. These discoveries have expanded our pool of knowledge as to the type of linguistic features involved in crosslinguistic transfer and the extent of their predictive ability in discerning L2 essays based on the L1 of the writer. All of these discoveries have led to theoretical advances in their explanation, but, perhaps more importantly, this volume has developed a set of methodological tools and statistical approaches to explain crosslinguistic influences in an empirical manner that affords hypothesis testing and the disambiguation of crosslinguistic influences that might otherwise be concealed from surface-level analyses.

From a L2 acquisition perspective, the studies reported in this volume are also enlightening. For example, in Chapter 2, Jarvis *et al.* provide evidence not only for language transfer at the lexical level, but also at the level of avoidance. Jarvis *et al.* demonstrate that it is not simply the production of lexical items that is predictive of the L1 of an L2 writer, but also the avoidance of forms that may not exist in the writers' L1. Thus, as Jarvis *et al.* demonstrate, Finnish writers are much less likely to use a third-person singular personal pronoun (e.g. 'he') because of the lack of pronominal gender in Finnish, which creates a need to rely on nouns more often for purposes of avoiding referential ambiguity. Similarly, Finnish writers are less likely to use articles in English, probably because an article system does not exist in Finnish. In a similar vein, in Chapter 5, Bestgen *et al.* demonstrate that Spanish speakers avoid subject position pronouns because such pronouns are generally elided in Spanish. Potential patterns of overuse were also common in the data reported in these studies. For instance, Spanish speakers seemed to depend on the overuse of *going to* when referring to future time (Jarvis & Paquot, this volume). Research findings such as these help to forward theories of L2 acquisition and provide evidence that L2 acquisition follows different developmental paths than L1 acquisition.

Practical applications for the research reported in this volume also exist in L2 pedagogy. The methodology used throughout this book has rendered findings that provide relatively clear results concerning the patterns that are specific to individual L1 groups. These predictable patterns may represent errors, avoidance, underuse or overuse that result from the L1 of an L2 learner and could be used to inform pedagogical practices. Such practices would permit language teachers to better understand and prepare for potential areas of learning difficulty for their students, affording early intervention and allowing teachers to focus on attested areas of interference. Addressing the transfer of patterns from an L1 to an L2 early in a pedagogical environment might improve an L2 learner's accuracy in both form and function. Such patterns could also influence the development of curriculum, the development of functional activities, and the development of naturalistic assessments.

Additionally, the models developed and discussed in this volume could be of value in developing scoring algorithms to assess learner proficiency at the spoken or the written level. Such algorithms have already been developed using Coh-Metrix indices (Crossley & McNamara, in press; Crossley et al., 2011, in press), but indices assessing n-gram accuracy are yet to be tested. Such algorithms would provide objective measures of language proficiency and language development and allow teachers and administrators to more quickly place students in proficiency level-based classrooms or assess the efficacy of various pedagogical interventions.

The exclusion of error analysis in our discussion on automated assessments of language proficiency and language progress indicates another area of future development: the automated quantification of additional linguistic features. Currently, only the n-gram analyses and the Coh-Metrix analyses were automated to the point where human assessment of text quality was unnecessary. There is much work to be accomplished in other linguistic areas involving the automation of linguistic features. The most obvious component suitable for development is error analysis. While past studies have used automated error analysis to classify the L1 background of L2 writers, the accuracy of such analyses has been less than optimal with Wong and Dras (2009) reporting an accuracy of around 50% in determining misuse errors. The errors that have been automated have also been relatively restricted and have generally focused on formal and syntactic error types (see Bestgen et al., this volume, for further discussion). In addition to error identification, there are a variety of other linguistic features that lend themselves to automation that might prove important in L1 text classification studies emphasizing crosslinguistic influences. These include, but are not limited to, measures of lexical equilibrium, lexical rarity, lexical disparity, lexical dispersion, (see Jarvis, 2010), collocational accuracy (Crossley & Salsbury, 2011), word association norms, basic category usage, semantic categories, global and local coherence measures, part of speech diversity and part of speech collocations.

In closing, this volume has demonstrated the practical advantages of using advanced theories and methods common in computer sciences and mathematical modeling for investigating intergroup heterogeneity and intragroup homogeneity. These advances in machine learning, artificial intelligence and pattern recognition have led to powerful data-mining tools that allow for the rapid and accurate categorization of information. These same tools have been adopted and further developed by linguists working on classification problems related to language use and have resulted in functional applications for identifying texts by type (e.g. spoken or written, fiction or nonfiction, original or translated texts, original or plagiarized texts; Baroni & Bernardini, 2006; Sebastiani, 2002; Stamatatos, 2009; Stamatatos et al., 2001) and by topic (e.g. business, medicine, politics, sports, communication; Jo et al., 2000). Additional studies have also identified texts by the characteristics of the people who produced them (e.g. male or female, American or British, native or nonnative speaker of English; Crossley & McNamara, 2009; Koppel et al., 2002; Mayfield Tomokiyo & Jones, 2001). Recently, these tools and techniques have been further refined to enable the relatively accurate detection of the native languages (L1s) of nonnative speakers of English according to various language features found in samples of their writing, including emails (Estival et al., 2007), written narratives (Jarvis et al., 2004), and argumentative essays (Koppel et al., 2005). The chapters in this volume have expanded the potential of these tools and methods for identifying the L1 of L2 writers. These approaches not only provide promising results for machine-learning algorithms and computational tools, but also provide exciting and promising findings that have direct applications for studies of crosslinguistic influence, L2 acquisition, L2 pedagogy and L2 assessment.

References

Baroni, M. and Bernardini, S. (2006) A new approach to the study of translationese: Machine-learning the difference between original and translated text. *Literary and Linguistic Computing* 21, 259–274.

Corder, S.P. (1967) The significance of learners' errors. *International Review of Applied Linguistics* 9, 147–159.

Crossley, S.A. and McNamara, D.S. (2009) Computational assessment of lexical differences in L1 and L2 writing. *Journal of Second Language Writing* 18, 119–135.

Crossley, S.A. and Salsbury, T. (2011) The development of lexical bundle accuracy and production in English second language speakers. *IRAL: International Review of Applied Linguistics in Language Teaching* 49, 1–26.

Crossley, S.A. and McNamara, D.S. (in press) Predicting second language writing proficiency: The role of cohesion, readability, and lexical difficulty. *Journal of Research in Reading*.

Crossley, S.A., Salsbury, T., McNamara, D.S. and Jarvis, S. (2011) What is lexical proficiency? Some answers from computational models of speech data. *TESOL Quarterly* 45, 182–193.

Crossley, S.A., Salsbury, T., McNamara, D.S. and Jarvis, S. (in press) Predicting lexical proficiency in language learners using computational indices. *Language Testing*.

Estival, D., Gaustad, T., Pham, S.B., Radford, W. and Hutchinson, B. (2007) Author profiling for English emails. In *Proceedings of the 10th Conference of the Pacific Association for Computational Linguistics (PACLING 2007)* (pp. 31–39). Melbourne, Australia.

George, H. (1972) *Common Errors in Language Learning*. Rowley, MA: Newbury House.

Granger, S., Dagneaux, E., Meunier, F. and Paquot, M. (2009) *The International Corpus of Learner English. Handbook and CD-ROM*. Version 2. Louvain-la-Neuve: Presses universitaires de Louvain.

Jarvis, S. (2010) Comparison-based and detection-based approaches to transfer research. In L. Roberts, M. Howard, M. Ó Laoire and D. Singleton (eds) *EUROSLA Yearbook 10* (pp. 169–192). Amsterdam: John Benjamins.

Jarvis, S., Castañeda-Jiménez, G. and Nielsen, R. (2004) Investigating L1 lexical transfer through learners' wordprints. Paper presented at the *2004 Second Language Research Forum*. State College, Pennsylvania.

Jo, T.C., Seo, J.H. and Kim, H. (2000) Topic spotting on news articles with topic repository by controlled indexing. In K.S. Leung, L.-W. Chan and H. Meng (eds) *IDEAL 2000*, LNCS 1983 (pp. 386–391). Berlin: Springer.

Koppel, M., Schler, J. and Zigdon, K. (2005) Determining an author's native language by mining a text for errors. In *Proceedings of the Eleventh ACM SIGKDD International Conference on Knowledge Discovery in Data Mining* (pp. 624–628). Chicago: Association for Computing Machinery.

Kubota, R. (1998) An investigation of L1–L2 transfer in writing among Japanese university students: Implications for contrastive rhetoric. *Journal of Second Language Writing* 7, 69–100.

Mayfield Tomokiyo, L. and Jones, R. (2001) You're not from 'round here, are you? Naive Bayes detection of non-native utterance text. In *Proceedings of the Second Meeting of the North American Chapter of the Association for Computational Linguistics (NAACL '01)*, unpaginated electronic document. Cambridge, MA: The Association for Computational Linguistics.

Mosteller, F. and Wallace, D.L. (1964) *Applied Bayesian and Classical Inference: The Case of the Federalist Papers*. Reading, MA: Addison-Wesley.

Montaño-Harmon, M. (1988) Discourse features in the compositions of Mexican English as a second language. Mexican-American Chicano, and Anglo high school students: Considerations for the formulation of educational policy. PhD thesis, University of Southern California, Los Angeles.

Odlin, T. (1989) *Language Transfer: Cross-Linguistic Influence in Language Learning*. Cambridge: Cambridge University Press.

Paquot, M. (2010) *Academic Vocabulary in Learner Writing: From Extraction to Analysis*. London: Continuum.

Poulisse, N. and Bongaerts, T. (1994) First language use in second language production. *Applied Linguistics* 15, 36–57.

Sebastiani, F. (2002) Machine learning in automated text categorization. *ACM Computing Surveys* 34, 1–47.

Stamatatos, E. (2009) A survey of modern authorship attribution methods. *Journal of the American Society for Information Science and Technology* 60, 538–556.

Stamatatos, E., Fakotakis, N. and Kokkinakis, G. (2001) Automatic text categorization in terms of genre and author. *Computational Linguistics* 26, 461–485.

Tsur, O. and Rappoport, A. (2007) Using classifier features for studying the effect of native language on the choice of written second language words. In *Proceedings of the Workshop on Cognitive Aspects of Computational Language Acquisition* (pp. 9–16). Cambridge, MA: The Association for Computational Linguistics.

Ventola, E. and Mauranen, A. (1991) Non-native writing and native revising of scientific articles. In E. Ventola (ed.) *Functional and Systemic Linguistics: Approaches and Uses* (pp. 457–492). Berlin: Mouton de Gruyter.

Wong, S-M.J. and Dras, M. (2009) Contrastive analysis and native language identification. In *Proceedings of the Australasian Language Technology Association* (pp. 53–61). Cambridge, MA: The Association for Computational Linguistics.

For Product Safety Concerns and Information please contact our EU Authorised Representative:

Easy Access System Europe

Mustamäe tee 50

10621 Tallinn

Estonia

gpsr.requests@easproject.com